Dedicated to my husband Smiley,
and sons Sean and Craig,
who I carried on the trail with me in my heart.

THE RANGE OF LIGHT IN THE SIERRA

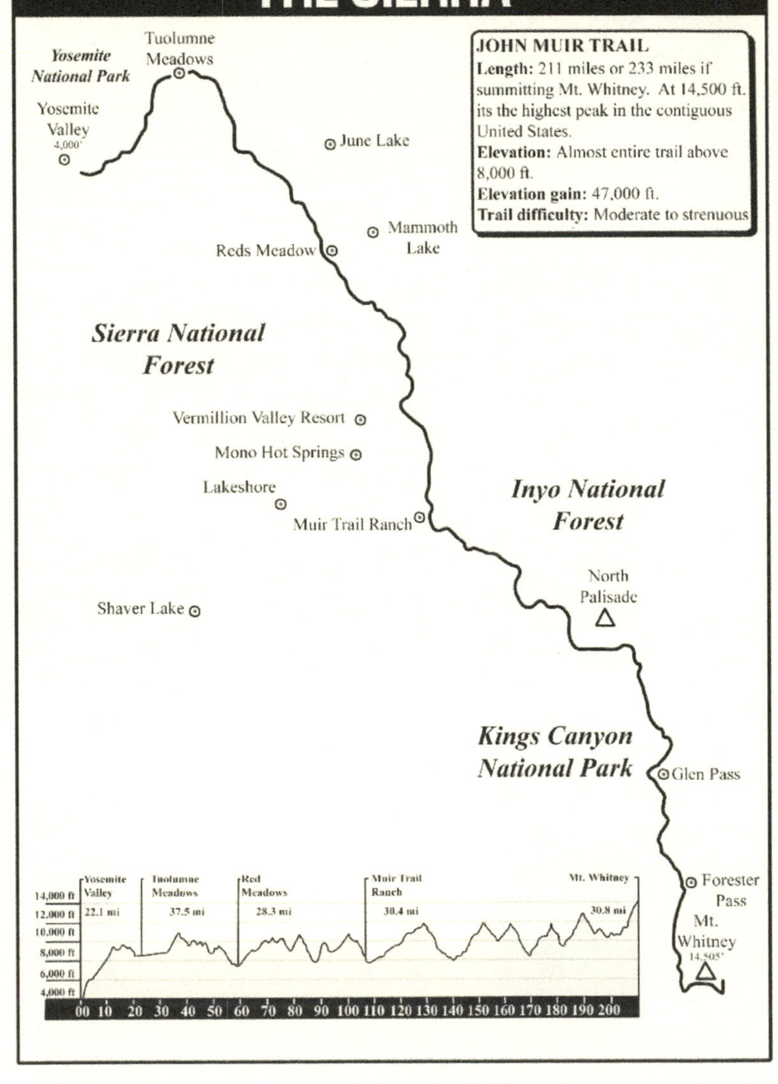

Preview Hike One: Day 1
July 11, 2004

I could barely breathe. My knees were killing me in spite of the braces and the hiking poles I'd almost left behind. When I fell backwards, my heavy backpack cushioned the blow. It had also left me pinned to the ground like a turtle trapped upside down in its own shell, my arms and legs thrashing for freedom.

What the hell was I, an out of shape, fifty-year-old woman with bad knees and asthma, doing on the top of a mountain at an elevation of 9,360 feet? Hiking long distances in the high Sierra, surrounded by sheer granite cliffs and glorious blue skies, had been my dream for decades. Judging by my precarious position, however, I had to wonder if perhaps I'd waited too long.

White ballooning clouds changed in form and substance. They danced around the jagged-toothed mountains teasing the earth with the promise of a summer rain. Thousands of pungent pine trees, loomed like green sentinels dotting the landscape, witnessing my disgrace. Their branches shook with the wind, sending oxygen I couldn't seem to pull in. Shifting my body weight from side-to-side, I struggled to get myself upright.

Somewhere along the way in my life, I'd lost the spirited, red-headed girl inside me who'd thrived on adventure and thrills. I needed to find her again. Maybe a rugged, twenty-seven-day hike in the wilderness was taking it a bit too far. A woman with a grandmother's face cannot easily revisit her youth in action.

The John Muir Trail (JMT) is said to resemble a heart monitor chart. After hiking only eight of the total two-hundred and eleven miles, my entire body was screaming. I felt alone, afraid, and found it increasingly difficult to breathe. In spite of a steady alpine breeze, thick trails of sweat rolled down my face. I licked my lips, tasting salt. It added to my thirst. I reached for a happier thought.

Motherhood had been one of the highlights of my life. The first laugh of my infant sons, the word *Mamma* they still use to call me, and those tight, squishy hugs and sweet kisses they be-stowed on me were my rewards for time well spent.

Yet, I'd traded parts of myself by becoming a parent. I no longer had the energy or nerve to rock climb lofty mountains, or to practice twirls and high jumps while ice skating. I knew all the words to nursery rhymes but had forgotten the lyrics to the Carol King songs I'd loved to play on my guitar. My hiking trip had been planned in the hope it would help me find some of those lost pieces.

Famished, I realized the extra thirty-five pounds I'd packed onto my body wasn't helping. Like a song in my head that wouldn't go away, I kept remembering the words: "You'll have to get in shape and lose weight, Mamma, if you want to hike that trail." Sean, my rock-solid, buff-bodied firefighter son had told me that when I'd proudly boasted I was going to hike the John Muir Trail.

I'd been slim and toned before having children and letting go of that part of me was a mistake. My sons weren't the cause, but I'd used birthing them as an excuse to become lazy and complacent.

Perhaps Sean had been right. If I'd followed his advice eleven months prior, I might not have been suffering. Maybe I wouldn't have tripped so easily over that large boulder and fallen backward onto my pack. But there I was, stuck to the ground, my legs and arms flailing to tip me over.

I wished I could hide my head inside my shell. No such luck. If I'd felt any sense of achievement when I arrived at the top of the mountain, it was shattered. Unable to free myself from my load, I stared at the sky and contemplated my next course of action.

One of the many guidebooks I'd researched mentioned something about *common sense* going a long way. It also said that concentration, when you are on rough ground, will reduce the risk of a fall with a heavy pack. OK. I was obviously short on common sense, concentration, or both. It occurred to me I might not be able to dislodge myself from my pack without help.

When I started this trip, I had been with two other middle-aged women and a teenager. The being together thing was short-lived. I estimated they were at least a mile ahead. To be honest, I was glad they weren't around to revel in my shame. Instead of being proactive and trying to help myself, I fantasized about one of the constants in my life—food.

Food had become a great source of comfort. Each step my sons took toward adulthood found me shoveling cookies, crackers, or sometimes leftover peanut butter and jelly sandwiches in my face in order to fill the empty spaces. I had told myself my metabolism had slowed. Or maybe it was my thyroid—like Oprah's.

The dehydrated cuisine in my pack wasn't appealing to me in the least and I envisioned myself enjoying a delectable In-N-Out Burger including the grilled sweet onions and crispy fries. Make that a Double Double Burger, with a creamy chocolate shake.

Comfort eating I didn't need but desperately wanted.

I'd worked hard to convince myself those burgers were the healthiest offerings of the fast food joints we'd frequented the last few years. My growing sons were always ravenous. We needed to eat something after shuttling them to various events in cities outside our small mountain town of Mariposa, California. I also liked the feeling I got when my family was all snuggled safely in those shiny plastic booths. My sons would open up and share stories while eating out, which had made me feel important in their lives.

A heavy sap-filled pinecone, which seemed to fall from the sky, returned my thoughts to the present. It bounced off the top of my forehead like a basketball hitting the court. *Ouch!*

Searching the branches of a nearby tree I noticed two fat, bushy-tailed gray squirrels scampering from limb to limb. They reminded me of my sons wrestling together when they were younger. The mischievous rodents chewed and dug, gaining access to the nuts encased in the cones before hurling them at me. Luckily, most missed their mark. I smiled in spite of myself. When they scurried off and left me alone, I felt the familiar tug of loneliness. I missed my boys.

Still, for some reason I found it comical I couldn't dislodge myself from the ground. I heard myself giggling maniacally with no one around. If a woman laughs in the forest and no one is around to hear, does it mean she's nuts?

I imagined the sweat making muddy tracks across my face and I could feel the itching mosquito bites covering my body. I'd foolishly left behind the three-ounce bottle of mosquito repellent to save weight in my pack. How had I forgotten about the persistent whining of mosquitoes? Their torturous little bites made me crazy.

Debra, the leader of our hellish hike, constantly badgered me about *light gear packing.* Her bitching had made me leave behind things essential to my personal well-being. I knew after this three-day preview hike—a trek we had arranged around Debra's hectic work schedule—bug repellent would be one of the things I'd make sure and return to my pack.

The heavy, horrible, bitter-tasting energy bars she'd insisted we bring added at least two pounds to my forty-five pound load. I never ate pretend chocolate. So why did I feel afraid to tell her how I felt? When had I become such a coward?

The active humming of mosquitoes and ever-present need to gasp for air, along with my throbbing headache, reminded my body it was time to take some course of action. I needed to dislodge myself from my predicament. Before I could act, I heard what sounded like a panting, rasping dog charging toward me. My eyes widened in alert:; my body stiffened in panic.

It couldn't be a dog. I was in the part of the woods where domesticated animals weren't allowed. I was, however, in the natural home of wild predators, including black bears.

Bears loved the food humans brought into the wilderness. Laying there on my back made me an easy target. The panting grew louder. I wriggled violently from side to side, tangling myself in the hiking poles lying beside me. This couldn't be the way it ended.

As I lay below the crisp cerulean blue sky, I prayed for a second chance. Horrified, I gasped for breath. Perched above me with menacing teeth and a ferocious expression, I saw not a canine nor bear, but my friend Jane Smith's lowered brow and flared nostrils.

"Where in the fuck have you been, and what on earth made me decide it was a good idea to hike ahead with that crazy woman?" she asked.

Jane, with her sassy smile and bright blue eyes, was one of the two women who had hiked ahead of me. She'd come on this first three-day preview part of our trip after I begged her to keep me company. After that, I would have to face the remaining twenty-four days on my own with Debra and her sixteen-year-old daughter Jenny.

Jane's eyes glazed. Her scowling face made it clear she wasn't a happy hiker. "How in the world," she asked, "did you think you could hike with that lunatic all summer?"

Startled, but finally able to breathe, I tried to kick my feet in the air imitating bicycle-peddling action. I hoped maybe she'd get the idea I was in a precarious position. No such luck. She simply stood there with her hands on her hips.

"Well, it's obvious I'm stuck, so help me get up and maybe we can talk about it."

"OK, but only if you let me talk shit about your little friend Debra." She pushed me over onto my side and freed me from my pack.

"Good heavens," I gasped. Unless you've been attached to something cutting into your shoulders like the weight of fifty bra straps pushing and squishing against your stomach and hipbones like a mammography machine does to your boobs, you probably have no idea how good it felt to finally rid myself of that hellish burden. "Thank God you came back, Jane."

She breathed hot and heavy air on my neck while helping me up, then stomped around, kicked up loose dirt and pebbles, and threw her pack down. "Debra's a nutcase. Certifiable. Thank God I've been working out all summer riding horses on trails. If she thinks she can outdo me she's got another thing coming. It might be my first-time backpacking, but I can beat her skinny ass in a minute and plan to do exactly that."

Dragging my backpack behind me by pulling it with my foot, I limped toward a large boulder. "Wish I had your confidence,

Jane," I stammered. "My big ass, along with every other part of my body, is killing me. I'll be lucky to make it through the day."

I plopped down on the boulder and lay my head in my hands. In a previous life—B.C.(before children)—I'd spent two summers in my twenties as a wilderness ranger. In fact, it's where I first met my husband, Smiley.

But after motherhood, and fifteen years spent in a classroom teaching second graders, those days were long gone. I'd gone soft in every way. The mosquitoes tormented me, and my right knee burned and continued to make snapping sounds. In sympathy, the left one also ached. An orthopedic specialist had already told me I was only a few years from a knee replacement.

I waved my red bandana in the air like a flag of surrender. "Debra said this trip would be a fun walk in the woods with friends and we'd do poetry, yoga, and laugh a lot. What a joke."

"Well, so far the joke's on you," Jane said.

I smoothed out my bandana, which had the entire 211-mile John Muir Trail printed on it. Studying it, I saw I'd covered about 1/20th of an inch on that scale. It made me even more miserable to realize how ashamed I'd feel when I quit this trip after doing only the first miniscule section.

Jane kept pacing back and forth, kicking up dust, which didn't help the situation. I kept my mouth shut even as dust aggravated my throat and bronchial tubes. I didn't think it would be wise to ask my only friend in the wilderness to stop doing something that might make this nightmare situation even worse for me.

"How long do you think you can be out here in this fucking wilderness without killing her?" Jane asked.

I couldn't muster the energy to answer.

What would I do without Jane's humor and help on the rest of the trip? I wondered how I could convince her to come back. I'd made plans with Debra and Jenny to take a four-day break at home before our next leg of the journey. It would give me several days off to doctor my blistered, bleeding feet and figure out what equipment worked, and what needed to be swapped out or dumped all together. Unfortunately, I wasn't so sure I'd find the courage to get back on the trail.

"She's a control freak." Jane kicked sticks as we walked. "I can't believe I let her take my camping dress out of my backpack. It's my lucky charm. I always wear it when I camp."

I shook my head in frustration. "We've spent months in planning. I've had so many dreams about the new me I was going to discover on this trail."

The JMT is rumored to be the prettiest part of the much longer 2,650-mile Pacific Crest Trail. It has the highest peaks and wide expansive vistas. There are many ways to hike it; purists think the only way that counts is hiking all 211 miles consecutively. Other hikers do it a section at a time and take years to finish the whole thing.

Debra and I had made the choice to hike the entire trail in one summer. We agreed to not do it all at once but instead take three separate hikes during different times the same summer. The first two trips would be short. They'd help us know what worked for us and what didn't. We talked about learning from our mistakes and seeing if our gear and supplies were chosen wisely. We had also wanted to see how the high altitude affected us and try to acclimate to it. The two preview hikes would make the final three-week backpack easier—at least in theory.

I sighed in dismay. I wanted to be known for something other than being a wife, mom, and teacher. Maybe, too, I wanted to prove I wasn't old, I still had what it took. Too bad my body wasn't cooperating with my soul. "We better get going before Debra and

Jenny get so far ahead of us they forget we exist."

"I think they've already forgotten about you. Debra makes it clear every chance she gets that this is her trip and you're just her pack mule. What's up with that chick anyway? Do you think she could be bipolar? You might want to re-evaluate this whole situation, girlfriend."

I shook my head. "I know it might seem funny to you now, seeing the person I've become, but I've always dreamed about hiking this trail. It's been part of me for a long time and I've waited for the right moment to do it."

"Being a middle-aged woman, I can relate, but whatever made you decide to hike over two-hundred miles in the wilderness with such a bitchy, tight-ass broad?" Jane asked.

"She was a different person. Funny, happy, full of life. This is a side of her I didn't expect." I shrugged.

I'd met Debra through Smiley. Her ex-husband, Jim, and Smiley had been the untamed fallers who cut down burning trees of up to 150 feet tall in raging wildfires. They were the guys who chose the most dangerous and exciting jobs. We all lived together for about a month before Smiley and I were married. I hadn't known much about Debra then either, but I did enjoy the fun times we'd shared.

It was sad to see how different she was from that young girl. Maybe she was trying to find the part of her she'd lost, too. Divorce hadn't been kind to her. She had to buy out Jim's portion of the house equity, realized he'd been cheating on her with younger women, and, worst of all, he got most weekends with the kids.

I remembered I had already bought two pairs of costly footwear on the Internet and trial-tested them by taking short hikes around Mariposa. After each time my feet throbbed in pain. Those boots were not my friends so they all found a new home at the local thrift shop. Afterwards I drove seventy miles to a Hi-Tech shoe store and bought the pair I was wearing. The first problem was letting the salesman talk me into getting heavier ones than I'd previously owned.

I knew a good pair of boots and socks can make or break a backpack trip. If I had listened to my gut, I wouldn't have been persuaded to purchase three pairs of useless boots. The current pair wouldn't even make it to the thrift store. When I arrived home, they would be tossed directly into the trash. I didn't want to impose their torture on anyone else.

"Do you think you could stop for a minute and help put some moleskin on my feet? I think I have some monster blisters," I mumbled.

As evidenced when I peeled my socks off, that was not an understatement. Bloody skin stuck to my socks, and the whole back edge of both heels was encased with blisters. Several more had sprouted on my toes, making me wince in pain.

"Holy shit," Jane said. "How're you going to hike with those feet? Here, let me see what I can do."

She went straight to work. Jane was a good old cowgirl and knew how to doctor my feet. She was gentle yet efficient and padded them with gauze and tape.

"Well if nothing else those blisters give you an excuse to quit," she said.

"Can you please help me put my boots on now?" I asked.

Jane and I walked in companionable silence. We crested a hill and stopped short as the dramatic mountains of Yosemite National Park came into view—Columbia Finger, Tressider, Echo, and Cathedral Peaks.

Sunlight streamed through the trees at Cathedral Pass, making God-beam shafts of light shoot through the branches. A lone eagle soared above us stretching wide its wings and flying figure eights in a solo sky dance.

I was unable to speak. Jane, never at a loss for words, seemed to feel the same wonder. We moved along reverently, bathed in silence. The Sierra wilderness had always been salve to my soul. Its constancy and beauty amazed me. My feet throbbed, but my spirit soared.

After a quarter of a mile or so, Jane stopped in her tracks and stared at me. "I see why you're doing it. This is some kind of holy place or something, isn't it? I've never seen anything like it."

"It gets better and better," I said softly. "This is my church, Jane, the only vision of God I've ever experienced except in the faces of my boys when they were babies. I've waited my whole life to hike this trail. Fantasized and dreamed about it. Not even Debra can take that away from me." I felt bad for slowing Jane down, but my feet throbbed with every step. "Remember my fiftieth birthday party when you and Debra came and we had such a blast? Didn't she seem like a lot of fun then?"

"Guess booze can loosen anybody up. Debra keeps saying she can't sleep. I've got some good sleeping pills I could give her. Do you want some, Lori? I've got extra if you need 'em."

"No, thanks." I shook my head. "I remember asking Debra why she wanted me to come on this trip. She jokingly said it was because I could go without booze or drugs for a month, and I can. Being up above 9,000 feet gives me a natural high. I just hope I don't get altitude sickness. I had it once. Puked my guts out and had a headache that wouldn't quit."

"It's getting late. I hope they saved us a campsite and are starting dinner." Jane slapped at a mosquito that had already bitten into her arm. "I'm not so sure I wanna cook in the dark."

"The true wilderness I'm seeking is beyond the High Sierra Camp where we'll be staying. At our campground, there'll be piped water and outhouses. This'll be one of our last chances on this leg of the journey to sit on a toilet."

"I'll take advantage of it. I like being with you—and this new adventure—but it'd be a miracle if Debra and I could be together more than two nights, even with all this wide-open space." Jane twirled and spread her arms wide. "Let's hope she lightens up a little. If she doesn't, maybe she'll be too tired to boss us around."

After the next curve of the seemingly endless trail, we saw camp spaces set up for backpackers. Despite twenty or more tents in a somewhat confined area the surrounding view was breathtaking. The sky blazed with rich red and orange color and the woodsy smell of cooking fires made my stomach growl. But where were Debra and Jenny? A little twist of anxiety spun in my stomach.

"There they are!" yelled Jane, moving as fast as she could with an attached pack. She headed toward a campsite sheltered by trees and rock outcroppings and set off from the others. Relieved, I shuffled behind her as quickly as my blistered feet would let me go. With each step, the raw areas on my heels attached more tightly to my socks, oozing pus through the bandages and spilling over the tops of my shoes.

"Great campsite. Where should we pitch our tent?" Jane asked, head darting from side to side.

Debra's freckled face resembled a ready to burst storm cloud. "Anywhere but here," she moved her hands all around. "I need some space and this area isn't big enough for two tents."

"I think we could make room," her daughter said. "There's a spot by the tree that looks good."

"That's where I cooked, and I'm planning on using it tomorrow for a kitchen area," Debra frowned. "What happened to you guys anyway? It's almost eight p.m."

"So nice of you to finally be interested. Lori has blisters all over her feet, and I'm not sure how she made it this far."

"You got me here, Jane," I talked loud enough for Debra to hear. "I can't thank you enough for waiting and helping me."

"You must've gone at a turtle's pace," Debra smirked.

My face heated and I told myself quite firmly not to tell her about falling backwards on my pack or letting her know how apt her analogy was.

"So much for the buddy system." Jane kicked some rocks they'd set up to put their stove on. "And what are we supposed to eat? Didn't we all pay for food? Where's our portion?"

"We didn't know when you'd be here and we were hungry, but we saved part of the bag for you to cook." Debra threw it at Jane before turning to her daughter. "What was I supposed to do, let Jenny go hungry while you two were out lollygaggin'? And now you ruined our kitchen area. I don't appreciate your attitude."

"I told you I could wait, Mom," Jenny stammered, biting her bottom lip with concern. "I thought it'd be better if we were all together."

Jane stepped toward Debra, putting her arms across her chest. "Talk about a shitty attitude, yours is as bad as they come. I couldn't care less about some damn old rocks you set up for a kitchen. There seems to be more than enough of them around here. I think it's food we might be short on."

"I'm 110 pounds and have to eat to keep up my energy." Debra stood up, running her hands down her slim athletic figure. "You might have some reserve on your bodies, but I don't. We could've used some energy bars, and Lori has them."

Being with Jane gave me courage. "Why don't you take them?" I felt myself revving up to give one of the tongue thrashings I'd been known to dish out to my sons when they misbehaved. "I hate the things, they taste awful, and they're weighing my pack down. I'm going to have a hard time when I don't have Jane with me to help divide the weight load from my pack. You told me Jenny's friend Christy was coming and would lend a hand, but that didn't happen. Now I've got a two-person tent when I only needed to buy and carry a one-person, a water filter, a cook stove, pots and pans. Someone else should help carry." I knew my ranting sounded like a whiney seven year old, but I couldn't stop. "Right now, my feet are covered with blisters. I couldn't have made it this far without Jane." For some reason my pack seemed lighter, and I felt like a grown up not a child after all.

"I told you to buy lightweight boots. You didn't, and now your feet are messed up," Debra said. "Jenny's and mine are fine. It's your own fault, and I don't feel the least bit sorry for you."

"Mom, my ankle's killing me," Jenny said, obviously trying to change the subject. "I think maybe I need some hiking poles."

"You shouldn't have played in those soccer scrimmages before our trip." Debra sat back down in a huff. "You've got a bad ankle and needed to keep it healthy. I don't feel sorry for you either. I'm going to bed to try and get some rest. I haven't slept for three nights getting things ready for this trip. Taking care of everybody isn't my idea of fun."

Jane and I looked at each other in disbelief then walked away. After a few feet, we simultaneously burst out laughing and couldn't stop. When we reached a spot with flat dirt and sheltering trees nearby, Jane turned to me, clumsily curtsied, and said, "Do you think we're far enough away from Her Majesty?"

We giggled and chatted while putting together our campsite and setting up our tent. After tripping over a few loose rocks and sticks, I was happy I'd taken the time to set it up in my backyard and knew how to do it efficiently.

With two poles and a single piece of fabric, my tent went up like an exploding popcorn kernel. It didn't have a rain fly and I hoped it wouldn't be necessary. A tent without a rain fly can be a big mistake, especially in the Sierra. Hikers in a lot better shape than I have been forced off the JMT by storms. When Jane wasn't around I'd use the extra space in the tent to store my pack.

Looking up over the ridge, I spied the one-and-a-half-person tent Debra and Jenny had crawled into. How is someone, even a skinny someone, considered half a person? It weighed in total about two pounds. Mine was three and a half pounds.

Jane skulked over and collected our part of the camp food, then, handing it to me, said, "Our portion looks puny."

"Me getting skinnier might be one of the good things about this trip. Hiking ten miles a day could help jump start a diet."

We cooked dinner on my new camp stove, which cost $142. It seemed like it might be worth the price. Water magically boiled at a 9,360-ft elevation. Dehydrated stew was my new best friend. The congealed gravy added salt to my body that had been depleted by the profuse sweat I'd released. We wolfed it down and were still ravenous.

"Well, if you want one, two, or three energy bars, be my guest." I tossed one to Jane. "Getting rid of these would be a great way for me to lessen my load."

Why did I still have them after I'd told Debra she needed to take them? I seemed to lack follow through, and this trip would require a great deal of that.

"Forget the fake stuff. Debra might have frisked me and taken out my camp dress, but she missed the Hershey bars and a container of Schnapps."

"Yum, sounds delicious," I said, licking my lips.

"Liquor is great in hot chocolate, and I've got marshmallows and graham crackers to add to the Hershey bars for s'mores. I learned how to camp right at horse camp. Only problem here is I'm the horse packin' the shit in. But, hey…it's all good." She chuckled as she poured the Schnapps into our tin cups. Hot chocolate combined with it made my head fuzzy but my stomach warm.

"Too bad for Debra and Jenny, but now we don't have to share. Besides, Jenny's too young to drink booze and I might offend Debra by using the F-word. I'm planning on saying it a lot tonight."

The Schnapps definitely took the edge off of the evening. After dinner, we stumbled over to use the outhouses. Turning around and facing me, Jane said, "I can see why people like riding to these places on horses. Beautiful shit around but what a workout to get here."

"Yea, shit is right, the horses leave it all over, and it pollutes the water with giardia. Years ago, I didn't have to use a water filter," I said while trying to find my way in the dark. Of course, we'd forgotten our flashlights. Where was Debra when we needed her?

"Horse shit is organic; helps the earth," Jane said.

"Bringing a horse in the wilderness is something we don't agree on. They do a lot of damage."

"So do people," she replied. "You might want to join me horse camping sometime."

I didn't want to tell her I was terrified of horses.

Some people spend thousands of dollars to go from one high sierra camp to the next riding animals. Food, water, a bed, and outhouses are provided. To me, it seemed contrary to the whole idea of wilderness. I wondered if I'd feel the same when I was in my sixties or seventies and still wanted to be able to reach mountain areas I could no longer get to by foot.

My feet were numb and no longer throbbing, my hunger was appeased, but there was still one major problem: constipation. I never had an easy time taking care of business in the woods. The constant bloat bothered me almost as much as Debra's disdain.

I sat in the pungent outhouse a lot longer than the average camper, covering my face with a bandana and trying not to breathe while contemplating my fate for the next month. Parts of me no longer worked as well as they used to. In spite of my attempts to mask it, the smell was not pretty, but neither was the extended outlook for the hike.

Back at camp, Jane and I sat on enormous and strangely comfortable granite boulders watching the stars come out and blanket the inky sky like a million fireflies. Our disagreement over horses didn't seem to have affected our relationship. I found myself relaxing, full of food, friendship, and a feeling of accomplishment after a strenuous ten-mile backpack. I might not have done it as well or as fast as Debra, but I was there, and that was enough for now.

Jane sang at the top of her lungs, *Oh Lord Won't You Buy Me a Mercedes Benz*. Tall, jagged peaks to the east and west of our campsite reached to the heavens. Bathed in moonlight, I had the feeling of oneness that always filled me when I was in the wilderness. I lacked nothing.

Joining Jane in her unadulterated joy, I sang loudly and probably off-key. The mean girl part of me secretly hoped the sound was keeping Debra awake for her fourth night in a row. Maybe being exhausted would make her forget about trying to hike more miles a day. Alternatively, God forbid, it could just make her bitchier. I hoped Jenny was sleeping peacefully, dreaming of boys, fun, and, of course, good food.

Sucking up the last liquid at the bottom of our tin cups, Jane loudly said, "I'm fuckin' tired."

"I'm fuckin' tired, too." I giggled, finding the word 'fuck' coming out of my mouth more easily since being around Jane. We did a high-five slap and tossed our arms around each other in a bear hug. I felt warm from the inside out. Yawning, we crawled into our tent and sleeping bags.

"I gotta get some sleep and be ready for tomorrow. I'll show Debra who the better hiker is," Jane murmured from somewhere inside her bag.

"I'll be happy to wake up and be able to walk," I said in a tired wheezy voice. "I'm not even going to try and keep up, but *you go girl*." I reached under my coat I was using for a pillow and found my inhaler, then sucked on it long and hard as if slurping a soda. I did it three times even though I knew I was only supposed to use it twice. "Would it bother you if I wrote in my journal?"

"Nothing, including a fuckin' bear attack, could keep me awake, but you're going to need more than a journal to get you through this trip, girlfriend." She patted my shoulder and handed me a small paperback pamphlet with a picture of praying hands on it, *Science of Your Mind, Change Your Thinking Change Your Life.*

"Thanks," I said. I'd never known Jane to be religious, but there are lots of things friends don't know about each other.

"You can keep it," she said shyly. "You don't know when a little dose of God can come in handy."

"I'll need all the help I can get," I replied.

I listened carefully as my unconventionally spiritual friend mumbled while drifting off to sleep. "I'll pray for you, girlfriend, hoping you can do this journey for all us middle-aged women who need something or someone to believe in. Good night, good luck. You'll fuckin' need it."

Dear Diary,

Today was the first day of a seemingly impossible twenty-seven-day journey. I teach my second-grade students not to use the word can't. Instead, say "I'll try." Maybe that's all I can do.

Only hiked ten miles and I'm exhausted. Whatever made me think I could do this? All I did today was trudge along. I think that's what I'll be doing the whole journey if I find enough grit to go on. TRUDGE, TRUDGE, TRUDGE.

Need all the prayers, good thoughts, and support my friends and family can give me. My whole life Mom has told me I can do anything and be anybody I want. I mostly believe her. Hope I told my sons that enough times so they believe it, too. I want to be that kind of a mom. Smiley said I'm on a journey for every woman who is ordinary and wants to do something extraordinary. Where will I find the grit, health, and desire to continue? SCARED!

Preview Hike One: Day 2
July 12, 2004

I'm not sure it's a good sign when you go to sleep hungry and wake up feeling the same way. I've never been a morning person, but my tentmate was. She was up shaking me, "This place is fuckin' beautiful, Lori. You've got to get up and see it."

I tried to be enthusiastic. Wriggling out of my sleeping bag, I bumped my head when I sat up. I remembered the signs in car mirrors that said *Be careful as things may appear bigger than they are.* I had thought the tent was much bigger the night before.

Jane flailed around grabbing her clothes and toothbrush, getting ready to go out and greet the day. She poked her head out of the flap yelling, "Hey, you two up there trying to hide from us, what's for breakfast? Let's eat. I can hardly wait to see what's next on the agenda."

Jane could have been a phone sex operator; her voice has a raspy deep-throated quality, and her laugh was seductive, making men and women listen intently to what she said.

It surprised me when I heard no response from either Debra

or Jenny. I followed Jane out of the tent, beginning to feel some of her enthusiasm. Brilliant Sierra blue skies surrounded us. A red-tailed hawk made figure eights above the towering pines, and the crisp mountain air made me gasp. I tingled with anticipation of new adventures, and it helped numb the nagging pain in my back and feet.

Looking up the hill I spotted Debra. Even at a distance, she seemed to be glaring. She stomped toward us. I wondered what type of conversation she would have with Jane that morning. However, I had no interest in being the target of Debra's apparent anger and slunk back into the tent. Not wanting to miss any of the action, I peeped out of the flap. I'd learned long ago that avoidance served me well.

Standing alongside a massive pine tree with her hands on her slim hips, Debra barked, "You don't need to yell and bother everybody. We've been up for hours. I couldn't sleep so figured I'd get Jenny up and we'd get an early start."

"So, what's for breakfast? I'll be glad to prepare it," Jane said in her friendliest *eat shit* voice.

"You guys have the oatmeal in the bear canister inside your tent, so we couldn't cook it. I was trying to be nice and not disturb you. Apparently, you don't know much about the etiquette of backpacking or you wouldn't be hollering in the woods. Get Lori up and let's get going. We're losing the best part of the day."

Jane took an equally definitive stance, planting her hands on her hips, which she swayed while looking Debra straight in the eye. I raised the tent door a little bit higher, shamelessly enjoying the drama. Jane, who never ceased to amaze me, calmly and slowly stated in an even lower voice than usual, "Well, and a good morning to you, too. Isn't this just the most magnifico spot God ever created? I'm so glad to be a part of your little adventure. It was real nice of you to let us sleep in."

"I didn't *let* you do anything. I'm not in charge and don't want to be responsible for you." Debra stomped her foot.

"We'll make breakfast, then we can head out and see more of what I can only say is some of the most breathtaking land I've ever been privileged to walk. Lori told me about all the complex planning you did to make this happen, and I can't thank you enough. She's explained to me how much this hike means to her and how you've worked so hard to make it happen. So, girlfriend, let's eat." Without missing a beat, Jane pulled the stove out of my pack.

Even from where I so cowardly watched, I could see Debra was taken off guard. I silently cheered Jane on.

"Sounds good. Jenny and I'll be down in a few minutes," Debra mumbled.

I poked my head out of the tent and sheepishly looked up at Jane, "Thanks a lot. I'm sorry I wasn't there for you. I guess Debra intimidates me."

"Who can blame you? She's got big issues. I figure I'll try to kill her with kindness for a while and see how it works. I've got a feeling something really bad happened to her. Do you have any idea what it was?"

"Honestly, I don't know her that well, which is good and bad," I replied. "The bad part is if I'd known what she was like I might not have come on this trip. However, that's the good part, too. I think that's how life is, the good in something can also be the bad, and vice versa."

"You can say that again," Jane nodded.

"Her divorce wasn't pretty. She was stunned when her husband left her a couple of years ago. Maybe that's part of the problem. I know from seeing my mom raise us alone that it isn't easy."

Jane and I hurriedly prepared for the day. We worked well together in taking down camp and fixing a breakfast of oatmeal and dried fruit. Jane whistled as she worked and was fun to be around.

Her good cheer, combined with the feeling of exhilaration I got from being in the high country, made me actually look forward to hiking. I couldn't stop thinking about how much I wished Jane could be with me on more of the trip. Debra, Jenny, and I had one more three-day leg planned and then the last stretch of our journey was twenty-one continuous days. I had begged her to join us, unsure how I could make it without her. But she had previous commitments making it impossible for her to go any farther than the first three days would take us.

I could even see Debra succumbing to her charm while we were eating breakfast. "I've been on hundreds of horse rides, but this country can't be beat. The lakes, the mountains, the critters are incredible. I would love for some of my horse friends to see it," Jane said. "What do you guys think will be the hardest part of the hike?"

"For me, it's the passes," I said, "but it's such a treat when you get over them. The view yesterday when we went over Cathedral Pass was incredible. Heaven on earth."

"What was the elevation?" Jane asked.

"About 9,700 feet, isn't it, Debra?"

"I think so, but it's the lowest one we'll be going over, so don't be too sure of yourself."

"Making it over the pass made me confident I can do the others. The pinnacle of Cathedral Peak jutting toward the sky like a gothic spire reminded me of the man-made churches I've seen in Europe, but in my estimation, there's no contest. Cathedral Peak's the winner."

"The part I hate is getting up so early." Jenny tucked a loose strand of hair behind her ear. "But I liked the sunset and hearing you and Jane singing last night."

"The alpenglow was a great finale to the first day," Debra admitted.

"I missed my horse, but it surprised me how good it felt to

use my feet." Jane's blue eyes twinkled.

Remembering the good stuff, like the high-country high, made the blisters on my feet and the aching in my back a little easier to deal with. Jane talking nicely to Debra seemed to improve our situation. I figured I'd try to proceed along the same lines.

"I appreciate all the advance planning you've done for us, Debra. You were right to have us start the JMT in Tuolumne Meadows rather than go down to the valley," I said.

"I gave it lots of thought." Debra cracked a smile. Her lightly freckled face and warm brown eyes looked so much better when she wasn't angry. "It seemed smartest to start out easy."

"I couldn't agree more."

Starting preview hike one in Tuolumne Meadows and going down to the Yosemite Valley floor was the easiest. Many people did it the opposite way starting from Yosemite Valley and going up to Tuolumne. The route we were on for the first three days started at 8,400-ft and went up to 9,700-ft but then we got to hike down to Happy Isles which is in Yosemite Valley at about 4,000-ft. This meant most of preview one was going downhill.

I stretched my legs and took in the view, once again struck by the beauty surrounding us. I knew if I had to start in Yosemite Valley and gain that 5,000 foot elevation I'd never make it. Even with bad knees, I was a much better hiker going downhill than climbing uphill, in part because of my asthma. I again heard Sean's voice in my head, "You better get in shape if you want to hike that trail."

My knees throbbed going down hills but the hiking poles and knee braces seemed to be helping. The truth was I wasn't very good at walking either up or down. At times, I wondered why I enjoyed backpacking at all. I'd need something more than my ability to put one foot in front of the other to help me complete our two previews and the long haul.

My recent blisters were another matter. I rubbed my heels,

dreading what new damage I would do to my tattered feet as the day wore on. It was foolish to have started a hike with expensive new boots. I'd make sure to use my trusty old ones on the next leg of the trip. The only problem was, I had about a hundred miles of hiking on them and wasn't sure they'd last.

Like so many things that worked for me, my old hiking boot model had been discontinued. Equally frustrating, every comfortable bra I'd ever owned was no longer manufactured. So, I packed shirts that best disguised I wasn't wearing one while hiking.

Mom wouldn't have been happy about the no bra thing. She claimed going braless made for sagging boobs later in life. So far, I'd proved her wrong. Smiley often remarked, "You sure have perky boobs. Nobody'd ever guess you're married to an old fart like me."

The disgust on my son's faces when I whipped my bra off as soon as we got in our van to drive anywhere flashed through my mind. I remembered when Craig told me, "Hey Mamma, I found out you were lying. Not everybody's mom rips off their bra as soon as they enter a vehicle."

"I'm not everybody's mom, I'm yours," I said. Going braless helped me live a little on the wild side in my tame world.

That first part of the hike certainly showed me I'd over-estimated my abilities. However, I had my husband's words ringing in my head: "You can do it if you want to." At that point, with Jane's help, I wanted to. Debra not believing I could do the trip made me want to succeed even more.

As much as I wanted to linger, I got up and joined the others in making haste to get our campsites cleaned up after breakfast. Debra and Jenny came down the hill. Jane was ready to go and was fidgeting with the weight in her backpack, shifting from one foot to the other. Debra's fingers wrapped through her shoulder straps, her eyes darting back and forth between Jane and the trail.

I couldn't help but notice the two women sizing each other up. Obviously, I was no threat to Debra's alpha status. Jane was another matter altogether. Her barely contained animal energy and enthusiasm for the hike seemed to alternately amuse, agitate, and challenge Debra.

We swaggered toward the trailhead. It felt like the start of a race, the two of them strutting about like bantam roosters. I raised my eyebrows and looked at Jenny. She looked back and raised hers at me. I wondered if she was as curious as I was to see what would happen between her mom and Jane.

"We have a little more than ten miles to hike today." Debra began to pace. "If yesterday was any indication, you two will need all the daylight there is."

"I'll need the daylight, but Jane could hike this trail with the best of 'em," I said.

"Well, we're all in this together, right?" Jane turned toward me, her blue eyes sparkling. "I'm not planning on leaving you behind." Jane started pacing, too. "I'm sure Debra understands the issues with your feet. It won't hurt any of us to slow down."

"I'd be happier if you didn't," I said. "I'm very familiar with this part of the trail. I did it several times when I worked in Yosemite before I was married. You guys go ahead. I'll join you for lunch."

"Sounds good. Come on Jenny." Debra proceeded down the trail.

"I'll stay here. We'll take our time," Jane said, as we watched Debra and Jenny power hike off.

"Don't worry about me. I'd love to see you catch and out hike her. You'd be doing me a favor. Go for it." I could see Jane was torn between her loyalty to me and her desire to challenge Debra's cockiness. "Just save me some lunch. Anything besides those godforsaken energy bars."

"Are you sure?"

"Positive, girlfriend. Go," I pleaded. It was fun and rewarding to see Jane head out in a cloud of dust. It was even better seeing her catch and then blow past Debra and Jenny on the trail. I'd love to have seen Debra's face as Jane whizzed by.

I'd told Jane the truth: I didn't mind hiking alone. In fact, I enjoyed the time to think and daydream. It never bothered me to be at the end of a group. Staying back, you often got to see and experience things others missed. The old cliché *It's not a race but a journey* was my personal motto.

I'd earned my degree in parks and recreation and worked as a ranger for the Sierra National Forest at Big Sandy campground. I lived at Bass Lake in a tent before I met Smiley and got married. At twenty-five years old, we weren't parents yet, and I was in the best physical shape of my life.

Twice I'd gone on a solo backpack for a week. The rangers were supposed to go out with a partner, but one of the guys quit midseason. That meant I had to go out alone a couple of times during the summer. Those weeks tested my skills. The lonely howl of the coyotes, and sometimes not talking to anyone for days unnerved me. But remembering the good parts helped fuel my hunger to return to the wilderness I loved. I'd never been able to recapture the peace it afforded me.

Even with my physically challenged body, those memories reminded me I had what it took to hike the trail. As my three hiking partners left my view, the realization hit me that this just might be the way I traveled much of the JMT—alone, but not lonely.

Attitude is a huge factor in being able to do anything difficult, so I decided to enjoy the first part of the hike as much as I could. I had the uneasy feeling Debra would make up her mind that she didn't want me with her after all. My blisters made me walk slowly. I became lost in thought about all the money, time, and energy I'd spent getting ready for the trip.

As a teacher I got summers off, even though in the last few years that time was reduced to about two months. We spent part of our vacation cleaning up classrooms, getting caught up on curriculum, and working on getting ready for the next year. I also tried to rest, read books, and work on home projects I'd put off.

I also spent a lot of summertime in Utah visiting my mom who was fighting a second round of breast cancer. Living in Mariposa meant at least two days of driving or an expensive plane ticket to be with her. My feelings were torn about spending so much time away from her that summer. The doctors made it clear her time was limited.

At twenty-one-years-old, my mother found herself raising four kids. She'd given up most of her dreams to make us her priority. She never finished high school and had to pocket extra food at the grocery store. She dodged creditors by never answering the phone and often worked two or three menial jobs as a waitress and maid to provide for us. She wanted better for me. She had insisted I follow my dreams.

To keep my mind off the pain of my blisters and the ache in my knee, I focused on Mom and the other people I was missing this summer. While my boots ticked off miles, I ticked off memories. I remembered some of the comments people made when I said I was going to hike the JMT.

After telling Mom I'd be walking it for her, she laughed. "Follow your heart. Do it for yourself, dear. I never liked hiking. Sitting on a beach drinking a margarita in Hawaii is more my idea of a vacation."

My sister Rhonda said in no uncertain terms, "Don't tell me it is all fun, in your usual Pollyanna style. It's gonna be hell. But I know you'll do it."

Smiley laughed, "Better you than me. You'll be a whole different person when you return. I'm interested in seeing who that person will be."

Sean, my twenty-three-year-old son who had forewarned me to "get in shape," bragged to his firefighting buddies about his mom hiking the JMT. Those memories helped ease my foot pain and gave me incentive. Craig, who was twenty and in college, groaned when I called his dorm apartment the previous spring. I heard his comments (in response to my asking him to backpack fifteen miles to bring us a restock of food) repeatedly in my head as I trudged along, "Oh, God, no, not another nature hike to hell, Mamma. I hate hiking, but I guess I'll have to bring in the food. I can't let my mom backpack more than 200 miles and not even bring her food. This sucks!"

My boots kicked up dust and my poles dragged behind me as I kept putting one foot in front of the other. In spite of everything I felt good. Inhaling the sweet mountain air cleared my sinuses. Dry crisp pine needles crunched under my feet and for a while I forgot about my aches and pains. Two rotund fluffy marmots wrestled and played tag on the slippery granite rocks about fifty yards away.

I envied their carefree attitude. I couldn't help wondering where they'd found all that food to keep them so fat and happy. The trail blazed with color and even if I knew all the names of the flowers I'd never be able to recite them. A richness much greater than money surrounded me.

My stomach started rumbling. Hopefully Jane had waited for me farther up the trail. I had no illusions Debra or Jenny would be there.

I continued to think about the people in my life and what they'd said about my journey. Most of the teachers I worked with thought I was a little crazy anyway. One of them said, "That's nuts. The nearest I come to backpacking is condo camping."

Sharon, my most Zen teacher friend, told me, "I'll pray for you. What a wonderful spiritual journey you're going on. I'll be with you in prayer and thought."

"Hike the trail for me, feel the wind, see the blue skies, and keep it in your heart to share," Connie, my friend battling multiple myeloma, a rare form of cancer, beseeched me.

I plodded along remembering the courage she'd given me and the inspiration. Before the trip, we swam together daily in the town pool. She was on huge doses of chemo and, at first, could only do one lap. Every day she increased her distance. She was up to doing ten. She told me I inspired her, that if I could hike the JMT, she would at least get in shape and swim across Tenaya Lake, a small Sierra lake near Tuolumne Meadows in Yosemite. It was her long-time dream to swim it. I felt Connie's words guiding me.

I passed the part of the trail leading off to the right toward Half Dome. If it had been up to me, we would have taken time to go up the cables to the top. Most people hiking the JMT take time to climb it. The top of Half Dome gives an amazing 360-degree view of Yosemite Valley. But we weren't like most people. Debra clearly told us since she, Jenny, and I had ascended it previously we would not waste our energy doing it again.

The boys and I had gone to the top of Half Dome when they were teenagers. Craig and I pulled ourselves laboriously up the cables during the last 400 vertical feet on the east slope. Sean did somersaults in front of us. He was always my risktaker. If he slipped while on the cable section he would likely fall to his death. It was a calculated risk. When we arrived at the top, stunning views of Yosemite Valley unfolded like a miniature village. Glacier-formed granite slabs had glistened in the sunlight with only a trickle of water flowing from the famous Yosemite Falls.

It was worth seeing again. As I lamented the fact that Jane would miss it, I looked up and almost bumped into her. She was only about ten feet in front of me.

"Hey, girlfriend, I was beginning to worry about you. How're the feet? Ms. Mary Sunshine and her daughter went ahead and said they'd meet us in Little Yosemite Valley. Is that where we're doing our wilderness camping?"

"That's the place, all right, but don't bet on it being much of a wilderness experience. You'll see tons of people and likely lots of bears because of 'em."

Little Yosemite is the most highly impacted campground on the JMT because it's so close to Yosemite, the most populated national park in the United States. I couldn't blame the crowds. With its incredibly beautiful lush green meadows, cascading white foamed waterfalls, and massive granite cliffs enveloping it, Yosemite was something special. There are more sheer granite faces in Yosemite than anywhere else on earth. People from all over the globe come to climb and visit the amazing monoliths.

"I'd love to see some bears. Have you ever seen any?" Jane's eyes glowed in anticipation.

"Believe it or not, a bear touched me in Little Yosemite," I told her.

"No way. Did it attack you?"

"Luckily no. I was twenty and sleeping outside. It wanted the food I'd foolishly left in a bag next to me. At first, I thought my guy friend sleeping beside me was touching me but his hands felt very hairy. I also wondered why he was hitting on me in the middle of the night. We'd always been just friends and it seemed weird."

"What in the hell did you do?"

"I woke up and heard Ken whispering in my ear, telling me to be quiet for a minute, that a bear was touching me. I don't know how, but I managed to stay still. It finally took its paw off and mercifully didn't hurt me."

"Oh my God, then what happened?"

"There was chomping, ripping, and groaning as it ate up our rations. Ken got a pot and lid and banged them together, shouting at the bear to leave us alone."

"How cool." She smiled wide, her white teeth gleaming. "Have you ever seen another one?"

"I've seen lots of them. Most were on the trail we will be going on to Little Yosemite."

"Were you scared?"

"Sure. Once, hiking with my sons, coming down from Half Dome, we saw one and we were all so tired we could barely muster up the energy to scream and holler at him so he'd leave us alone. That's what you're supposed to do. Make lots of noise and scare them off."

"I thought bears didn't like people. I haven't seen any on my horse rides. Maybe the horses and dogs we bring keep them away."

"You're probably right. However, the thing attracting bears isn't people, it's their food. One night at Little Yosemite there was another very funny bear scare, one I'll never forget."

"Tell me," Jane insisted, as we continued along at a pace I could maintain. I was slowing her down, but she didn't seem to mind.

"Well," I continued, "my friend Nan and I had taken our kids to the campground and we were finally bedded down. There were hundreds of people camped all around. It resembled a big urban campground including outhouses and some campers who partied well into the wee hours of the night."

"I like a good party, but there's a time and a place." Jane squinted in the bright sunshine rubbing her hands together.

"I always have to get up to go to the bathroom. At midnight, I headed for the john, shivering. I heard all sorts of stomping feet, loud voices, and rustling branches."

"What was it?"

"Reaching the outhouse, I saw a naked man with a hot dog raised above his head. He was running through the trees and shouting, "There's a bear after me!"

"Calm down. Maybe you've lost him," I said, looking around.

"I think he wants my hot dog," the man stammered.

"Why didn't he drop the damn thing?" Jane asked.

"I think he was too scared. He lowered the hot dog to about waist level. I couldn't help seeing other parts of his anatomy while I gazed at the piece of meat. I was laughing so hard I started crying."

"What a hoot," Jane chuckled.

"My boys came running from our tent, and I heard lots of thudding footsteps. People were joining me, curious to see what all the ruckus was about. Several of them shined flashlights at the man, who froze in his tracks."

"What are you doing out here naked?" one of the campers demanded, holding his sides in laughter.

Looking around with crazed eyes, the man replied, "This is *not* what I thought a wilderness experience would be like. This is certainly *not* the wilderness."

Another man snickered. "No shit, Sherlock. So, take your hot dog and beat it."

"What a great story."

"Sean and Craig still talk about it to this day. *This is not a wilderness experience* are words that honestly convey what Little Yosemite is like. I just wanted to warn you."

"Can't wait to join in the fun. Do you think Debra will save us a campsite?"

"Hope so. It isn't easy to find one. We should get there soon. Have you noticed all the people we've seen on the trail? That's a pretty good indicator we're near."

"They're sure friendly, though. Hope Debra has been taking some Happy Camper lessons from them." Jane began whistling and swinging her arms as she walked over and sat down on a boulder. "Let's have some lunch. I'm starved."

"You know me, always ready to eat." I threw my pack on the ground.

Because this trip was only three days long, we brought some fresh food. That morning we had taken it out of the bear canisters and put our own individual lunches in our backpacks.

Lunch consisted of dried jerky, cheese, oranges, and trail mix. I also poured my amazing orange flavored Emergen-C powder packets into our water.

Jane guzzled it down. "I don't know if it's because I want to believe it, but this shit actually makes me feel peppier."

"It works for me."

After traveling a bit farther, we noticed a group of young people working along the trail. The winter rains had made a mess of the wooden water bars that helped make the trails navigable. Their shovels clinked and banged tossing rocks to the side. A voice called out, "Hey, is that really you, Mrs. Tierney?"

I turned towards the voice and wondered which one of my previous students it was. My sons regularly complained they couldn't go anywhere without someone knowing me. We live in a small town and I had taught hundreds of kids and met many of their parents. Sean often commented that it was nearly impossible for him to get away with anything.

A teenage girl with a dirty face, lopsided grin, and long swinging brown braids ran over and put her arms around me, or at least as much of me as she could since I was still encased in my pack. "It's so good to see you up here. I didn't know you backpacked."

"Yup, I actually do other things besides teach. I haven't done a lot of it since my boys were born, but I'm here now, hiking the JMT," I bragged. As soon as I said it, I knew I shouldn't have. The short portion we'd done didn't mean I'd finish the whole thing. I could feel my face flush in embarrassment and exertion from the few miles of hiking I'd accomplished that day. To top it off I heard my lungs making wheezing kitten sounds.

"Wow," the girl said, wiping sweat off her face with a tie-dye bandana she took from her hair. "I haven't seen you since second grade. I'm working on the trail crew to get out of my house. I have five brothers and sisters, and when I'm home all I do is babysit and clean. My friends call me Cinderella."

"How could I forget you? You worked so hard in class and gave the best hugs."

"You were always my favorite teacher. I loved the hugs you gave me, too, and the way you played your guitar. It reminded me of singing around the campfire."

"Thanks, Josie. It's always good to see one of my students outside of school." She had grown lanky and was swinging her arms from side to side.

"You even remembered my name," she smiled. "Where you headed?"

"Little Yosemite. We should almost be there."

"That's where we're stationed. It's about a mile. There's a campfire tonight, you'd have fun. Come sing with us," Josie said.

"Well, shucks," Jane said in her deepest voice. "We love singin' so you can count on us. I'm particularly good at doin' cowpoke songs. I'm a horse person, but this teacher of yours dragged me out here. It's sure different usin' your own two feet."

Josie swung her shovel back and forth while running toward her coworkers. "It starts at eight. Hope you can make it," she said over her shoulder.

Thank heavens we only had another mile or so to go. If my throbbing feet could talk they would have been swearing at me. When I thought I couldn't take another step, I noticed the trail marker showing us the cut off to Little Yosemite. We could also hear lots of people which was a clue, too. I had a bad feeling in my gut about getting a site. Jane looked at me expectantly.

"Let's wander through. Maybe we'll find Debra and Jenny,"

I said.

Friendly people waved and said "hi" as we strolled through the area.

Almost at the end, someone yelled, "Hey Lori, we're over here." I recognized Jenny's voice and smiled. She ran toward me, her brown ponytail swinging. "I saved you guys a site by us. Hope it's OK."

"I'm sure it'll be great." I looked around and saw that the campground was jam packed with people. Clothes were strung on trees and ensolite pads were strewn about. Only the beauty of the area kept it from being mistaken for a homeless camp. Jenny had done us a favor saving us a spot. "Thanks. Where's your mom?"

"She's down at the river bathing." Jenny rolled her eyes.

"Let's put our stuff down and join her," Jane said.

We pulled swimsuits from our packs and followed Jenny to the swirling icy blue river meandering through the campground. People were fishing and lounging all along the edge of it. Temperatures soared around 90 degrees, and we were eager to cool down and relax by joining other hikers in the water. The river would be the best place to wash off trail dirt. I couldn't wait to jump in.

We changed into our suits behind some trees. Jane's bright multi-colored bikini made me feel dowdy in my worn black matronly one piece. She had birthed two sons, but it didn't stop her from strutting about. We didn't have the flat stomachs of our youth, but she wasn't letting anything bother her. She squealed, laughing and running toward the water. I followed.

About forty feet to the left, we spotted Debra. She'd gone one step further than Jane and was bathing nude. She kept busy washing her hair using the regular shampoo she'd insisted on bringing even though I'd pleaded with her not to. It was bad for the environment. But, Debra lived by her own standards. If a rule served her purpose, she followed it. Otherwise, forget it. If I had the guts, I would have thrown her the biodegradable stuff Jane and I brought. I personally didn't even use that on my hair in the water. It was best to use only in campsites.

I had to admit Debra was the fittest of us all and had managed to maintain her youthful figure. She was as skinny as the day I met her, and I couldn't help but feel beyond frumpy next to her. Smiley claimed she needed some more meat on her bones.

I suspected he said those things to make me feel better. I remembered how he'd patted my ample butt when he told me that maybe my hiking the JMT would help me stop asking the boys and him to hike with me. He had said this while munching on a cookie, "You know dear, we hate backpacking but love you. I've been a firefighter too long to find sleeping on the ground appealing. Even your voluptuous body can't entice me."

"That's the spirit," said Jane, flinging off her swimsuit. "My birthday suit will serve me well out here." She dove gracefully off of a nearby rock outcropping.

I looked longingly at the two of them free from the confinement of clothing, the water rushing over their bare bodies. The men, women, and children around the river seemed to care less if Jane and Debra were nude. I'd never thought of myself as a prude, but even in my top form during my younger years, I couldn't have been coaxed to bathe naked with an audience. That day was no exception.

I jumped in. Jenny joined me in the water, wearing a suit, too. My boys often commented on the fact that people who should swim nude don't, and those who shouldn't do. I'm sure I belonged in the category of those who shouldn't and Jenny with those who should.

The cool water felt delicious and made goosebumps rise on my skin. We swam, played, and splashed until the sun slunk behind the trees. Climbing out of the sparkling water, we lay on our backs to dry. Debra joined us, and I admired her lack of modesty. After basking for a few minutes in what was left of the day's warmth we put our clothes on and headed back to set up camp.

"We met one of Lori's previous students working on the trail. She told us there's a campfire tonight," Jane told Debra and Jenny as we walked.

"That might be fun." Debra squeezed the water out of her hair with her hands.

"I'd like to go," Jenny said with a sparkle of yearning in her eyes. She probably wanted to hang around people her own age. "What was her name?"

"Josie Collier," I replied.

"Oh, I know her from school." Jenny smiled.

Dinner went well until Jane decided to make some pudding for us in the same pan we'd cooked stew. Debra narrowed her eyes in irritation. She informed us in her most patronizing voice that it was not OK to cook dessert in the same container other food had been cooked in.

"We washed the damn pan first. What are you so pissed about?" Jane said while drying it.

"Once again, you're doing a no-no," Debra said. "You don't know anything about backpacking, do you?"

I wasn't sure if she was talking to Jane, me, or both of us. The *not cooking dessert in the same pan as other food* was an addendum to the camping I was used to. Weren't we supposed to be packing light?

Jane ignored Debra and finished cooking. She passed me some pudding in a Sierra cup and proceeded to chow down on hers from the pan.

"I want my share. Don't forget to wash the pan again since you're the ones who had to have dessert," Debra said reaching out for her portion.

"I'll be glad to wash it," replied Jane, handing Debra the rest of her pudding. I continued eating mine without offering to share. It tasted better than anything we'd eaten in the last forty-eight hours. Without comment, Debra took the pan and scooped some out with her spoon. "For not wanting any you sure seem to be liking it. How about sharing with Jenny?"

"Give me a chance." Debra took several more bites and handed it to Jenny.

"I'm not hungry." Jenny turned away and headed toward their camp. Debra followed, leaving the dirty pan.

Jane banged it loudly on a rock several times before washing it. We then walked over to Debra and Jenny's campsite. "We're ready to go. Wanna join us?" I asked.

"We'll come later. I don't want to feel responsible if you lose your flashlight or anything else. I'm sick of telling you two what to do. I don't want to be in charge," Debra said.

Jane and I shook our heads in unison and left.

It was a full moon, so we hadn't packed a flashlight. That put some bite into Debra's bark, making me feel foolish.

"My God, do you think she's bipolar or something?" whispered Jane as we continued to head to the campfire.

"I'm not aware of it," I replied. "People do change over the years. She's certainly not the happy-go-lucky girl I used to know. We always had time for a laugh when we worked for the forest service and rode on the back of Smiley and her ex's motorcycles. She laughed the loudest and had the best jokes. I can't remember a punch line to save my life."

At the campfire, the wood crackled and red flames licked the evening air. Teenagers on the trail crew sang loudly and sounded good. One of them strummed a guitar. Josie convinced me to play a song I do for my second graders. It was a favorite of theirs, about a woman who had a crazy mixed up body. The title of the song had fifty-six letters and they always got a kick out of it: *Hagdalina Magdalena Hootenstiner Whatinhimer Hogan Logan Pogan.*

It felt good to be the one making music. Everyone clapped and joined in on the chorus. I looked around. I noticed Jenny and

Debra across from us; I was glad they had decided to come. Jenny had a smile on her face and was sitting with the kids singing along. She looked happier than I'd seen her on the whole trip. Debra sat next to her, arms folded across her chest.

The best part of the night was the s'mores. The gummy-burnt marshmallows melting the chocolate bars on graham crackers tasted every bit as good as the night before when Jane and I shared them. I couldn't seem to get food off my mind.

Debra and Jenny left the campfire early. My gut feeling was Debra didn't want to deal with us. I wasn't worried. The full, vibrant blue moon shone brightly and would pave the way to our campsite. Debra wouldn't have to find out we'd forgotten our flashlights.

At the end of the evening, Josie came over. Like a responsible camper, big sister, and the prepared student she'd been in my class, she held a flashlight in her hands. I had a feeling she knew we'd forgotten ours.

"Thanks for playing the guitar and singing with us, Mrs. Tierney. I'd be happy to walk you back to your campsite."

"You're a sweetheart, but we'll be fine. The moon and the stars will be our beacons." The only thing brighter than them might have been the joy filling me and warming my heart. I'd always loved and reveled in a Sierra moon hike. The trail glowed and shimmered, casting friendly guiding shadows on the trees and rocks surrounding us. How could we get lost?

Hugging me tightly and laying her head on my shoulder, Josie's muffled voice replied, "Have a great summer, Mrs. Tierney. You deserve one."

For the second night in a row, I went to sleep with the comforting taste of s'mores in my mouth, but I couldn't stop the knot in my stomach telling me I was in over my head. I knew the trail grew steeper, and after the first little part of the trip, there would be no more Jane. I rolled back over and pulled out my journal to write under the moonlight.

Dear Diary,

Feet hurt, back aches, and stomach tells me something isn't right. Had a chance to go to Hawaii for my 51st birthday. Why in the hell did I choose this trip instead? Must have been nuts. Smiley offered to use his overtime money to pay for it. He's tight with his money sometimes and it bothers me. I never had much growing up, but I had a mother who loved me unconditionally. Love makes me rich.

Smiley is a middle child with seven siblings and can't remember his mom ever saying she loved him. I get it that he equates money with security. Spending a little extra makes him nervous.

Maybe I could have brought Mom with us to Hawaii. She's always wanted to go and probably won't get another chance. Smiley loves her, says she's the mom he never had. Bet I could've convinced him to pay her way. One of her gifts is she never lets me talk shit about him to her. There's some shit I sure would have liked to talk about. Like maybe he could scour a toilet or pick up groceries once in a while? She said it's our own private business and she loves both of us just the way we are. Can't even imagine my life without her.

She can't die. I won't let her. If I close my eyes, mom's smiling face is chuckling at me. "Lori, you always were hard headed. Follow your dream. I'm proud of you."

Tomorrow's Jane's last day. Keep reminding myself 99% of doing something happens in your head. What you believe in, you become.

If I keep hiking the JMT, I need to bring pictures of my family. Miss them already. Reading the Science of Mind *book Jane gave me helps calm my spirit. Tonight, it told me to just BE. Embrace life. Guess I will. What other choice is there?*

Preview Hike One: Day 3
July 13, 2004

"Today's another day of livin' and hikin,'" Jane shouted as she rolled out of her sleeping bag like a sausage escaping its casing. She ducked, ready to escape the confines of our tent. She looked down at me with a wide lopsided grin and it was easy to see she was excited. I couldn't tell if it was because it was the last day she had to spend on the trail or if she was enjoying the whole backpacking scene. I wondered if this would be my last day, too. The blisters on my feet were screaming, and my back hollered with them.

Feeling even older than my fifty years made me question what I was doing out in the wilderness with a crazy woman and her sixteen-year-old daughter. Jane, on the other hand, was helpful, and made me laugh. She was my feel-good friend, one of those people who made life better. I felt certain the fun would stop after she left us. I couldn't imagine continuing the hike without her.

We crawled out of our tent. Debra and Jenny were stuffing sleeping bags. The pungent aroma of strong coffee filled the air.

Its taste had never appealed to me, but it smelled divine. I inhaled, hoping somehow the fumes would give me strength.

"Nothing better than a cup of coffee to get me goin,'" Jane strutted as I silently tagged along heading to Debra and Jenny's campsite.

"Well, you better make it yourself," Debra replied. "We already drank ours and are ready to go. I didn't get but maybe two hours of sleep."

"I could use some coffee and don't mind making my own. You're welcome to have some more if you want." Jane started up my stove that sat on the rock by their camp.

Not liking coffee was going to stand me in good stead if I decided to continue this trip. I'd be content smelling it, and Debra would be happy not having to share. A bargain. Needing some get up and go, I grabbed a container of Emergen-C from my pack. The little caffeine rush would be nice. I could already tell it was going to be a terrible, horrible, no good, very bad day.

"We're in a hurry to get to the bottom of the trail and won't be waiting around for you guys," Debra said, her thin lips snarled in contempt.

Jenny stood off to the side, saying nothing.

"So, what else is new?" Jane asked. "You're always in a hurry. I thought this was supposed to be a sightseein' trip."

"I've seen this part of the trail too many times, but I need to do this section so I can say I've done it while hiking the JMT." Debra shaded her eyes from the sun. She hadn't brought sunglasses. Probably thought the two ounces were needless weight.

"Jane's never been on this hike before. I know it's tourist infested, but it's still incredibly beautiful." I took a sip of my drink. "She shouldn't miss out."

"I've got to get back to work. Some of us don't have time to sightsee."

I looked over at Jane. "Let's stop and look at Nevada and Vernal Falls. We'll want to take pictures, especially if there's a rainbow over the path by Vernal."

"That'd be bitchin'. I'm up for it."

"No matter how many times I've been there, I still love it. When the mist from the falls splashes my face, I feel alive. It can caress you like baby's breath or can feel like a tropical storm pelting your skin. A rainbow arches from the top and plops itself across the trail as if waiting for a leprechaun to come hunting it." My hands and arms helped me tell the story as they flailed around.

"There's so much more of the trail. You're silly to waste time on this part," Debra interjected as she paced.

"It is a sight to see," I responded. "You might rethink bringing your camera along, Debra. This is a trip of a lifetime for you and Jenny."

"We'll remember it in our heads. A camera and film add too much weight. If you want to you can take some pictures for us in another area. Jenny and I've hiked this section a million times."

"I guess we'll see you in Yosemite Valley," I said as she swished off.

Turning around and staring at me, she nodded, "Don't take forever. We'll meet you at Curry Village noonish. If it takes much longer, you'll have to hitchhike. My truck won't be around after that."

Hitchhiking hadn't been in my repertoire since I was in my twenties. If I had to do it, it would be nice to have Jane along. Her Cheshire cat smile, sultry voice calling out to the cars, and the way she seemed to dance even when standing still would make getting a pick up easier. Alone, I didn't think I'd get a ride. Who would pick up a mosquito bitten, dirty, tired, fifty-year-old? Oh, to be twenty again. And skinny. A better idea was to pack our stuff and get out of Little Yosemite Valley so we wouldn't have to worry. I was certain Debra would keep her promise and leave us if we weren't there by noon.

All around us, Little Yosemite campground teemed with people, resembling a water park more than a wilderness area. Jane and I packed and were ready in about twenty minutes. Our breakfast of hot cereal and dried fruit gave me energy. Debra's threat of leaving us pushed me to put boots on in spite of the blisters. Pulling myself up with my hiking poles I began to plod along. While walking I remembered the details Debra had arranged for the trip and tried to convince myself they compensated for her less than pleasant company.

If you've ever had cactus needles sticking in your feet, you might have a good sense of the state of mine. My blisters had transformed from small pockets of pain to mountainous reservoirs of oozing pus. The moleskin wasn't helping much. The gooey yellow stuff stuck to my socks and shoes making it impossible to walk without limping like a lame dog.

"How're the feet, girlfriend?" Jane asked.

"Horrible, but thanks for asking. I'm trying not to think about them. It won't be easy, so if I whine, ignore it. I'm an idiot for wearing new boots."

I'm a lazy hiker and enjoy the flat parts best. I also like going downhill because it's easier on my breathing and requires less energy than going up. The seven miles we'd be hiking that day were all downhill. The bad thing about descending is the amount of pressure it puts on your feet and knees. I remembered reading that for every extra pound you had on your body it put five pounds on your knees. I did the calculation in my head and packing 175 pounds beyond what I was already carrying was not a pleasant thought. My knees were supporting a whole extra person. No wonder they creaked and moaned.

We hiked away from the campground and proceeded down the unpopulated trail. The sudden quiet soothed my senses.

"It's only a little way until we spot Nevada Falls, Jane. I bet there's not a waterfall as pretty anywhere else in the world, and there should be lots of water. We had good snowpack last year."

Each step felt more miserable than the last. I couldn't believe I hadn't packed flip-flops to wear in camp. They'd exited from my pack when Debra flung them aside after her light gear inspection. "These are extra weight. You don't need two pair of shoes," she'd said. Wishing fervently I still had them, I realized I might end up hiking barefoot. Definitely not advised in the guidebooks.

"I hear water ahead," Jane said.

"You're right."

A few minutes later, we rounded a corner and caught our first glance of the falls.

"Fuckin' A. What an orgasmic sight!" Jane stopped in her tracks. Wide, pulsing, and voluptuous, its sound alone was enough to make you breathless. Cascading water sent volumes of spray into our faces as we hiked, refreshing my body and spirit.

A mile or so farther we found ourselves at Vernal Falls. We peered over the ledge, holding onto the metal rail, and taking in the rushing falls cascading below. My breath caught in my throat, and not from asthma. The cables on the narrow rock ledge helped maintain our balance as we scurried down the steep trail.

Approximately halfway to the bottom of the falls we stopped to look behind us. Jane gasped. Mist surrounded emerald green mossy rocks on each side of the path. A rainbow starting at the top of Vernal Falls arched over the trail like a postcard picture of Ireland at its most lush.

Somewhere Over the Rainbow played in my mind. Jane clearly had the same thought. She spread her arms wide and lifted her head to the heavens. Her throaty contralto resonated in the canyon. I liked singing on the trail but usually felt too embarrassed.

I looked around. *What the hell.* I lifted my head and arms, singing along. Several people with large smiles on their faces chimed in as they passed by. I sang louder. Being with Jane did that for me.

After getting a fit older woman on the trail to take our picture, we hiked the mile and a half to the bottom in record time. Arriving in Yosemite Valley, Debra and Jenny were nowhere to be seen. Luckily, I knew where the truck was parked. Jane and I scrambled onto a shuttle that dropped us at Curry Village. I was surprised when I saw Debra and Jenny at the truck waiting.

"Hurry up and load your gear so we can get home. Some of us have to work tomorrow. I'm beat," Debra said.

"We need to pee. We'll be right back." Taking off my pack I headed to the bathroom doing the best rendition of running I could under the circumstances. Jane soon caught up.

"Don't breathe while peeing," Jane admonished, as we went into the bathroom stalls. "The hiking Nazi waits for no one."

We didn't talk much on the ride to Debra's house. I was exhausted. When we arrived, Jane broached the subject of my talking to Debra as we unloaded our gear and put it into my car.

"I'm worried. I hate to have you out there with Debra acting the way she does. Ask her what the problem is, or I will."

"Give me a few minutes."

We went into Debra's home and used the toilet and made some phone calls.

Afterwards, I stepped into the living room to confront Debra, my nerves taut. "Can I talk to you?" I asked. Jane stayed in the other room, petting the dogs.

Debra crossed her arms over her chest, glaring at me from her seat on her padded leather couch. "I don't have a lot of time or energy, so make it fast."

Forcing myself to look back at her while speaking I said, "I have the feeling you're sorry you asked me on this backpack trip. You act as if you think I can't do it, and that makes me feel awful. Let me know if you want me to quit. You and Jenny can hike the trail without me."

"I think you can do it, but do you?"

"I thought we'd kind of worked things out last winter when we had those planning meetings. It seems like lots of things we discussed you've now decided to change. Not bringing a map bothers me the most, so if I go on, I'll get my own."

"This whole thing has been a lot harder to plan than I thought. You're right, if you want maps, you need to bring them," Debra said.

"I know both of us spent a lot of time and money, but I wish you'd tell me now if you don't want me with you."

"Jenny and I aren't quitting. You shouldn't either. I thought things went pretty well under the circumstances. Some of Jane's language bothered me. Honestly, I'm glad she won't be coming with us."

I shifted my weight, gaining traction. I wouldn't let her talk about my friend without responding. "I'm not. There were times if Jane hadn't been there I wouldn't have been able to go on. I'm having a hard time imagining carrying all the gear and hiking without her to cheer me up. "

She sighed. "You've got to be the one to decide if you want to come or not, but don't expect any money back. I'm broke."

"I'll see how my blisters are in the next four days and let you know."

"Sounds good. For what it's worth, Jenny said she's glad you're with us. Good luck with the blisters. Drive safe." She stood up and started toward the bathroom. Jenny appeared and followed us outside.

As we were driving away, Jane leaned out the window and blew kisses. "These are for you, Jenny. Hang tough."

That night at home, after I'd caught Smiley up on all the news, I plopped down on our squishy couch with my two tiny terriers snuggled next to me.

Dear Diary,

Coming home to a broken-down fridge with smelly rotten fish inside was not pleasant. However, Jane, her husband Wes, Smiley, and I drinking beer and wine and eating dinner together was fun. A minor miracle: Wes, before being a cop, had been a refrigerator repairman and could fix it. In a roundabout way, Jane helped make things right for me at home as she'd done on the trail.

The trip didn't sound nearly as formidable when we were laughing, drinking, and eating. We all got drunk. Unusual for me. Felt great, and I wasn't sorry. God, it'll be good to sleep in a bed with Smiley next to me snoring his head off. Fresh food, water to drink without filtering, a toilet, and a warm shower did much to improve my mood. IT'S ALL GOOD. That's Jane's favorite saying. Think I'll make it one of mine.

First Set of Interim Days at Home
July 14, 2004

I woke up in the morning almost as stiff and sore as I'd been on the trail. Smiling lazily, I remembered the best part of the night before, and the fun Smiley and I had together. As mad as Smiley sometimes made me, the way he communicated so poorly, and had such a difficult time ever being wrong or saying he's sorry, we still enjoyed lots of things as a couple, not the least of which was sex. Would I miss it on the trail hiking for thirty days or would I be too exhausted to care?

The two of us met when we were in our mid-twenties. I was working a summer job for the Forest Service near Yosemite; he was a firefighter for them. He was the weirdest man I ever met. This guy with long hair, a climber. A crazy man. He drove motor-cycles. I thought, my gosh, I'm not interested in a relationship. I wanted to be free. I was twenty-five. I wanted to travel.

But, we fell crazy in love. Back then, living in a small conservative town, Smiley didn't think it was a good idea for us to just live together. We knew each other only five months before getting married. People asked us if we were insane or if I was pregnant. Since I wasn't pregnant, maybe I'd been a little rash, surely more than a bit infatuated.

My beer drinking, cigarette smoking, wild mountain hubby had not been anything like the man I'd imagined myself marrying. We'd defied the odds, though some days I wondered how. He was stubborn. When he said he was going to do or not do something, there was no backing down. After I told him my last boyfriend tried to make me feel guilty by crying all the time, I asked him to please not cry. From there forward, no matter what, he hid his sadness from me. He refused to share the stories of his service when he was a sniper in the Vietnam War. Said it didn't matter anymore because he was living a different life. I respected those parts of him but these things exacted a toll on our marriage.

He didn't know how to argue and often times walked away in the heat of a disagreement, leaving me screaming to an empty room. That morning I couldn't decide if I wanted to stick close by him or brave the JMT again with Debra the Nightmare.

Groaning, I contemplated the fact there were only four days to get ready for the second part of our trip. My blisters didn't let me forget about them for a moment. I headed to the bathroom and glanced at the clock—9:30 a.m. What a luxury to sleep in after rising with the sun and hurrying onto the trail.

Only the idea that maybe I'd lost some weight got me out of bed. I yanked off my nightgown. Every woman knows it's better to weigh yourself first thing in the morning, naked. I ran to use the toilet and rid myself of every extra ounce of fluid.

I took the scale from the closet and placed in on the tiled bathroom floor. Holding my breath, I inched my toes forward, stepping on its cool smooth glass as lightly as possible. Sucking in my stomach, and closing my eyes, I gave the numbers time to adjust. I looked down and gasped.

Not only had I not lost weight, I'd gained a pound. How

could this have happened? Then I remembered the night before—all the food and booze—and was more than a little pissed off I couldn't continue to indulge after so much hard work on the trail.

Since I hadn't lost any weight, I tromped over to raid the fridge. Luckily, most of the food was still good, even after the fridge had broken down. Three pancakes, large glasses of milk and juice, and six sausages made the day seem brighter. Plans for the morning were to doctor my feet and meet my friend Nan for a swim.

With age sometimes comes wisdom, and two of my favorite sages were the Seeleys, Ralph and Flo. They had an outdoor pool where I was meeting Nan, my longtime hiking buddy with a head of spiral curls like mine. To celebrate their forty-sixth wedding anniversary, they'd hiked to Cathedral Lakes, a ten-mile hike in the Sierra at 9,000 ft. They also ambled daily along Mariposa roads picking up trash along the way.

Ralph was working in his vegetable garden when we arrived. He dropped his hammer and waved in our direction then slowly made his way over to greet us, his body curled over like a C from arthritis. Nan and I joined them at the side of the pool. "Hi." He clasped our hands. "So good to see you."

He and Flo disappeared inside the house for a few minutes before reappearing in swimsuits. Ralph lowered himself slowly and deliberately into the water, resembling an old turtle with limbs spread. Flo's white hair shimmered in the sunlight like new-fallen snow as she dived in. She swam laps in a way I'd never been able to, her stroke a pleasure to watch.

With great humor, they told Nan and me stories about their lifetime adventures. They were seventy-five, still vibrant, and excited about life. Their tales gave me hope, and Flo's comment made me chuckle, "We might get a little lap dog when we get old."

"I need to tell you something, Lori." Flo looked over at me while dogpaddling. "I told some people at the Methodist church about your JMT journey, and a few folks asked me who you were going with. When I told them Debra they were aghast. They said she's tried to get other folks to hike with her, but nobody else would go because of her temperament. I hope it's OK, but I asked everyone to pray for you."

"Thanks. I take help wherever I can get it. My Mormon friends are saying prayers for me in Utah, and Nan, who's Jewish, and Carol, a Buddhist, are doing the same. You know they say it takes a village to raise a child. I think for me to finish the JMT it will take all my friends and family, of every faith or nonfaith praying for me or sending out good thoughts."

"Good for you. That's the spirit." Ralph swam with slow deliberation toward the edge of the pool. We all joined him.

"I'm not sure I can do it. I can't keep up."

Ralph's thick white eyebrows arched over his deeply lined face. "Why try? If you'll indulge me, I'll tell you about the 3,000-mile cross-country bike trip Flo and I took. We were sixty-two years old."

"Oh, I remember reading about it in the paper. What an accomplishment," I said, getting out of the pool and wrapping my towel around me. I sat in a well-worn deck chair.

"You two are my heroes," Nan inserted.

"Well, believe me, it wasn't a piece of cake," Ralph continued, "Was it Flo?"

"No. A lot was just plain hard work," Flo said. "There were people biking who didn't want us to be there. One in particular was a mean, unlikeable man half our age. We thought of him as *Scowling Richard.* He told us we were holding everybody back because we were just too old."

"He kept waiting for us to drop out. I think his lousy attitude made us try harder. Maybe that's what you should do, prove Debra wrong and don't let her negative thinking get to you," Ralph said.

"As an older woman and a hiker, I would love to see you do

it," Flo said.

"I would feel like a quitter if I stopped now," I replied.

"It'd give me hope. I'm already forty-three but look forward to finding the time and energy to hike it myself someday," inserted Nan. "You're my role model."

"Connie, my friend battling cancer, asked me to do it for her. To see, feel, taste everything, and bring it home to share with her. My son Craig has arranged his work schedule to lug in food for me, and my dear friend Trisha will check on my dogs and house."

"Sounds like you're better off than you think." Flo handed out plums we munched on.

"I'll take it easy and hope my feet get better. If that happens I'll take it as a sign I'm supposed to continue. Things always look better after a good night's rest. None of us slept well on the trail. I've noticed as I get older the thing I like least about backpacking is not being able to sleep. I can't ever seem to make it through the night."

"Yup, I can relate," Nan said.

"Getting up to go to the bathroom is another thing. I have a friend who carries a plastic bottle and just goes in it. I haven't done it yet, besides Debra would probably ding me for the extra weight of the bottle. Does anyone in their fifties or older get through the night without peeing?" I asked.

"Nope," Flo said. We all plopped back into the pool and continued to swim.

My resting days flew by. I continued to nurse my feet and, amazingly, they were healing. The pain lessened and the oozing pus slowly diminished. I tended my garden, walked my dogs, slept late, and ate lots of food I wouldn't have on the trail.

Nan, Jane, and Trisha phoned, cheering me on. Jane even offered me her horse. Mom called, saying, "I'm fine dear, just get tired a little easier. Be strong for both of us."

My boys were enjoying all the food we were eating. They frequently joined us for meals. The gooey calorie laden desserts were their favorite part of my interim stay. "It's fine with me if you want to quit, Mom. I'm not too hot on packing stuff into you anyway. You'd get us both off the hook," Craig said one night at dinner.

"Maybe you're right," I replied.

Sean, who usually remained silent, stopped eating and looked me straight in the eye. "You never let us quit anything easily. You said if things get tough, the tough get going. I believed you. I know you can do it, if you want to."

I glanced at my son, who was then more a man than a boy and realized how much he looked and thought like his dad. Smiley had said almost those exact words to me.

My husband was called out for a fire assignment my third day home. We had slept in each other's arms surrounded by warm puppy breath and the small curled fur-bodies of our two little terriers.

Smiley woke me up, leaned over, took me in his arms, and administered a long, sweet kiss, nonchalantly saying, "Since you won't be here when I get back that'll have to keep you for a while. Have fun." He then pursed his lips, rounding them, making loud sucking noises while trying to fish kiss me. He knew how much that irritated me.

"I'm not so sure how much fun I'll have." I wriggled away from his carp mouth. "I'll miss you."

"I love you three times more." He walked out the door without a backward glance.

I realized I had in essence told him I'd be going on. His confidence in me was a mixed blessing, but Sean was right. I was not a quitter.

That night, I climbed into bed and pulled out my journal. Writing helped me get in touch with my thoughts.

Dear Diary,

I've gone a bit mad thinking about going back on the trail. Should bring a picture of my family. Bought some new, lighter boots and hope my feet will be OK in them. Debra and Jenny are hiking in tennis shoes although I think Jenny's ankle could use something more substantial. Have now spent $280 on footwear, more than my shoe allowance for a year. Don't know what else to do. Old boots almost worn out and don't think they'll make it, so I'm leaving them home. Could be a mistake. Should've thought it through better.

I'm a lucky woman. I have family and friends who believe in me. It's also a burden. Have to believe in myself. Oh, shit. I am nuts. It is said that inside of us is every age we ever were. Can I find that young girl inside me on the JMT, or is she lost forever?

First Day of Second Part of Journey
Going on the Trail Again: Day 4
July 16, 2004

I ate a huge bowl of Rocky Road ice cream for breakfast. The benefits of being a grownup. Maybe the nuts were nutritious.

Next, I sprayed *Liquid Fence* all over my yard in hopes the deer wouldn't devour my flowers. Boy did that stuff stink, but it worked.

I called my mom. She spoke in her chirpy little voice. I know what that meant—something was wrong. "I'm getting lumps all over my body, they think the cancer may have spread. But don't worry, I'm not going anywhere."

My heart thudded against my ribcage and my chest became so tight it hurt to breathe. Mom was always there for me; I should be there for her.

As a teen when I was getting a drink from a water fountain a friend had jokingly pushed my head down. I bashed my front teeth against the metal spigot, breaking off parts of both of them. With no dental insurance and a minimum wage job Mom marched me off to the one dentist willing to see us. Then, in an *eat shit* voice stated, "My fourteen-year-old daughter is NOT going to have silver front teeth. I don't care how much cheaper they are."

Mom worked extra hours as a bar maid during the evenings to earn money to finance my porcelain caps. There was a four-month period I sported two stubs as teeth in my upper jaw before she accumulated enough money to pay the dentist. I was 5'6" and weighed one hundred pounds, making me the brunt of jokes and giving me the nickname Lollipop. Mom, however, was my biggest fan. "Lori, you are beautiful no matter what." The truth was she believed it, which made me question her sanity, but love her even more.

Being a non-Mormon in Utah with divorced parents made me a misfit. Leaving Utah my senior year of high school with my mom and stepdad allowed me to finally feel comfortable letting my wild red hair curl naturally and wear bell-bottoms and crop tops. Moving to California had saved me from a state–and a state of mind—where I never belonged. It was my way out of institutionalized religion. I was free. I didn't have to be a Mormon like most of my friends, or a Catholic like my dad's family.

Mom was a rebel and had denounced being a Mormon when she'd married my father at seventeen as a pregnant bride. She never converted to Catholicism and eventually shied away from all churches. The leaders of both religions had warned her the marriage would never work. They were right.

"I'm only a kid myself, how am I supposed to raise four of them?" my dad would ask anybody willing to listen.

He eventually ran away, leaving mom penniless, with no education. She kept going. Mom had grit and did what she had to do. She raised us, but more than that, she loved us all just the way we were.

Mom cried when my stepfather's business failed and California's exorbitant cost of living forced them out. At twenty-one years old, I chose to stay behind when they moved back to Salt Lake City. California was my adopted home. I had only wished it included Mom.

As much as I wanted to be there for her, I knew her wishes. She wanted me to hike the trail. I needed to do it for myself, and for Mom as well. Mom was fortunate my two brothers, Craig Sr. and Kevin, lived in Utah and helped her out. My sister-in-law Brenda loved my mom and whenever necessary did the personal stuff Mom wasn't comfortable having my brothers do. My sister Rhonda had a demanding job as an executive secretary in Fresno CA. She did her best to fly to Utah every two months to do whatever she could. It helped knowing there were people available if needed. The unconditional love Mom showed us was paying forward.

After one last hot shower, a carb filled breakfast, and kisses for the doggies, I marched toward my destiny. Promptly at 7:00 a.m., I drove to meet Debra and Jenny in Tuolumne, the high country in Yosemite. I'd been looking forward to the second leg of our journey even though I'd hiked that section of the trail in the past. Its scenery flip-flopped from stark to lush, always leaving me in awe of the contradictory beauty.

At the trail, I started unloading my stuff. Debra's car was already parked and she sauntered over. This was the first time I'd ever seen Debra meander slowly through the woods. John Muir had said the only real way to see the wilderness is to saunter, not to hike. Most of the time I just trudged along. Forgive me, John.

Without as much as a hello, Debra put her hands on her hips and said, "There's about a two-mile-long stretch of the JMT along the road we won't be going on. If you want bragging rights to the trail you better get back and do it sometime. I already have."

I continued about my business. I wanted to leave so I wouldn't have to think about being a lousy hiker.

Jenny stood by Debra's truck laughing and telling jokes with a friend. I'd originally thought that was what would happen on the trip—fun stuff. My throat felt like cotton, and my stomach twisted in a knot. I was capable of enjoying hiking. I wasn't so sure I was capable of having fun with Debra.

Lani, Jenny's friend, sporting a bright tie-dye bandana on her brown bobbed hair, approached me with a big smile, "Want me to carry some of the extra gear?"

I liked her already. "Sure," I said.

I took out the water filter and some poles for the tent and handed them over. Debra and I would bunk together and Lani and Jenny in the other tent. I noticed Debra hadn't offered to carry anything extra and that Jenny was carrying their entire tent and cooking supplies. I reminded myself to mind my own business and enjoy having Jenny's friend help me.

Being with teenagers buoyed my spirits. Many of my friends complained when their kids were that age, but I loved the energy and hilarity my boys and their friends brought to our home. I missed it. Having youthful hormones on the trail would make everything a little brighter. I found a spring in my step I hadn't experienced the whole first part of the trip, even with Jane.

Debra busied herself by adjusting the straps on her backpack. "We have nine miles to hike, so we'd better hightail it. See ya' later," she said to me. She began moving her hand in a swift back and forth movement. "Come on you two, hurry up. I told your mom I'd take good care of you, Lani."

"I thought we'd walk with Lori awhile. Go ahead, Mom. We can catch up later."

Debra narrowed her eyes at Jenny and me. She was not pleased. "Don't worry about me. I've done this part of the trail before and it's almost flat. Walking through Lyell Canyon will bring back special memories to keep me company."

"Are you sure?" Lani asked.

"Flo and Ralph, a wise old married couple I visited while I was home, told me as long as I make it in time to have dinner with you guys I shouldn't feel bad. That'll be my mantra. *I might be late, but I'll be there for dinner.*" Damn I was already hungry.

"Come on let's get going." Debra motioned, her tone reminiscent of a drill sergeant.

"Sure you don't mind?" Lani kicked a pile of sticks. "I'll be glad to wait for you. My mom wouldn't care."

"Just save me some chow when you get to the horse camp. That'll give me something to look forward to," I said.

I used to make fun of freeze-dried food. On that morning, I couldn't wait for dinner to eat my portion. If anyone asked my opinion, I'd tell them the *Mountain House* brand is the best. "Go on, I'll be fine," I continued, trying to sound cheery.

I took a deep breath, sad to see them go. The girls had brought some lightness that rubbed off on me. They took their time getting ready to leave, which gave the impression they wanted to hike with me. I created my best beauty pageant wave and smiled as they headed down the trail.

I surprised myself by walking along at a steady pace. Lyell Canyon was a vision of beauty anytime, and that day was no exception. The open, emerald green meadows, the river cascading through the canyon's enormous craggy granite boulders, and a tapestry of wild flowers all around made it a scenic wonder. I found myself humming as I hiked.

I'd been in the Sierra Mountains many times and still didn't know the names of most of the flowers. It wasn't something I was proud of. The only ones that came easily to me were Indian Paintbrush and Shooting Stars. I liked to let the wilderness soak into me and become part of who I am. I could tell you what things looked like, their smell, and how they made me feel. I often couldn't tell you my exact location or the name of something. I wasn't great at reading maps and even worse with a compass. I wished I'd taken time to become better at both.

Rounding a corner, Mt. Lyell came into view. The mountain was timeless. The gray monolith, with its glistening white rivers of snow cascading down, made me shiver. It jutted into the skyline and I could see the glacier atop. The extinct wooly mammoth would have been at home there in the wilderness. Throwing back my shoulders, my footsteps became lighter. The soft, sensuous wind, and the azure blue sky enveloped me. I could feel my mouth lift in a grin.

She was coming back, the young girl inside. She fueled me, reminded me of who I used to be and could still become. Feelings I had when I was nineteen years old and climbed Mt. Lyell crept back into my soul. It didn't matter if my face was becoming laced with wrinkles, that I was dressed in the attire of an older woman with kneepads and hiking poles. The emotions were real. Once more, I was in love.

To love a person is one thing. To love a place and have a deep soul connection with it is as real and intimate in a different way. I was lucky in love. It came in the form of my husband and sons. I felt a similar connection with Mt. Lyell.

Thirty years ago, my friends, Barbara and Ken, and I had scurried to the top with the freshness of youth. We had riotous fun sliding down on our butts with backpacks lying on our laps. It felt like riding a toboggan chute. Ken said my curly red hair bounced around so much it looked like copper coils dancing in the sunlight. The fierce wind that bit my face and the exhilaration I felt when I signed the climber's book on top of Mt. Lyell were memories that sustained me through the more mundane tasks of motherhood and teaching second grade. I always knew somewhere inside of me the wilderness lived on.

Unfortunately, my new boots started to bother me. Not to

the extent the last ones had, but enough to irritate and remind me of past and present blisters. I took a break to filter water and put moleskin on my feet. I once again wondered why I carried energy bars. I couldn't bring myself to eat one. I poured my trusty secret weapon—powdered Emergen-C mixed in water—and took out one of the three real chocolate bars I'd sneaked past Debra. She'd been too rushed to bother me much about my gear this time.

I needed a plan to help me carry on during the hard parts of the hike. I had eight more miles left to go, and the trail grew steeper. My breath became shallower. Wheezing forced me to stop and use my inhaler. I'd forgotten to take my asthma medicine. A bad mistake. I made a mental note to take it every morning with my gooey oatmeal breakfast.

Stopping about every ten steps, I got nowhere fast. I forced myself to up the count and move ahead 100 steps, then allowed myself the reward of a drink from my water bladder. Once again, I was glad I hadn't listened to Debra's advice. She'd said it would be better to carry a canteen in my pack, as she and Jenny were doing. Every sweaty, bone aching, one hundred steps I felt thankful that bladder was hanging right out there. I could sip through the large plastic tube hanging over my shoulder and take a drink without having to remove my heavy backpack.

Looking ahead, I saw three other groups and one lone hiker. One group stopped and talked, and I took another water break. The lone hiker and I merely nodded at one another. We seemed to share the feeling—*reserve your energy.*

I finished the nine miles by 6:00 p.m. and found Debra and the girls at the horse camp. Despite my nose being filled with concrete trail boogers, I smelled the camp's pungent scent several hundred feet away.

Not only were the mosquitoes biting, but the flies from the horses found me as well. Whacking and splattering their bodies until red blood was squished all over my arms, I stopped for a moment, pulled out my mosquito net hat, and placed it over my head and face. I imagined I was not a pretty sight. I couldn't care less.

Several other campsites had seemed a lot more suitable. Wasn't that one of the nice things about backpacking? You could get away from stuff like horseshit. I knew even Jane, fierce lover and defender of horses, would have agreed with me. It dawned on me this was the first place I'd seen a lot of people all day. I realized I disliked seeing tons of people and enjoyed my own company.

Food, however, was most welcomed. The lasagna and blueberry pudding the girls had waiting for me tasted better than most of what I fed my family. Cooking wasn't one of my strong suits.

I'd done too much of it as a kid when I tried to take my mom's place in the kitchen while she made a living. There were at least twenty easy things you can make from ground beef, and I'd fixed them all. I was sure my sons got tired of my meals. I did. Still, I usually hadn't hiked nine miles before dinner, so the exhaustion could have accounted for some of the freeze-dried food's appeal.

I visualized serving the lasagna to Smiley, in its foil package, on a candlelit table at home. I imagined the grin on his face as he ate it and heard his voice, "Thanks for dinner, Hon. Hope you didn't tire yourself out with the prep work."

Thanking them for the meal, I told Jenny and Lani I'd wash the dishes and clean up. They crept into their tent. Debra hadn't bothered to stay awake for us.

Dear Diary,

Took a peek in my tin mirror and looked like hell when finally made it to camp, but it was fun jumping in the stream and splashing water all over my dirty body. Felt better than a long shower at home. I take too much for granted.

Having Jenny and Lani here helps. They remind me what it was like to be young.

This campsite was OK after all. Lying on a huge granite boulder and gazing into the dark to see almost invisible bats flying all around was mesmerizing. They used to creep me out. Their eyes glowed and their noises reminded me of leaves brushing against each other and rustling in the wind. Everything in the wilderness interconnects. The bats' job is to eat mosquitoes. They might become my new best friends.

Debra decided to sleep outside, so I get the tent to myself. Wonder if she hates me? Read some of my Science of Mind *book from Jane, looked at my family's picture. Now writing in my journal. Going to try and have some things to do at night to keep me sane. Heard if there are certain habits you can count on you'll be less afraid. I'm scared, but I'm here. Shouldn't that count for something?*

Second Part of Journey: Day 5
July 17, 2004

Not having a rain-fly for my tent was another mistake. I woke up to the sounds of waterdrops pounding on the roof and Debra's voice calling loudly, "Get your lazy butts up. Let's get going. Pack the tent before it gets drenched. I thought you told me you were the sunshine girl and it never rains on you, Lori."

I rubbed the sleep from my eyes. "I'm not the one who says that. Smiley is." I poked my head out of the tent. "We were in the rainforest in Washington for a week, and it never rained. Everyone told him I must be his sunshine girl and the nickname kind of stuck. My boys say it's because I try to see the good in things even if it isn't there. Smiley says it's just true; the rain stays away from me."

"Well it's raining now so I guess he was wrong," said Debra. "Trusting in that fairytale, I slept outside and my sleeping bag is soaked. Let's beat it before it gets worse. Get out some energy bars. We'll eat them on the way."

The prospect of eating an energy bar didn't entice me but losing the weight from my pack was a perk. I dug them out and passed them around. The label boasted, "Chocolate Peanut Butter Nutrition." It tasted as dry and chalky as ever, but I was glad I didn't have to cook oatmeal.

We packed, then I put on my $139 rain poncho. As I hiked, I noticed it breathed, didn't stick to me, and actually kept out the rain. Another good investment.

Rain was not a good sign. There were two mountain passes to climb that day. We'd camped as near as possible to them in order to go over the top early when we were fresh and the threat of thunderstorms was less. But a storm was brewing and we seemed to be in the thick of it.

It wasn't a good idea to stand on top of a mountain like a lightning rod in the middle of a storm. Donahue Pass was coming up in less than an hour. The top was 11,500 feet, the highest point in our trek so far. We'd have to decide whether to wait or go over it in the rain. Debra wouldn't be happy. To be truthful neither would I.

It wasn't the first time on our second trek I missed my buddy Jane. I was sure if she were there, she'd have cheered me on. I thought of her at home, cozy in bed, and wished I were there, too. Well, not actually in her bed.

With the rain pelting my poncho, I stopped for a minute and chuckled, remembering when Jane and I had zipped our sleeping bags together to keep warm and Debra had poked her head in our tent and shined a flashlight at us. Her face twisted in a horrified grimace, making me realize she may have thought we were lesbians.

Smiley and Jane's husband would have begged to differ. Jane and I had laughed a lot that night recalling how shocked Debra looked. I didn't care. We'd kept ourselves comfy and warm. Nothing better than body heat on a cold night.

The trip was stripping me of some middle-aged inhibitions. Maybe that was a good thing. I was trying hard to get more comfortable with myself.

Instead of moaning about how hard things were, I needed to remember people like my friend Connie, who was home fighting cancer. She was right: I was lucky to be healthy enough to get caught in a rainstorm while hiking in the Sierra.

As quickly as it started, the rain ceased. Not slowly and surely, but with magical immediacy. I glanced toward the sky and spotted a gigantic double rainbow. It arched over the mountain, its colors shimmering, and spilled onto the trail as we walked. I burst out singing *Somewhere Over the Rainbow* in honor of Jane. Jenny and Lani joined in. We put our packs down and started to dance and skip around. There I was horsing around with two teenagers and singing in the wilderness. Happiness!

"Maybe Smiley was right. You might be the sunshine girl after all," Debra exclaimed, waving her arms and singing along.

It was the greatest compliment she'd ever given me. I was thrilled she'd joined us in our exuberance. "That's one of the more flattering nicknames my family has for me. I don't think I'll share the others," I grinned.

Donahue Pass marked the boundary between Yosemite National Park and the Ansel Adams Wilderness. Although sad to be leaving Yosemite, we were excited to be entering the next phase of the journey. The land we'd walk on was full of myriads of mountain tarns and many large, high altitude lakes reputed to be some of the most beautiful on the JMT.

"We need to get to the top of the pass as quickly as possible. We still have one more to go over today," Debra said, looking at me skeptically. "Let's get going. We'll meet you at the top. I know what a tough time you have going uphill."

"I'll walk with you." Lani came over and stood by me. "I don't mind. This is going to be my only backpack of the season, and I want to enjoy it."

"You'd better stay with us. Lori 's slow, and I'm sure she

wouldn't want to hold you up."

Jenny looked at Debra. "I'll stay back with them. My ankle's bothering me. Could I use the hiking pole you brought, Mom?"

I hadn't been around teenage girls much, but if these two were examples of the next generation of women, I was impressed. Debra must've been doing something right to have Jenny for a daughter. I hoped my own sons would be as kind in the same situation.

"No way, you guys are with me. I'm not responsible for her but I am for you and Lani. Here's the pole, Jenny," she said, tossing it at her. "You can use it for a while. Let's get going."

"Thanks anyway," I said, "but Debra's right. I'd slow you down. I'll meet you at the top. I can't wait to see Mt. Banner and Mt. Ritter. I tried climbing those glaciers when I was about your age. I never made it to the top, but just thinking about those good times makes me happy."

"Sure you're OK?" Lani asked, squinting her hazel eyes in concern.

"I'm sure. But thanks for asking. See ya soon."

When they left I let out a sigh of relief. There was something I hadn't shared with anyone, not even Jane. Since the last fiasco, when I was out the first day and could barely breathe, I was careful to take my asthma pills every day and use my inhaler when necessary.

This still didn't prevent the torturous time I had walking uphill. I'd thought hiking would get easier every day. It hadn't. Climbing steep hills, I felt like my air supply was cut off, and when I could breathe I panted worse than my tiny terriers did after a long walk.

My secret, and the only way I'd made it to the top of the ascents, was to count one hundred steps and then take a long drink from my water bladder. It'd helped me on the first part of the hike and seemed to still work. I felt like a horse plodding after a carrot.

I could only imagine what Debra would say if she thought I couldn't hike uphill more than one hundred steps without gasping for air. I reminded myself that walking the trail was ninety percent mental attitude. Mom had taught me to not let my asthma define me as a child, and I'd be damned if I'd let it get the best of me this late in the game.

Starting out slowly I proceeded toward the pass. I'd gone barely fifty steps when I began panting for air and wondering if I should take a drink. Remembering the pact I'd made with myself, I continued on, in spite of my lungs swelling and constricting my oxygen intake, making sounds like a freight train. My doctor had warned me more than once I could pass out or worse if I didn't stop to get enough air during an attack. So far, that had never actually happened.

Only fifty more steps…then thirty-nine…then sixteen…. I was more concerned with my water supply. I'd talked to many hikers who had done long trips and they'd all said a water bladder was something they couldn't do without. I clasped the tube from it in my hand, forming a lifeline.

Debra and Jenny carried one small canteen each and had decided to not carry a water filter. They used mine whenever I was around. I'd reminded Debra I wasn't usually with them and they should think about taking their own filter on the next leg of the trip when we would be out for three weeks. Debra told me she'd rather risk getting giardia (a terrible disease some people get from drinking unfiltered water in the wilderness). While I thought it OK for her to choose to do that I was concerned about Jenny. I personally couldn't take the chance of getting sick. I needed my job. I had to go back and teach. Debra, a single mom, needed hers, too. In spite of this, she was dead set on the premise of *light gear packing*. I hoped for Jenny's sake the consequences wouldn't be grim.

Rewarding myself with a drink each one hundred steps made

my progress even slower. Trekking up the pass, I reminded myself to stop and look at the view, which dwarfed any IMAX movie vista. The voice in my head said, "What's the use of going on this journey if I don't take time to enjoy it, to look at things I'll probably never see again?"

About halfway to the top, I decided to take a break. I saw someone charging up behind me. It wasn't surprising. The John Muir Trail was a highly traveled route.

What amazed me was the person behind me was not walking the trail, but running it. With long lean legs and a full head of floppy brown hair, he appeared to be quite young, which made me feel better. He came upon me with a big smile, waving his hand. I thought he'd just shoot on by, but he stopped.

"How ya doin'? What a great day. Didn't you love the rain? This is quite a trail, isn't it? The passes are amazing! Running uphill is exhilarating. I feel so strong, don't you?" He ran forward and backward on the trail jabbering on.

His constant motion and the altitude made me dizzy, and I gasped, astonished he could say all that without pausing or passing out. "To be honest I hate going uphill. I don't feel strong. I feel like shit. Excuse the swearing, please. You're right, the passes are beautiful. This is a bitch of a trail and it's taking everything I have to get up it. I do love the view though. I'm impressed by your enthusiasm. What part of the JMT are you walking?" I asked, trying to mimic his enthusiasm if not his sentiments.

"I'm not walking any of it. I'm runnin'. My goal is to do the trail in five days."

"What part?" I asked incredulously with my mouth wide open. A mosquito flew in and was quickly devoured. It tasted amazingly good. I appreciated nourishment in any form. I was always hungry.

"All 211 miles." He smiled like an overgrown puppy dog.

"You've got to be kidding. I'll be lucky to make it out alive and you're running it? Do you ever sleep?"

"As little as possible. I can't stay long. Have to keep runnin.'"

"How old are you anyway?"

"Almost twenty-six...I have a deaf friend who ran the trail in seven days, so I'm not doing anything special. She had twelve dollars' worth of food and bummed the rest. The only time she slept was in bear boxes. Now that's something. Have a good trip. How old are you?" he asked, stopping for the briefest moment as he looked at me closely.

"I'm fifty and I'm doing this as a birthday gift to myself but I guess I'm not really doing anything special either. My friends are way ahead of me. This is a humbling experience."

"Well, you're here, aren't you? You'll probably see a lot more than the rest of us."

"Maybe I will. However, I'm sure having a hard time getting there while I'm seeing it. The trip to Hawaii my husband offered me is looking more and more appealing. Hey, would you like some energy bars? I'd love to get some weight off my pack, and I don't really like them."

"I don't either, but I could use the protein. Sure, I'll take some. If you'd hurry I'd appreciate it."

Digging them out of my pack as quickly as possible, I tossed him three.

"Thanks. Good luck," he hollered as he ran off.

"I'll probably need it. The luck that is," I yelled back.

It made me bone-tired watching him. I couldn't figure out why so many people were in such a hurry in the wilderness. Pausing for a few more minutes, I looked around.

The surrounding mountains resembled castles reaching to the sky. Puffy white clouds floated on and around them. The air had been washed clean by the rain and the space between receding clouds was filled with brilliant blue.

The fragrance of last night's storm filled and moistened my

nostrils. Millions of shimmering green trees were giving off the oxygen I so badly needed. For added insurance I took a puff on my inhaler and put some of my magic Emergen-C powder in water to help me make it to the top of the pass. I figured I'd just lie to Debra and tell her I ate those yucky energy bars. I felt clever getting rid of them.

I couldn't believe how hard it was for me to continue. It wasn't hot, yet I found myself mopping my eyes with my bandana, salty sweat pouring into them. I'd hoped hiking would get easier as the days progressed. That wasn't the case for me. I kept up my pattern of 100-steps-suck-water-100-steps… I needed to look at my map to see when the next water source was available. I would need some soon if I kept the 100-step-suck-thing up. For some reason I could hear Jane's voice in my head *100-steps-fuck-water-100-steps-fuck*…. I smiled in spite of it all.

Getting to the top seemed impossible, but after many sets of a hundred steps I had made quite a bit of progress. As long as I didn't think too much I was able to go on. Stopping to adjust my knee braces and the height of my hiking poles, I plugged along; 100-steps-suck….

The tightness in my chest was joined by a wheezy meowing sound coming from my lungs. I needed to stop and use my inhaler again or my asthma would get worse. I could pass out from lack of oxygen. Luckily, it was in my pocket. I pulled it out and puffed, feeling like a smoker in need of a fix. The inhaler and another suck of water did the trick and I lumbered on at my usual turtle pace. My heart beat rapidly from the medicine in the inhaler, pounding in my ears with every step.

Four more groups of hikers blew by. I smiled weakly and waved at them. They seemed to be whizzing up the trail.

A few minutes later, a spectacular view rewarded my efforts. Vistas of mountains and ancient, twisted hunchbacked trees surrounded me. An eagle soared, bouncing on air currents like laundry swaying in a breeze.

Breathless, I tried to take air in deeply so I wouldn't have to use my inhaler again. If I overused it my heart would beat faster and faster with the possibility of a heart attack. Plopping myself down on my butt against a tree—backpack and all—at the top ledge of the pass, I sat in dumbfounded amazement. "It's all good," Jane's voice echoed in my head.

I'd made it. It didn't matter how awkward I was or how long it took me or how out of breath I was. My boys would be proud of me. Smiley would be proud of me. I heard mom's voice saying, "Most of all be proud of yourself." And I was.

The wind was blowing and serenading me, *oohing* and *ahhing.* The cowboy lyrics to the song *Mariah* swirled in my head. It told me I wasn't alone; the ghosts of past hikers were there to help and guide me. Through that, I found the courage to go on.

"Hey there God, you must have been chuckling at the joke you played on JMT hikers when you put these passes so close together. The last two I had to hike over today hardly gave me time to think. We're not all angels sporting wings, you know. Some of us are mere mortals with sore blistered feet," I looked towards the heavens. "I also get the feeling that in order to make it over the next pass I might need a minor miracle. Could you maybe help me out a little?" The answer came in the form of more wind helping to push me along.

Billowing clouds threatened an afternoon storm. My friend Trisha always reminded me to follow the signs. Sighing and noting I wasn't the one in charge, I took one more look and scurried off.

My current lifestyle hadn't prepared me for the torturous climbs at over 10,000 feet. Unfortunately, my bad knees made hiking downhill on rocky pebbles or sandy trails not much better than going uphill. Even so, it was a pleasure to be moving more quickly along the narrow trail down the mountain. When I placed my hiking poles just right, I could feel they were helping take the pressure off my knees.

At the bottom, I realized I hadn't stopped to take a picture. I'd been too busy watching my feet to see much of anything. I reminded myself to take one on top of Island Pass. It was a good thing we'd had an early start. Debra was proven right again.

That would be the only time during our trip we'd planned to do two passes a day, thank heavens. Though apprehensive, I also felt a bit excited. I'd been able to get up the last two and knew they afforded amazing views. I would enjoy it when I got to the summit. Not if, but when.

After rewarding myself by resting against a tree and eating a piece of hard caramel candy from my pocket, I pushed on. Some part of me hoped Debra and the girls would be on top waiting for me. Another part knew they wouldn't. I was coming to the realization I'd be alone most of the trip except for the people I met along the way. There were worse scenarios. Smiley hadn't understood when I told him I felt like a puzzle with some pieces missing. Maybe I'd find some of those pieces during my exile.

Clearing my mind, I told myself if I was to be my most constant companion on this trip I needed to develop a mindset of joy, not fear. Fear had not served me well in the past. I constantly worried about Smiley when he was out fighting fires, turning me into an insomniac. I had many nights when I stayed up til' 2 or 3 a.m. until I finally was able to sleep. In the morning I had been less than a perfect mom for my sons and it really wasn't fair to them.

My worry hadn't kept him safe, it had just made me a grump. I put the words in my head, *I think I can, I think I can*, like "The Little Engine That Could," a story I read to my class each year to inspire them to do their best. I laughed at how second gradeish it sounded. My family said things to me like *get your head out of second grade*. I'd always asked, *why?*

It felt good to be thinking about my family. I hadn't taken a drink of water or been counting footsteps for a long time, maybe an hour or more. I didn't carry a watch and I wasn't very good at map reading, but I was a good sky reader. The sun and the moon were my allies and helped me with the rhythm and tides of the day. The earth was my timekeeper.

My steps grew lighter. I descended the grade more quickly than usual, dangling my poles at my sides, not really using them. Experiencing the same freedom that overcomes me while skiing downhill, my body was fluid and one with the earth, swishing smoothly from side to side. Smiling, I began to sing again. I wasn't thinking about being out of shape or overweight. I wasn't young or old; I just was.

After reaching the bottom of the ridge, getting to the top became easier than I'd thought. The gradual elevation gain was easy on my body and I continued singing. If ever there was a mountain pass more pleasant to go over and more rewarding than Island Pass, I'd like to know its name so I can visit it. Unlike Donahue Pass, it's not well defined. It's long and flat topped, offering the most exquisite view of a mountain tarn with Mount Banner jutting up behind it. I stopped the next group of hikers coming by and asked them to take my picture. I needed and wanted to remember this place.

The group looked a whole lot older than I. This gave me added courage. There were three of them, and one guy said, "Well, little missy, why do you have a shit-eating grin on your face?"

Without thinking, I blurted out, "Because one of you guys looks like my grandpa and the other two of you look like his friends." As soon as I said it, I felt embarrassed, but they laughed. "Oh, I didn't mean that the way it sounded. It's just so nice to see someone older out here."

"What are you, all of thirty-five?" said the one with the long white beard, as he winked.

Right then and there without thinking I threw my arms around him (no small task with a backpack attached) and said, "You made my day. I'm fifty. Most days I feel that or older. But today I'm feeling young."

"Hell, you are young," said the one with twinkly blue eyes like my grandpa's. "I'm eighty-nine."

"There's no way you can be that old carrying a backpack out here," I said, incredulously. "If you're eighty-nine, I'm a real wimp. I thought I was doing something special by being out here at my age."

"You are doing something special. You're a woman alone in the wilderness with a big smile on her face, getting your picture taken by three mangy mountain men. Most women your age wouldn't think of coming out here. They'd be getting their hair done or something equally stupid. You never know, we might steal your food or something."

"Not mine. I protect it with my life. However, you're more than welcome to take the energy bars I have left."

"We never touch that tasteless crap. Real men eat Hershey bars," Grandpa said, pulling one out of his pocket. "Want some?"

"Sure."

We removed our packs and sat against some rocks while taking in the view. The creamy texture slid around on my tongue and I didn't even take a drink of water. I wanted to embrace the smoothness as long as possible. I kept a small chunk in the side of my mouth and let it slowly dissolve. "Thanks so much for the chocolate. It's delicious. What brought you guys here anyway?"

"Pete here is the grandpa of our group," said the other guy. "I'm only eighty-five, and Jim here is eighty-six. We've been friends for over sixty years. We can't believe we're all still alive, so we come out here every summer to prove to ourselves we are."

"We're only hiking for a week this time, about seventy miles. We're not getting any younger but we're still kickin'. The alternative isn't good," Grandpa said.

"I'm the only one with a wife still alive," Jim said. "Every year she asks me if I'm going to go out in the woods and die on her. I tell her it'd be fine with me if I did. Can't think of a place I'd rather be when I kick the bucket. She always gets riled up when I say that and asks me how in the world I think she's going to be able to get somebody in here to haul my dead ass out. I tell her that's her problem." He chuckled. "You'll have to excuse our swearing. The woods bring out the best in us."

"I've been swearing a lot out here, too. I've dropped the F-bomb several times. My mom wouldn't be happy," I said. "She always told me a lady doesn't say *fuck*. Guess I'm not worried about being a lady out here on the trail. I just want to survive."

We went quiet as the sun surrendered to some clouds and the sky darkened. "Guess we better get going now that we've ate all the chocolate. We ain't getting any younger standing around," Pete said.

"We ain't getting anywhere, either," Jim chuckled. "Let's hit the trail." Chivalry was not dead. They pulled each other up and all three extended a hand to help me, too.

"Happy trails." I tightly embraced each one in turn. The human contact felt good. A lump formed in my throat seeing those guys head off. I thought of my grandpa, remembered his craggy face, smooth bald head, and scratchy beard tickling me whenever we hugged. He'd taught me to love the mountains and had been my first hiking buddy. I loved him with the same fierceness I loved the mountains. He was solid and constant, a giant in my life story.

I put on my pack and steadied it. I no longer walked alone, memories of Grandpa flooded me. "You can ride that bucking mule Lori…eat more of Grandma's pot roast, it'll fatten you up…

Your mom was the prettiest red-headed girl ever…hope you aren't still mad I let Sean drive my truck when he was twelve, I needed a driver…"

I was thankful to have summited those two passes and looked forward to making it to camp in one piece. It would be nice to feel safe and secure in my turtle shell tent.

Dear Diary,

Came into camp and Debra immediately started in on me asking what had taken so long. Told me girls wouldn't start dinner without me. Made me like them even more. I wonder at times who is the adult. She informed me she was not a happy camper. So, what else is new? Even her sour mood couldn't take away my happiness. I figured something out today. I AM HAPPY. Sang the song "Happy Trails" while hiking. Always sing it with my second graders at the end of day. Visualized their smiling faces singing along with me. On the trail I feel young. It took three men over eighty to make me feel that way. It wasn't because they're so much older than me. It was because they're still out here DOING IT at their age.

So grateful to feel healthy enough to be here. Made it over two passes by myself. Hiked over nine miles, going up and down GIANT mountains. Will put pictures of Sean, Craig, and Smiley under coat I use for pillow. I'm not alone. Walking in my head are entire strings of trail angels: Grandpa, Mom, friends, family, and a multitude of amazing folks I've met on this hike. God is here. I'm not classically religious nor can even say I'm a Christian but have always been blessed with faith. So many paths lead to the same glory. I lie here envisioning the grandeur of the mountains and hear the rushing rivers, fireflies dance and twirl around. I'm filled with light, even in the darkness of my tent. Life is good. God is good. All the time.

Second Part of Journey: Day 6
July 18, 2004

I shouldn't have been so cocky yesterday. When happiness finds you, disaster can be at its heels waiting to step on you.

After forcing down another bowl of oatmeal, I started cleaning up camp. Lani came striding toward me. "Would you like me to wait for you? I'm really not in a hurry."

I was tempted to say yes, but didn't want to subject either of us to Debra's wrath. "Thanks anyway, but I'm fine. I'll look forward to meeting you for dinner. Happy trails."

The girls took off, looking back and waving. I had a flu-like feeling in my stomach and realized I would miss the two of them. Debra followed without a backward glance.

And then it began: a hellish day almost from the start. I hated the mosquitoes, they loved me. I could only imagine how I looked hiking along with my net hat covering my face. Fortunately, it didn't matter much because people out in the wilderness are not in a fashion show. Truth be told, some of the people I ran into seemed to think the worse they looked the better they hiked.

Hiking alone made me feel sorry for myself. Not even the crested peaks or the clear blue Sierra sky seemed to cheer me up. My thoughts drifted heavier to my looks, and what I'd lost.

I remembered talking to my buddy Trisha about not being able to keep our hair in the places we wanted it, and growing hair in places we'd never want to have it. We were younger then and it had seemed funny. It didn't anymore.

Every morning I woke up and penciled on my eyebrows. When did they disappear? They were one of the things I missed most.

I tried to believe wrinkles showed character. I could cover the excess baggage on my body, but the fading eyebrows stole all the expression out of my face. Still, I couldn't believe that even out there in the wilderness, I used my little metal mirror to put them on each morning. I was positive they were crooked.

Debra had talked about the fork in the trail at the Reds Meadow turnoff. She mentioned that in order to do the Real John Muir Trail, I needed to hike uphill. I seemed to vaguely remember that a couple of other hikers we'd met had mentioned it was better to go downhill.

Since none of those people were around I decided to take Debra's advice. I hoped I wasn't being foolish. Debra had led me astray before, but this time I needed to believe her. I was too tired to think for myself.

It seemed like I'd hiked for hours and all I could do was look at my feet and place one foot in front of the other. The sun was beginning to set. My inner compass and clock seemed to have left me, confusing me about the time and the area. I hadn't seen anyone since the turnoff. All I could think about was making it to Reds Meadow to take a shower and get a burger. My head itched and I could smell myself. A steady stream of tears made their way down my cheeks and I began to hiccup.

The sun dropped lower, light giving way to darkness. I prayed fervently asking the universe to open up and show me the way. I realized I was lost and felt a huge black hole in my heart. I needed to back track. I went back to the last marker, a large flat rock with smaller rocks on top of it. They call these markers *duck*s when they are on hiking trails. I kept going back and forth to the same marker three times. Pulling myself together I told myself I needed to stop crying and make some sort of decision.

It seemed ludicrous that I hadn't seen another hiker. The JMT is said to be one of the most highly traveled wilderness trails in the U.S. but I had gone hours without seeing anyone. I decided to change direction and go downhill. The trail markers indicated I was still on the JMT. Thank God I could still read them in the fading light. Why had I never learned to use a compass or brought any maps? I felt beyond stupid.

My skin goose pimpled as the air grew colder, but I didn't want to waste time getting out my jacket. I should've been at home in my warm bed snuggled up with my dogs, and maybe even Smiley if he wasn't working a fire. The whole trip was becoming more like hell than the heaven I'd envisioned. Every step I took my feet throbbed and I could feel the blisters that lined my heels exploding.

HELLLLLLLLP! I hollered in the hopes that maybe somebody would hear. With every step I took I let my voice join in the fight to keep moving. Between crying and hiccupping I was barely able to voice the word.

Rounding the corner after hobbling over a ridge I finally saw some signs of civilization: a dirt road and some power lines. I rubbed my eyes and like a mirage, saw Lani running down that dirt road toward me. As if in slow motion, she reached me. I put my arms around her and sobbed. I wasn't even embarrassed. At that moment she was the adult, my savior.

"Oh Lori, I'm so glad to see you." She patted my back. "I thought you were lost or even dead."

"Well, at times I wasn't sure I was ever going to find my way here. I'm so glad to see you. Where are the others?"

"Debra got really mad at me and told me if I wanted to stay around and wait it wasn't her fault if something happened to me. She said she needed a shower and food. I told her we needed to wait for you."

"I don't know how to thank you. I'd almost given up hope."

"Why are you on this trip anyway Lori? Are you a masochist or what?"

"Maybe. But I like to think I'm just somebody who wants to hike the trail and live a dream. I'm so impressed you stood up to Debra. I could still be roaming around otherwise."

Lani let me hold onto her shoulder as I limped along. My knees throbbed and my shoulders sent shoots of pain to my head, which was working on a major migraine. Off in the distance a pair of headlights glared. When they finally reached us, I recognized the truck as an old Ford pickup. I knew that because Smiley was a Ford man. Some people like Chevys but Smiley always swore that Fords were the best. I missed him even more when I peered inside the cab and a Texas style cowboy hat looked at us. Inside of it lived a man with a smile as wide as his wrinkles were deep.

"Hey little ladies, would you like a ride somewhere? I'm thinking with those backpacks on you might be headed to Reds Meadow?"

"We sure are and we'd love a ride." I threw my pack in the back of his truck before he had a chance to jump out and help. Lani did the same.

After a short ride and thanking our Texas hat guy profusely, Lani and I headed to the campground. The store was closed so any hope of a burger was gone.

"I'm so sorry you won't get a hamburger, Lani. You really were my trail angel today and I can't thank you enough."

"It's OK. But I think if we hurry we might get a shower."

Lani threw her pack down at the campground. She didn't even bother to talk to Debra, who stood at a camp space, hands on hips, her brown eyes narrowed.

"What took you so long? We saved you guys some mac and cheese but you sure took your turtle time. You could have got Lani lost, too."

Following Lani's example I ignored Debra. Instead I took out my trail towel and scurried over to the showers. We made it just in time and hot water had never felt so good.

Walking back to our campsite after the shower, Lani and I figured I'd hiked about 15 miles. I felt like I'd been an unwilling participant in a marathon. Every bone in my fifty-year-old body ached. I climbed into my tent without even looking at the stars. My hellish day had finally come to an end.

Dear Diary,

Because of Lani I'm able to write in this journal and I'm alive. Need to let that girl's mom and dad know what kind of stuff their daughter is made of. I love her. She's my new best friend.

Exhausted! Fell asleep for a while then heard all sorts of ruckus. Looked outside my tent and a mama bear and cubs were ransacking the campground. Hearing them going for my pack I wasn't even scared. Had enough of scared. Just plain pissed off. Jumped out of my tent, banged pots and pans together swearing at the bears to leave all my shit and all of us alone, or they'd be sorry. Helping myself was a good feeling. So much better than being in the woods lost and crying.

The young woman camping next to us told me I looked like Medusa with red hair flying all around and arms flapping in circles as I cursed and yelled for that mama bear to leave all our stuff alone and go back into the woods where she belonged. The woman thanked me for my bravery. I told her

I wasn't brave just tired and mad.

Going to try and fall back asleep. Maybe I'm brave. Probably just dumb. Don't know. Don't care. I'm alive and didn't get eaten by a bear.

Fourth Day- Second Part of Journey: Day 7
July 19, 2004

About 6:00 a.m., we finished packing and went to the shuttle bus stop by Reds Meadow Store. It was so cold my breath looked like smoke blasting out of a chimney as I paced around waiting for the bus. I slept for most of the hour ride to Mammoth. When we arrived, Debra's nineteen-year-old son Jason waited with the Ram pickup truck to take us on the two and a half-hour ride home. The plan was to rest up for three days before we continued on the last leg of our trip.

My legs wobbled like limp spaghetti noodles, and my fingers felt like ice cubes. I made a mental note to purchase gloves. It got cold in July at 9,000 feet.

While riding in the truck my shivering was made worse by the freezing looks Debra kept shooting at me. She started in telling her son, "I can't believe Lori actually got lost. I told her where we'd be and how to get there..."

Jason laughed. "It seems to have worked out. She's here now. Maybe she just needed a break from being bossed around, Mom."

I had to admit Debra had great kids.

"She wasn't lost, just took her time and saw a lot," Lani dug at some dirt under her fingernail.

"Lani's my hero. Without her who knows where I'd be. I wasn't sure I could walk another step. Seeing her on the dirt road was a miracle. She's one of my trail angels."

"Wow, a hero and a trail angel, Lani. Can't wait to tell the guys." Jason took one hand off the steering wheel and patted her on the back.

"She helped me get a ride to Reds Meadow campsite in time for a hot shower. If she hadn't you probably wouldn't want me in your truck, Jason. The smell wouldn't be pretty."

The girls talked about friends they'd hang out with, eating cheeseburgers and pizza, listening to music, and sleeping 'til noon. They were particularly excited about seeing a couple of boys.

Jason peered through his Oakley sunglasses into the rearview mirror. "Well Sis, you better clean up before thinking about meeting anybody. You're still grungy and smelly, even after your shower at Reds Meadow. I'm surprised you didn't attract bears. Not even my friends would be interested in you."

"Hey, speaking of bears, did we tell you about the mama with the cubs at our campground last night?" Jenny asked, ignoring her brother's teasing.

"Yeah," Lani said. "Lori jumped out of bed screaming and swearing and scared them off. Everybody in the campground was impressed."

"She was stupid. The mother bear could've got really pissed and come after us," said Debra, shaking her head.

I tried scrunching down in my little area of the back seat and said nothing. Debra was right. I'd been an idiot for a lot of the trip. It was naïve to think I could hike two hundred and eleven miles in the wilderness. I'd have to make some changes if I planned to go on.

While they talked I constructed all kinds of fake and real excuses for not continuing the hike. My boots were a mess. I had horrible blisters. Craig couldn't get off work to help bring the food in. My asthma was getting worse. My family needed me. I was sick.

Differing thoughts emerged as the alpine glow over the Sierra splashed the vistas in technicolor. I remembered the elderly men I'd met, hiking and living their dreams. They made me feel young.

I visualized the stars exploding and lighting up the wilderness in the night sky, and the warm feeling I had inside at the end of each day. I knew I'd probably never have another chance to hike the trail. These things produced doubts in my mind about giving up.

"I'm worried about getting lost again," I said. The last time I went home Smiley suggested I bring some road flagging tape. His thought was you could tie it on a tree at intersections, so I'd know which way to go if I'm lagging behind."

"That's a lousy idea," Debra replied. "What will the other hikers think?"

"I don't care. Would it hurt you to put some up along the trail so I'd feel more confident that I'm heading in the right direction? I'd clean it up." It felt good to stick up for myself.

"The JMT is so well-marked only an idiot could get lost on it. I'm not even bringing a map. Sounds like work, and that's something I don't need more of," Debra said.

"I don't mind. I'll do it," Jenny said. "I heard about a Boy Scout leader who got disoriented on the JMT and was found about a half mile from his group. Lori's not the only one who's gotten lost out there."

"Neither of us needs more weight in our packs. She can find her own way."

"A roll of flagging tape won't weigh Jenny down, Mom," Jason put his hand on his mom's shoulder. "It sounds like a good idea. We use tape on the trail crew to help each other out."

"Smiley says all the firefighters carry it," I said.

"Lori has a lot more weight in her pack than we do. I don't mind carrying the stupid tape," Jenny said.

"Suit yourself. I'm not carrying it," Debra crossed her arms over her chest.

"I'm planning to bring maps and getting a lot more acquainted with them if I continue. My big concern is my boots. They're not working out."

"I hope you come back," Jenny said shyly. "The next part of the trip lasts three weeks. That's a long time. I like having you with us."

I inhaled the increasingly familiar scent of body odor and earth. "Your mom might not feel the same way. I know I'm a lot slower than you two."

"You hiked fifteen miles in a day. That's more than I can do," Lani said.

"Me too," Jenny said.

"It wasn't on purpose. Doing those miles the other day didn't kill me, but it took a lot of the fun out of hiking. All I did was walk. I can't remember seeing anything and didn't take one picture."

Debra stared straight ahead. "Well, sort out your boot problem and figure out how to avoid getting lost. I've got to go back to work for the next three days, then we're back on the trail."

"I'm a lot more comfortable with the ten miles a day we decided on in our planning meetings. After doing fifteen once, I know doing that again would do me in."

"You getting lost made the trip longer. We can't always stop after ten miles. We have to plan around campsites, passes, and other things. Every day is different."

"I know. Like I said, I'll have to think about it."

"If you quit, I can't pay you back for your portion of the supplies."

"The money we spent was more than I budgeted for. I hate to admit it but I think I may have bitten off more than I can chew. I'm not sure I can hike the whole JMT."

"You can if you want to. You're always saying ninety percent of doing the trip is in your mind. You might not be in the best shape but seeing those men in their eighties the other day should've given you some inspiration," Debra said.

The trip back to my little Ford Escort in Tuolumne was long. The kids, however, listened to music and talked non-stop. This surprised me, as Jenny always seemed so quiet.

"You sure you can't go on the rest of the trip with us, Lani?" I interjected into the conversation. "It'd be a lot more fun for Jenny."

"No thanks."

"We could share my equipment." It had been so nice to divvy it up with her the last couple of days.

"It's neat you want to finish, but I like short backpacks. The next three weeks sound like more work than fun."

I'd been thinking the same thing. The lots of work and not much fun factor stayed in my head, even after picking up my car. I had about an hour and a half to mull things over in my mind while I shuttled myself home.

Driving in the late afternoon from Tuolumne to Mariposa is a scenic wonder. People from all over the world come to drive Tioga Road. Bits of recycled glass were placed in the asphalt when it was being built. As a result, the highway sparkles like tiny diamond chips scattered across the ground.

I buzzed by emerald green meadows and gigantic granite mountains jutting into the horizon. The snaking, narrow road dropped off thousands of feet. My heart still pounded each time I made the treacherous ride. Driving past deep blue cobalt lakes surrounded by multicolored wildflowers helped calm my nerves.

After having children, I found it difficult to navigate and was often terrified in the car, whether I was the passenger or driving. Many years ago, while easing down a steep embankment, my brakes failed. Three-year-old Sean and baby Craig were with me in a thirteen-year-old Plymouth Reliant station wagon. We drove into the side of the hill and onto the rock ledge. If I had been on the other side of the road we would have gone off a sheer cliff and rolled at least 600 feet. We'd probably be dead.

I had a friend who called 911 for a helicopter to bring her down from Tuolumne, as she claimed her husband was surely trying to murder her by making her ride passenger on the road. Of course, helicopters were unavailable for terrified wives and saved for honest rescues. As a result, she had waited until Xanax could be delivered making it possible for her to sedate herself before making the drive down.

She never returned. No matter how frightened the road made me I always got beyond my terror because of the extreme beauty the ride offered. I felt empowered after finishing the second leg of my hike, turned on some John Denver tunes, and soaked in the wild and majestic scenery as I drove.

My two little terriers wiggled in rapture when I returned home. Their tails thumped the ground as I rubbed their tummies and picked each of them up, letting them give me wet dog kisses. After being out in the woods, their slobbery saliva didn't bother me. Their adoration was a gift.

We went outside, and the sun tickled my skin with warmth. I sat down on the chaise lounge. It felt rapturous to be motionless, warm, and loved unconditionally. My big, white, friendly mutt Lily scampered over eager to be recognized. I stroked her briskly all over. She was the guard dog for our five acres and protector of the terriers. At sixty-five pounds, she would jump up and gently wrap her arms around my waist and lay her head against me. Her big hug made me feel warm and cherished.

I lounged outside for a long while, petting and being adored by my doggy family. All three of them nudged my hand when they thought it was their turn. They were a pack and knew their positions. Lily was the undisputed leader. Prada and Sweet Pea waited patiently for their pats.

The fridge was my next target of attack. I devoured a crisp apple, an orange, two glasses of cold milk, and a peanut butter and jelly sandwich. Next, I bit off a big chunk of cheddar cheese, inhaled some sliced turkey and finished off five oatmeal cookies. Finally, I felt full.

A shower was on the agenda. The hot, stinging spray on my skin felt like a sensuous massage. Streams of dirt rolled off my body and poured into the drain. Taking the pumice stone I usually used only on my heels, I rubbed it all over the caked dirt on my extremities. Skin slid down the drain like a shedding snake. The shower at Reds Meadow had only taken off the first layer of trail dust.

After getting the gunk out of my hair and off my body, I jumped into bed for a nap. Sweet Pea nestled in my arms, and Prada curled up in the bend of my legs. Heaven. It was nice to be away from dirt. A soft mattress felt divine. With my head encased in a clean, cushy white pillow and all the soft doggy parts protecting me, I sighed, closed my eyes, and slipped into nirvana.

When I awoke several hours later, I inspected the house. Smiley and Craig had done a good job. I felt blessed.

Smiley arrived home later that evening after working on a fire. I was sleeping when he crept into bed nudging my side. Still half encased in sleep, I felt—more than saw—his body next to mine. He smelled musty and good enough to eat, like the roasted s'mores that had been my favorite food on the trail.

After lovemaking, I felt warm and safe. It hadn't been fun

being scared on the trail. Smiley made me feel protected when we spooned in bed. He cradled me in his arms, resting his head atop mine. His loud snoring didn't bother me. That night it sounded better than any of my favorite songs.

Dear Diary,
There's no place like home.

Second Set of Interim Days: First Full Day Home
July 20, 2004

The next day, I was dead to the world. It was 1:20 p.m. when I finally dragged myself out of bed. I hadn't awakened once during the night. On the trail, I woke up at least two or three times a night; I had to pee, I couldn't get comfortable, or I was cold. Debra said she never slept for more than an hour at a time and was up most of the night. I believed it accounted for part of her grumpiness. Smiley had left me a note on the kitchen counter.

Dear Lori,

Enjoy your day and do nothing if you want to. We've missed you. I fed the dogs. Can't wait to hear more about your adventures. Did you pick up some pieces of your puzzle along the way?

Luv ya 3x more, Smiley

The good and the bad are often the same. My friends and

family called me all day long. I appreciated their concern but avoided some of their questions. Many of them thought I was crazy and encouraged me to quit the trip.

My longtime buddy Trisha laughed. I could picture her purple glasses sliding down her nose as she shook her head from side to side. "I think it's cool you're doing it, but I never would. I'll pray for you."

I knew I could count on her. We'd been prayer buddies for years, helping our marriages and sons through some hard times.

Even though I grew up in Utah and 99% of the population in our town was Mormon, my mom had me baptized Catholic to please my dad's Italian family. Mom would not let any of Dad's family be my godparents because she said they hated her for getting pregnant at seventeen and eventually saddling my dad with four kids total before he was even a grownup. Didn't it take two to tango?

Instead of family, Mom had selected a nun and a priest who offered to be my godparents. They'd told her they wouldn't be able to give me material presents but would always pray for me. Although my prayers weren't always answered the way I'd thought they should and my faith had been tested, I'd been given another gift by Mom, the knowledge that prayer is mighty in any form. Even my atheist friend Ann would chant the Saint Anthony's prayer, *Dear St. Anthony, please come around, something's lost but can't be found.* I used it, too, and most of the time found the lost item. Who can argue with success?

My sister Rhonda called. "I told you it would be hellish, but I know you'll finish. I believe in you." She was my little sister and along with Mom had always been my cheerleader. I felt lucky she was not only my sister but also my best friend.

Then Dad called. "I'm really excited for you." I bet he was rubbing his bald head as he talked. "I'm planning on meeting you at Whitney Portal at the end of your adventure. What day do you think you'll arrive?"

"I'm not sure, Dad. We're tentatively planning to be there in about three weeks but nothing's certain." I didn't want to tell him I'd thought of quitting. I loved my dad, and had forgiven him, but didn't want to believe I'd inherited his tendency to quit when the going got rough. I needed to search deep inside myself for Mom's grit.

I phoned Mom, since she hadn't contacted me. Her voice sounded raspy and faded. "How're things going, Mom?"

"About the same, dear. But I'm getting more bumps on my head, and I'm continually tired."

"I should be staying home and helping you. It's selfish of me to spend my whole summer hiking."

"You've never been selfish. You're here when I need you. How's the hike going? Are you wishing you'd gone to Hawaii yet?" she asked, changing the subject. We both knew the end of her trail would be sooner rather than later, and my journey was taking away time I could be spending with her.

"I'm not having much fun, but I love the scenery and being in the wilderness. There's a sense of freedom I thought I'd lost. The young girl hiking with us reminds me of how I used to be."

Mom took a soft breath. "Life's never exactly what we think it's supposed to be. But then, it is what it is. I know who you are and what you're made of. I hope you know it, too."

"It hasn't been the journey I thought it would be."

"I know you can do it."

"But I'm worried about you. Please take care of yourself. I love you."

"I love you, too, dear," she said so quietly I had to strain to hear the words.

It reminded me how lucky I was. I'd always had a mom who believed in me. When I was a child that knowledge was powerful; as an adult it was priceless. There wasn't another woman I knew whose mom made her believe in herself the way mine did.

"I know you said you're coming for my seventieth birthday at the end of August. Your brother even invited your dad and Shirley. It's funny how we like each other after I hated her so much when your dad married her."

Mom had a classic, beautiful look even after the ravages of cancer. Stunning red hair and high cheek bones had been her trademarks. It hit her hard when her hair had grown back in dull and frizzy after chemo. Shirley was a round, brisk English woman. She had grown on me and I loved the fact that she took such good care of my dad. He was a funny, full of life man who thrived on attention. She was able to supply it.

"Yeah, after all the women he cheated on you with, it's weird he chose her. He certainly dated younger and more attractive girls."

"Her big boobs got him. He's still a big baby. I raised you kids and I'm glad she has to take care of him, and I don't. After all the narcissistic men I dated before meeting your stepdad Charlie I realized maybe your Dad wasn't the worst of the lot. She's welcome to him. I've got my kids and I can't wait to see you."

"I've already bought my plane ticket. I wouldn't miss it for the world."

"We'll have fun."

"Thinking about it will keep me going while I'm hiking," I said, holding back tears. I missed my mom. The thought of losing her terrified me.

"I'm so proud of you."

"Mom, I'll walk the trail for you, see everything for you."

"Oh, no, dear, I have no desire to hike it. I would have gone to Hawaii. Do it for yourself. I can count on you to do the unusual."

Mom could always make me smile. "To be honest I don't think I want to finish. I'm in bad shape. Debra, my hiking partner, doesn't like me. I can't keep up, and I'm having trouble controlling my asthma. Continuing will mean walking it mostly on my own. I'm not sure I'm strong enough."

"Sure, you are."

"I'm just so scared, tired, and fat."

"Don't let anybody or anything make you feel less than you are. Walking that trail has been a dream of yours, and you have the chance to make it happen."

"Dreams can sometimes become nightmares."

"I'd hate to see you give up on something just because it's hard. You've given me a lot of courage in my cancer treatments. If you decide you need to quit, I'll understand, but think long and hard about it."

We continued to talk about her dogs, my dogs, her grandsons, my sons, Utah weather, California weather, her flowers, my flowers, all the things we shared and loved. Hanging up the phone, her unconditional love enveloped me like a comfortable, old quilt, making me feel safe and warm for the third time that day.

It was amazing my feet didn't have more blisters. There were a few small ones lined up on my toes and heels, and they throbbed periodically. Hopefully they'd heal in the next three days. The second pair of new boots, the ones I'd just hiked in, hadn't worked much better than the first.

My old tried and true pair would have to be the ones I took. I got them out of the garage and wiped the dust off. Looking at them, I realized they probably didn't have enough tread on their soles to finish the last three weeks of the trip. I reminded myself that's why I hadn't taken them in the first place. They had seen and done too much and had earned their retirement. I wasn't sure how to remedy the situation. There was no time left to break in new footwear. During the first two short trips I'd already learned how painful it was to walk with blisters oozing pus and rubbing against my boots.

It would be a nightmare to get blisters on the last part of the backpack. We'd be hiking continuously for the first time without a break for at least eighteen to twenty-one days. It would be impossible for me to hike that long with injured feet. Not having suitable boots was a solid reason to not continue the JMT. Maybe it was time to quit.

Jane called and we laughed about Debra *moments* on the trail. She understood them like nobody else could. "I've no doubt you can hike that trail. I have no doubt I could, too."

"I believe Debra can hike it as well. But I'm sure she'd rather do it without me."

"Debra would love for you to quit. Fuck. To be honest, I need you to do it for both of us. I wish I had the time and resources to go with you."

"Jane, thanks for the little book you gave me. It's been a big comfort for me at night. That, and pictures of my family, have gotten me through some rough times. Just remembering how much fun we had makes me smile. It isn't the same without you."

"You rock. I'm with you in spirit. The pictures I have of us hiking are on my fridge, and they're priceless. I can't wait to hear the stories you'll bring back. It's all good."

Dear Diary,

My friend Bonnie had us over to dinner in celebration of the part of the hike I've already done. Real food-delicious. I felt proud. It was fun telling stories about my adventures. The trail didn't seem so daunting over wine and beer. Hedonistic eating in between trips is probably not helping my hoped for weight loss.

Smiley had to check out a control burn near Yosemite after dinner and isn't home in bed with me tonight. Miss him, but the dogs are here to keep me company. Craig was home. He let me know he isn't thrilled about having to bring supplies up to Kearsarge Pass to restock us. Reminded me he would be a lot happier if I decide to stay home. He also said he understood if I continued. "After all," he said, "I'll bet you did a lot of stuff for me you didn't want to do when I was growing up."

Sean called today and said he bragged about me at the fire station where he works. Promised to try and get home to visit before I went out on the trail again. For some reason he seems certain I'll finish. I told him I wasn't very fit and the trip was harder than I'd expected. He reminded me he'd warned me. He also said when he was growing up he knew when I made a commitment I kept it. This long speech was high praise from my son who is usually a man of few words. How can I quit when he believes in me?

Smiley left a voicemail. "See you tomorrow night when we have dinner with Connie and Glenn. You'd better enjoy all these decadent feasts with your friends. I don't envy you your freeze-dried food on the trail, even the lasagna. Luv ya 3 times more."

Funny, I'm missing the shimmering stars in the wilderness. They saturate your being with their luster and streak across the sky like vagabond fireworks. I see them even behind closed eyelids. Dreamed about some of the mountain passes I've been on top of on this journey. Don't have to fantasize anymore. It's real. Nothing in the civilized world gives as much satisfaction as going over a high Sierra pass above the timberline with crystal blue sparkling water below.

I'm confused. As they say, tomorrow is another day. I'll decide then.

Second Set of Interim Days: Day Two
July 21, 2004

I thought I'd sleep late, but ended up out of bed at 8:00 a.m. There were too many things I wanted to do. Our friends Connie and Glen Rothell were coming for dinner. Smiley had picked up a tri-tip, and I planned on making potato salad.

Spending time in our flower garden always improved my mood. It was therapeutic to go outside and pull weeds. One of the things I shared with my mom was a love of plants. It seemed the older I got the more things she and I had in common.

Smiley and Craig took good care of the yard and flowers while I was gone. The war we had going with the gophers in our lawn was beginning to slow down a bit. I noticed two traps Smiley had set. Those darn rodents were determined to destroy the $3,000 patch of sod I got as a gift for our twenty-fifth wedding anniversary. I'd chosen sod instead of the belated diamond ring Smiley offered me, and I'd lived to regret it. Kinda like hiking the JMT, which I'd picked instead of Hawaii.

Before becoming personally acquainted with gophers, I'd

considered myself a pacifist. Now I supported my husband in doing just about anything short of bombing the yard to keep them at bay, even applauded him for it. An amazing thing happens when you defend your own land.

I remembered standing at the end of a gopher hole with a shovel to smash their heads after trying to flood the little suckers out. I was somewhat relieved it didn't work. I wasn't sure what I'd do if I came face-to-face with one.

My sons and their dad had set up gas lines in the yard to try to force the intruders out. I had to leave the house in fear my guys would blow themselves to smithereens. Smiley had a tally chart with him, comparing himself to the terriers. He wanted to see who killed the most gophers. This summer it was Smiley 14, dogs 8. The only problem was the deceased had apparently invited their families to visit before they died, so the gopher explosion continued.

The phone rang. It was Connie. We met about four years ago through Sean who worked with Connie's daughter on the search and rescue team. Common ground.

Sometimes you meet someone you have an instant connection with. That's the way it was for Connie and me. She'd been battling cancer for as long as I'd known her. The prognosis wasn't good, yet mentally she was one of the healthiest people I knew. Even though she'd lost about fifty pounds and all her hair, she hadn't lost her zest for living.

She didn't let cancer define her. The twinkle in her eyes and the smile on her face produced a shimmering aura surrounding her. She'd been one of my greatest supporters of my JMT backpacking trip.

Connie met me at the town pool all of June and July as we readied ourselves for our own personal journeys. I was a terrible swimmer, but Connie loved it. Every day she would struggle, breathing heavily, holding onto a paddleboard, and each day she went another half lap or so. Her peach fuzz hair would peek out of the water and a smile spread across her face as she cheered me on, telling me to push hard and get in shape.

Her goal was to swim across Tenaya Lake, a small high Sierra lake in Yosemite that was reached by car. She'd been tallying up the lakes she swam for several years and wanted to do as many as she could. Since her illness, she hadn't been able to go backpacking and was unable to swim in the sparkling waters the wilderness provided. "Do you know how lucky you are to be healthy enough to hike the JMT?" She panted and gasped as she kicked on her paddle board. "I'd love to be there with you."

I vowed to myself every lake I swam in the Sierra would be in honor of Connie. She'd promised herself if I finished the John Muir Trail, she'd swim across Tenaya Lake. I believed in her. She believed in me. Connie had told me, "I have visions about hiking the trail with you. In them, my body is no longer my enemy, it's young and fit."

Last spring after hearing Sean's words, "*You better get in shape if you want to hike that trail,*" I'd joined a gym with Connie. I enjoyed it most when we worked out together. She'd pedal hard on the stationery bike while I'd try to use the treadmill for at least forty-five minutes. The best part of our experience was the margaritas we drank at her pool afterwards. Someone once told me, *calories consumed within one hour of a workout are free.* I was living that lie.

"Hearing about your journey will be the next best thing to being out there," Connie would say as we slurped on the icy drinks.

Sometimes after Connie's chemo she wasn't able to get out of bed. Other times were better. On a particularly good spring day, she'd gone to see the flowers along the Hites Cove Trail in El Portal. Rumor had it the Mariposa poppies along the way were so plentiful it looked as if gallons of gold paint had spilled across the canyon. It was one of her favorite hikes and she didn't want to miss it. She talked Glenn into going with her. About a quarter of a mile in, she got winded and told him, "I'd love to sit here, rest awhile, and enjoy the flowers. You go ahead without me."

Glen hadn't wanted to leave her, but Connie could be very convincing. As she relaxed and enjoyed the colorful flower extravaganza, she saw a person running toward her. Connie reflected on the fact that she'd always wanted to be a trail runner. She waved at the woman. After she'd passed by, Connie stood. She started running very slowly and went about a hundred feet. Her voice resonated with wonder and joy when she relived it for me. "I was free, Lori. Cancer couldn't stop me; age couldn't get in my way. That hundred feet felt like a hundred-mile victory." She'd stopped after she was breathless. She sat down and said aloud, "Now I'm a trail runner."

It was funny. I'd just been thinking about Connie and she telephoned. Ah, lovely synchronicity. "How are you doing, Lori? Are the blisters improving?"

I had blisters. She had cancer. I'd never heard her complain about her situation and when I said, "They're getting better," I couldn't help myself and continued, "God, Connie, there really is no fairness in the world if people like you get cancer."

"It's just the way it is. I can't change things. I do the best I can," Connie replied. "It's Glenn and the girls I worry about."

I told her lots of funny Jane and Debra stories. Talking and laughing with Connie made me realize even without walking a step on the JMT she was one of my Trail Angels.

"What can I bring for dinner?" she asked.

"Just you and your encouragement for me to finish the hike."

"I can't do that. I've decided to release you from the promise you made to walk the trail for me. I don't think you should finish."

"Why?" I asked incredulously.

"I've talked to a lot of people who said they think Debra would be a terrible hiking partner. Truth is, even if I was healthy and in top shape, I wouldn't hike with her. I can't think of another person who would do the trail with Debra. So, quit. You've done enough."

"Thanks, Connie, I'll think about it. There are lots of reasons I might quit, but only one reason to continue. This is my chance, and it may never happen again."

"But is it worth it?"

"I need to figure that out. Come over and we'll drink lots of wine, the guys can guzzle beer, and I can forget about my aches and pains for a while. You're a great friend, Connie. I love you."

"I love you, too. No matter what you decide, you're my hero."

"No, Connie, you're my hero," I murmured as I hung up the phone.

Dear Diary,

What a fun dinner. Was great to relax and laugh a lot. Loved being able to go to the bathroom whenever I needed to. A couple of times I went in and sat on the toilet just because it was there. Smiley cooked the meat just right. He usually chars food on the grill, but never admits it. Sometimes I'm mean and go on and on about him burning things. I am not the perfect wife.

Getting to sleep in a real bed was great. Having sex was even better. Smiley says sometimes I AM the perfect wife. Too tired on the trail to think about anything but how I'm going to make it through the next day. Wonder if it will get easier if I go out for the last three weeks. Maybe like Connie when she ran the trail for a while and felt she was a trail runner, I could believe the part of the JMT I've done is enough? I could tell myself, "I've hiked the JMT." Nevertheless, there's still so much more I want to see and do. I don't have cancer, my body is healthy. Maybe the truth is in doing what you can and realizing that's enough.

Second Set of Interim Days: Day Three
Last Day Home Before BIG Hike
July, 22 2004

Last night at dinner Craig reminded me I could bail out and come home with him after he hiked in our resupply at Kearsarge Pass. He also said he was now kind of looking forward to it. His friend Devan, who was coming with him, had time off work and so had Craig. His coworkers were impressed he was hiking eight miles starting from 9,208-ft in Onion Valley off Hwy 395. Kearsarge Pass is a climb of about 2,000-ft and about fifty miles from the end of the JMT. I thought if I made it that far it would be nothing short of a miracle. Knowing I would be seeing Craig would give me something to look forward to.

Smiley leaned over the bed and threw me a roll of yellow flagging tape and some maps. "These are your going away presents. Make sure you flag the trail. You might wanna sit up so I can go over the maps with you." He had a red marker in his hand to trace the route, so I knew he was serious. He got busy marking the way.

"It would be so much better if you were coming with me," I whined.

"No way. It's your dream, not mine. I'd have killed Debra by now."

"We could keep each other warm at night. I get lonely in my tent all alone," I continued in the sexiest voice I could muster.

"Think about it. I don't like sleeping on the ground, hate hiking, and freeze-dried food is something I can live without no matter how much you keep telling me it tastes good. I've ate enough MRI's on fires to hold me for life. I'll live this little adventure through you."

"Don't you want me to stay home? Don't you need me here?"

"Quit whining. Yeah, I need you, but want you to do what makes you happy."

"Well, I'm not always happy hiking. It's not what I expected."

"Things never are. But, I bet you go on. I know how you are."

"I think I bit off more than I can chew."

"Trying things that are hard make us grow," he chanted, in a singsong falsetto voice. "I've heard you say that at least a hundred times to our boys. See you later. Have fun getting ready to go." He kissed me solidly.

Dear Diary,

Can't believe I called Debra and told her I'd meet her tomorrow. What's possessing me? Spent half the day lying in bed, other part eating as much as I could, and the remainder of the day figuring out what I needed to bring and what I could throw out of my pack. My pack is still way too heavy. Guess I'll have to hope and pray my old boots make it. Couldn't think of any other way to solve that problem, so they're coming with me. Every bone in my body aches.

Wow, big deal, lost a whole pound. Bet I gained it back. Looked over and over the map Smiley gave me. What a fucking long trip. Can't seem to quit using that word since hiking with Jane.

The next part of the trip will be different. Going out for three weeks is a lot harder than going out for three or four days. Not sure I have what it takes. Think I'll do a day at a time.

Last Part of Journey: Day 8
July 23, 2004

I kept waking up all night thinking about the fact I'd decided to tackle the rest of the hike. When I did sleep I had nightmares where I couldn't breathe while climbing up giant mountains made of ice cream that keep melting and never end. Puffing hard on my inhaler, I dropped to the ground clutching my heart. I woke up sweating and gasping, relieved it wasn't real. I put my hand on my heart and felt it beating. I convinced myself to forget it and go back to sleep. Not a good idea since in the next dream I was walking downhill and feeling so smug that I start running to catch Debra. I ran so fast my knee popped out and I fell to the ground no longer able to walk. Waking abruptly, I reached down to feel my legs and knees. They were intact, but my left knee was miserably sore. I shouldn't have gone to bed.

I reminded myself to do one day at a time like the Alcoholics Anonymous pledge. If I committed to the trail, it would be hard to get off.

Getting out of bed, I looked at my map. There were places

where it would be easier to leave the trail and get home. I put a mark by Muir Campground, the place we would be getting our first restock. It was about a hundred miles into the trail. If I made it that far I wouldn't feel like a complete failure if I quit. Florence Lake, which was five miles from the campground, had a ferry that could take me across to the other side and I could have someone pick me up there. Another option would be to leave with Craig. He would be joining me about 180 miles into the JMT, and I could always hike back to the car with him. It never hurt to have a backup plan.

I'd said goodbye to Sean and Craig the night before. They both gave me a big, long hug. I held them tight, like they used to hold on to me. "I love you forever," I told them, and they said it back.

Smiley was leaving early, so he came back to bed to wake me up. "Get up lazybones," he leaned over puckering his lips and giving me his fish lips kiss.

"I want a real kiss, I need something to remember you by." I stuck my tongue in his mouth. He followed suit and I cupped his head in my hands as we sucked air.

"Hey, I thought we took care of that last night." He put his hand on my boob.

"Your hand is like a magnet always going for boobs. I'm trying to talk about love, not lust."

"One and the same for me with you, my dear."

"Am I really going to leave my warm bed and go out into the wilderness with a woman who hates me? Please talk me out of it."

"I've never been able to talk you out of anything you wanted to do in our twenty-five years of marriage. What makes you think I can now?"

"What makes you think I want to go? I have so many reasons not to."

"Well, your fully loaded backpack in the front room's a clue."

"What if Debra keeps leaving me behind? What if I can't do it all alone? I'm afraid."

"You're not alone," he said, reaching for my hand and placing a small polished heart shaped rock in it. "My heart will be with you. My body, however, would never want to hike the damn trail. Way too much work," he shook his head.

"You're right. It's way too much work." I covered my head with a pillow.

Smiley plucked the pillow off my head, swatted my butt, and said, "You could always stay home and clean house. Time to get up."

"I don't want to."

"I'll be waiting to hear all about your amazing journey. I love you three times more. You go Big Red."

He leaned down to kiss me. It was a good one, not a fish lips one.

"See you in three weeks," he said, walking out the door without even looking back.

"I love you, too," I hollered at his back, as I clenched my polished heart rock tightly in my hand.

I still couldn't believe I was continuing. I climbed in my old Chevy station wagon to meet Debra in El Portal, the small community she lived in outside Yosemite National Park. It was only 6:00 a.m. and I wished I was a coffee drinker. My head was fuzzy from waking up so many times during the night. I wasn't a morning person, and I always looked forward to my summers when I slept in till at least 8:00 or 9:00 a.m. I realized now I'd have to be up at the crack of dawn each morning. That was not a pleasant thought. Ahead of me was a forty-five-minute ride to Debra's house then a two-hour ride to Mammoth where we'd be starting our hike. Plans were to be on the trail by 1:00 p.m. Our goal was to cover seven miles to arrive at the campsite.

Debra and Jenny weren't ready when I arrived. I knocked on

the door then let myself in. I could hear them arguing in the back room. I couldn't understand it all, and didn't want to, but I heard enough to let me know Jenny wasn't excited about the long last leg of the trip ". . . and my friends and I have plans. . . I don't like hiking. . . can't you just leave me alone…"

". . . too bad, you're going no matter what. . ."

I felt like an intruder and fervently wished Jenny's friend Lani had been willing to do this last part of the trip with us. I wasn't the only one who needed an ally. What happened to Jenny's other friend who was supposed to come with us? Thinking about it made me pissed off once again. I was carrying the gear that should have been shared by two. I remembered Jane's saying, *It's all good.* I missed her. The arguing continued until I started making noise to indicate my arrival. "Hey guys, I'm here and ready to go. How about you two?"

Debra came in from the back room and gave me a look that should have sent me home. I tried to ignore it. "How long have you been here?"

"A minute or so," I lied. "I'm eager to get going," I lied some more.

"Well, give us a few minutes and help yourself to some coffee or tea. Are you ready for the long haul? Jenny and I are excited. Hope you are, too."

"I sure am," I lied again. If this trip didn't make me into a hiker, it could make me into a damned good liar.

Debra's son and his girlfriend were going to drive us to the place we stopped four days before. Debra was a stickler about logistics. She insisted we must hike each part of the trail exactly as marked on the JMT official route or we couldn't count it.

While Debra and Jenny continued to pack, I went outside with a cup of caffeinated tea, hoping to suck up some energy. I sat down on what was left of a picnic table. I was already tired, and the day had just begun. A few minutes later, Debra's boyfriend,

Todd, joined me. I'd met him before, liked him, and wondered how the two of them had gotten together. Todd came over with a big smile on his face. He was a very fit, handsome, lanky, Asian man, ten years Debra's junior, which made him about thirty-five. He worked on the Yosemite trail crew. During the planning stages of our trip I had met him at Debra's house. He'd been full of animated conversation, and a lot of enthusiasm concerning our upcoming backpack. Once again, I had to admire some of Debra's choices.

Todd sat down by me, "So you're going to go for it? I give you a lot of credit. Debra isn't always easy to be with. She does, however, know a lot about backpacking and is very determined."

"That's for sure. Without her, I would never have even thought of doing the JMT. She's done most of the planning and legwork to get this hike going. She made sure we got our resupply sent off to Muir Ranch so it'll be waiting for us. She arranged for you and your friend Steve, and Craig and his friend Devan to bring in our last provisions. I appreciate all she's done."

"She can be controlling. I have a hard time with that part of her, but she does know her stuff."

"Without her I'd never be able to do it."

"I know it's been a huge relief to have you share costs with her. I try to help when I can, but being a single mom isn't easy. She'd do anything for her kids. She loves 'em like a mama bear."

"Her kids are great, and she's lucky to have you. Thanks for bringing in our resupply to Charlotte Lake. Craig told me he's excited to hike with you. We packed extra stuff in the resupply stock for all of us to share when we meet up."

"Craig's cool. It'll be fun hiking with him. We talked on the phone and have it all arranged. Do you think you'll be OK?"

"Hope so. This trip's a dream come true. Although to be honest, sometimes I feel like I'm living a nightmare. I've fallen down so many times I'm not sure I'll ever get up. I'm half-assed scared a lot of the time."

"I'm sure you'll be fine. You've made it this far, you'll make it all the way."

"Thanks. Can I ask you a favor? Would you please watch out for my son and Devan? Craig's backpacked, but it isn't his favorite thing. Devan's a great kid, but he's never backpacked before. They're both nineteen and in good shape, so I don't foresee any problems. It'd make me feel so much better though, knowing you'll keep an eye on them."

"No problem. Wish I didn't have to work so I could hike the whole trip."

"I wish you could, too," I replied as Debra came outside to join us.

"Let's get this show on the road. What're we waiting for?" Debra said, as she ran over to the truck with her fully-loaded backpack and tossed it in over the tailgate as if it were an oversized pillow.

"I think it's you we've been waiting for," I mumbled, grunting as I pushed and pulled, inching my pack over to the truck. Debra rolled her eyes as I struggled to put it in the back. She sighed, disgusted, as Todd picked it up and threw it in for me. I was soooo tired. And it was only 9:00 a.m.

Debra's son, Jason, and his girlfriend, Mia, joined us outside. Jenny came slowly behind them dragging her pack in much the same way I'd dragged mine. Todd also threw Jenny's pack over the side of the truck. Debra gave Jenny one of those looks I give my kids when they've done something awful. I made a note to self to eliminate those looks as much as possible. I smiled at Jenny and said, "He threw mine in, too. What a guy." It helped knowing even the young grew weary.

"Well, I guess we're ready." Debra sounded more cheerful than I could remember her being on the former trip. She smiled, leaned over, and gave Todd a huge hug and kiss. He returned it. I was envious, wishing I was home safe and warm in Smiley's arms.

We crammed tightly into the truck. It should have been very uncomfortable, but it wasn't. I felt strangely secure nestled by the side rear door next to Jenny. I smiled to myself. It was odd a teenager could make me feel safe, but Jenny did. Having both of her kids in the truck brought out the best in Debra. Seeing that part of her was encouraging. Telling jokes, laughing, and talking about the exciting things that might happen on the trip made the ride seem short. It was fun reviewing all the stuff we'd already seen and done. It brought back memories of the good times on the trail.

Jason and Mia sitting close together in the front seat were darling, and obviously in love. "I wish I could help Craig bring in the food," Jason said. "Too bad I can't get off work." Craig knew Jason from high school and was more than a little pissed he wouldn't be helping bring in the resupply.

When we were planning the trip, Debra had said Jason would come with Craig, Devan, and Todd. That changed and they now had to carry the extra weight Jason would have brought in. It was interesting how things had shifted. For example, Debra was no longer carrying any maps, she wasn't bringing a camera, or a water filter (she said they would borrow mine or do without). I tried not to fixate on those things, but they bugged me. I worked on returning my mind to the conversation in the truck where everyone but Jenny was talking and laughing.

Jason and Mia dropped us off at Reds Meadow at 1:05 p.m. It was the same place we'd come out of four days prior. A stickler on doing the trail *right,* Debra had calculated the time we would arrive at the trailhead almost to the minute. Impressive.

After Todd and Mia left, we decided to fuel up by eating before we started hiking the seven miles we'd planned for the day. We each ate one of the bitter tasting energy bars. I didn't have the nerve to remind Debra I thought it unfair I was carrying them.

What happened? I'd turned back into the wimpy person who

refused to stand up for herself. I rationalized if I ate it there would be less weight in my pack. It left a burnt, rubbery taste in my mouth, and I took a large drink of water I should have saved for the trail.

Thank God for the peanut butter and jelly sandwiches and oranges we'd brought. We wouldn't be having any more fresh food for a long time. When Craig brought supplies to Charlotte Lake, I hoped he'd remember to include the oranges and Snickers bars I'd asked him to get.

Debra was like a tiny Energizer Bunny ready to zing off immediately. It was a crisp day with the sweet scent of wildflowers entering my nostrils. The jays cawed and played havoc in the nearby trees. Debra's excitement was contagious, and we started out hiking together. This part began gentle and flat, helping me out. After a short distance, the trail started uphill, but it was such a gradual slope I enjoyed it.

We came to an area that was severely burned in 1992. The charred and twisted trees contrasted with the beautiful greenery. I was beginning to feel a bit depressed by the blackened forest when we saw an area of mature, green, towering pine trees and crossed over two gurgling, full-bodied streams. It refreshed my spirit. I stopped, ready to filter and get a cold drink.

"Would you mind letting me use the filter first? I need to get going. I'm enjoying being out here and starting the real part of our trip," Debra said. "You're sure walking slow, Jenny. Lori's keeping up with you."

"For your information, Mom, I'm trying to keep up with her. I'm tired. Why don't you just go ahead. If it's OK with Lori I'll hike with her."

I waited for Debra to veto the idea and when she didn't, I

said, "I'd like that, Jenny. It'd be nice to have company. We shouldn't have any trouble reaching our campsite by dark. Haven't we gone about four miles already?"

"I think so. You'll find Deer Creek Campground easily," Debra nodded, her thin lips pursing in resentful agreement.

"Just to be safe would you mind flagging the forks on the trail for us so I'm sure where you're headed? After I got lost in the woods, Smiley made me promise I'd ask you to mark them."

"Sure, just give me the flagging." She shot out her hand for the bright yellow non-adhesive tape. "Maybe you should come with me, Jenny. I don't want you to get lost."

"I'm fine, Mom. Just be glad I'm here." She tugged at her thick brown sock and brushed off her knees.

"All right, see you guys in a couple of hours or so." Debra turned and marched on ahead of us.

I was surprised Debra hadn't put up more of a fuss about Jenny walking with me. After living in a house full of men it would be interesting to spend time with some extra estrogen.

"Do you like being out here? I don't," she said, before I could answer.

"What don't you like about it?" I asked.

"I hate mostly everything. The mosquitoes are awful, hiking's not my thing, I miss my friends, and the food is crappy." I'd never heard Jenny say so much at one time. She started in again before I could say a thing. "I guess the scenery's pretty and I like hearing you say how much you like it. You're lucky you get to hike alone so much."

"Most of the time it's nice being here by myself," I said, walking steadily. "It gives me some time to think about what I want to do with the rest of my life."

"I can think of lots of things I'd rather be doing." Jenny pulled on her brown braids.

"Hiking alone isn't bad, but it's nice to have company. Your mom is lucky you agreed to hike the JMT with her. Sometimes I have to beg my sons to even go to the movies. It'd be great to have them here. I can't wait to see Craig."

"Do you worry about dumb stuff happening out here?"

"What kind of dumb stuff?"

"Stuff like…well…stuff like…having a period?"

"I don't have periods anymore. I had my ovaries removed last year because of some precancerous cysts."

Her eyes widened. "That's scary."

"It turned out fine, but I understand why you'd worry. I used to get horrible cramps when I was your age and just wanted to lie on a heating pad and sleep when I had my period."

"I get bad cramps, too."

"Not fun. Let me know if I can help."

The trail grew steeper, and I had to perform my 100-step-suck-water thing. For some reason it didn't bother me when Jenny saw me doing this. The mosquitoes buzzed and bit at us. We used any extra energy we had swatting them off. Neither of us seemed to want to stop and get out the insect repellent or our net hats. Trying to avoid the pesky things helped me move faster along the trail.

We finished hiking in the Ansel Adam's Wilderness and saw wood trail markers telling us we'd made it into The John Muir Wilderness. It was an area I'd never been in before.

Entering a meadow my eyes widened from the brilliance of the emerald grass and multi-colored wildflowers shining bright in the alpenglow. Debra had painstakingly identified the names of the flowers on the first part of our hike, but it didn't matter what they were called; I loved how they made me feel and how they looked. I asked Jenny to take a picture of me in the midst of them. Sitting in the middle of the field, I inhaled the sweet aroma and felt the stems tickling my sundrenched skin.

Then I snapped a picture of Jenny. Her long braids wound

around her head and she wore a lopsided grin. She personified youth and tenderness, while looking lovely and wild. Feeling a pang of jealousy at not having a daughter, I hoped Debra appreciated her. My sons' faces leaped into my heart and mind. Envy left. Joy replaced it.

True to her word, Debra had flagged the forks on the trail and Jenny and I saw where we needed to turn. I was careful about removing the flagging. Debra had told me repeatedly to make sure and remove every piece of it. Unnecessary. I had no intention of leaving my mark in the wilderness by dispensing yellow flagging all around. I might forget the names of flowers, but I was not about to litter sacred ground.

We arrived at camp about 6:00 p.m., the sun still shining bright in the summer sky. Debra had a watch and made it her business to keep track of time. I'd left mine behind on purpose. The rhythm of my day and the clues Mother Nature gave me would be my compass and time keeper on the trail.

Our campsite was set back from the main trail and surrounded by majestic shadowy pines. We used our bear canisters (which resembled small black plastic beer kegs) for chairs by the fire. At the beginning of our planning stage I was not a happy camper when I found out I had to carry one. It took up the majority of the room inside the top compartment and added weight to an already overloaded pack. The last time I'd bothered to weigh it—fully packed at home—it was almost fifty pounds.

I was glad I'd spent the $279 on my backpack. It had been on sale and was a bargain. It distributed the ten pounds of weight in the bear canister amazingly well and made it almost comfortable to carry the load. I thought about a time when covering food with rocks or hanging it from tree branches was enough to deter bears.

Times had changed since I'd backpacked nearly twenty-five years before. The water now had to be filtered, bear canisters were not just suggested but required in some areas, and many well-used campsites had bear boxes provided to store your food. The bear canister had set me back $74.

I imagined myself relaxing, sans blisters and constipation, on a white sand beach in Hawaii with the money I'd spent on this expedition.

That evening went better than I'd expected. Mother and daughter were at their funniest, cracking jokes about *Extreme Makeover* that aired on T.V.

"I'd be willing to go under the surgeon's knife for the results those women got. Wouldn't you jump at the chance?" Debra asked.

"Actually, no. I'm afraid of surgery. I've had two C-sections. I think I'll try to honor my scars and age as gracefully as possible."

"That's easy for you to say. You've got a husband who loves you."

"Maybe so. I still think it's important for women to accept themselves. I'd love to be thinner and fitter, and that's something I can control and work on, so I don't really have any excuses. Look at you, Debra. You have the body of a nineteen year old. I'm impressed."

"I'd trade it with you for a happy marriage any day," Debra said as she and Jenny retreated to their tent.

I loved being alone by a campfire, so I stayed awake. I heard them laughing and talking in their tiny tent. I smiled while the warm glow of the fire radiated my stomach.

The stars put on a twinkling light show, and I had a heart-to-heart with the Heavens. I gave thanks for the wonderful day. I asked that my mom and family stay safe, and for my worn-out boots to carry me. I fell asleep with thoughts of God and the mystery of the universe lassoing in my head.

Dear Diary,

Read my Science of Mind, *looked at my family's picture, talked to God, and now ready for sleep. For the first time, I can say I'm excited about the trip. I'm proud of myself. Didn't think about my weight, complain about the mosquitoes biting, or how far I walked. Looked for happiness and found it. Debra said I was lucky to have a happy marriage. I don't imagine she knows how hard we work on it. It hasn't been effortless, but it's been worth it. Smiley is a complicated man. He won't argue with me and clams up when I want to discuss things. He sees most things as black or white. Our friend Carol Holland says I'm the color in his life. Truth is a lot of a happy marriage is luck and hard work. It must be devastating to have someone leave you. Divorce is rarely amicable. It certainly has done something to Debra. Today was a good day. I'm a wife, a mom, a teacher, and I am hiking the JMT. I am me and I am HAPPY.*

Last Part of Journey: Day 9
July 24, 2004

The previous evening, a hiker reminded me to stock up on water for the first part of the day. "It's at least five miles to the next water," she'd told me. She was sixty years old, hiking the trail alone. The first time she'd walked it with her husband, they trekked hard and fast. "I want to take my time and enjoy the view this time," she had said. "I might not do it again." Boy, could I relate to that.

It seemed like many people were either running the trail, or hiking it furiously, trying to get from point A to point B as quickly as possible. It was nice to talk to someone who wanted to enjoy the journey.

Debra and Jenny got up at the crack of dawn, and I scurried around throwing things into my pack so I could join them. We wolfed down oatmeal. Debra pulled on her pack, "Hit the trail. Plans are to go about ten miles today and make Virginia Lake. We'll flag for you on the forks. It'll be a long day, so you'd better hurry. We'll need to use your filter before we leave. It's quite a while before any more water," Debra reached over and grabbed it from a rock. "I'll leave it by the stream so you can get it there."

"Should we meet at the next creek to filter water?" I asked.

"The way you hike, probably not. There's a lot of uphill today, so I think we'll just be heading out. We'll take our chances with the water we find on the trail. Good luck."

"See you tonight." I waved stupidly at the back of their heads and watched the sway of their packs. I could tell Jenny's ankle was bothering her. Her soccer injury didn't seem like it had totally healed. When she took off, she was using the hiking pole they shared. She was limping even more than I did when my knee was bothering me.

Watching her struggle reminded me to put on my knee braces, take my asthma pill, plop on my sunhat, shove my mosquito netting in my pocket, and adjust my hiking poles. I stuffed my inhaler in my pocket and checked to make sure my heart rock was in the other one. It was a good thing I didn't have a mirror. I was sure I wasn't a pretty sight.

Almost ready to go, I remembered to take a Citrucel pill. I'd brought them instead of the powder I usually used, and they weren't helping with my constipation at all. I felt bloated and unable to do much about it. I should've brought the sweet orange powder that always worked for me. I'd been afraid to pack too much of it because of the weight, having to mix it with water, and the bear problem. If I was honest with myself, I just didn't want to deal with Debra seeing me mixing it up and questioning me about my bathroom habits.

I'd always been weird about going to the bathroom in the woods. I know for some men and women this is a sign of being a real mountain person. I remember Bill Bryson writing in his book *A Walk in the Woods* that he just wanted to be able to talk with other men about shittin' in the woods. I didn't want to talk about shittin'. I wanted to actually perform the act. It was not happening.

It seemed like the uphill was never ending until I finally came to a stream where I filtered water. I'd never been a water nut, but the way a cold, refreshing drink of water made me feel on that day was beyond description. I drank a whole bag and filtered more to take with me.

Resting at a sunny spot, I proceeded to eat my lunch of gorp (a mixture of nuts, raisins and M & M's). As I gobbled down my food, I took note that my feet were finally pain free, but I tried to not look down at my boots. Whenever I did, their tongues flapped, chastising me for taking them on a journey they probably didn't have the soles to finish. I said a quick prayer asking for my shoes to stay in one piece.

Smelling ripe from a couple of days without any kind of bath, I decided to take the chance and jump in the stream. Every opportunity available in the middle of the day I tried to clean up. To save time I often rushed into the water fully clothed. That day I stripped off my clothes and fully immersed myself in a pocket of water.

Icy chills coursed through my body as I dunked my head under. Bliss. I played in the ripples the stream made as it progressed downhill making little hiccupping sounds. I floated awhile and did the best job possible washing my hair and body with the fresh, clean water. I'd become a new woman and wished Smiley was around to meet her. I was bold, I was naked, and I was taking care of myself.

After rinsing out my extra pair of underwear and socks, I tied them to my backpack and didn't even worry about people seeing them. Things like false modesty take a nosedive when you're struggling with basic sanitation issues. Besides, all the other *thru trail hikers* had underwear hanging out of their backpacks. I was just another JMT backpacker, and it felt great.

Giving up wearing a bra on the trip was a good idea. It

eliminated extra straps gouging my shoulders. My heavy backpack was enough; I didn't need a tight-fitting sweaty bra to add to my discomfort. Besides, nobody had the time or inclination to care if I was not sporting a slingshot, as my husband tagged it.

Getting to camp at a decent hour made me sing while approaching. I wasn't sure about the exact time, but I knew it was approximately 7:00 p.m. I was getting better at telling time from the sun. It was beginning to set and I was grateful for the light. The sun and I had become good friends on my solitary journey. It was something I could count on to keep me company. Maybe I was the sunshine girl after all. I found myself talking aloud to it at times. Perhaps the sun and God were intertwined.

"Please stay up and keep the clouds and rain away. Without you, my friend, I don't think I could go on. I've only so much stamina, and your shining brightens my day. I need you almost as much as the filtered water I drink. Please keep showing me the way." It seemed to be working, as we still hadn't had a day of real rain. Nature had become my religion and the wilderness my home. I continued along singing "You Are My Sunshine," Jane's big grin flooding my mind and urging me on.

Hiking up the hills that afternoon, I'd realized how well my system of hiking one hundred steps and sucking water worked. I'd used my inhaler only once. It gave me the adrenaline I needed to finish climbing up a vertical incline. It brought me to my destination: Virginia Lake.

Ice blue with surrounding jagged mountains, Virginia Lake overlooked a cornucopia of wildflowers surrounding its shore. Two squirrels sprung from rock to rock. They seemed to be involved in a carefree game of tag. My mother's sweet face surfaced in the recesses of my mind. She reminded me I didn't need to do the hike for her. She was wrong; I not only needed to do it for her, but I needed to do it for me. Taking off my shoes and soaking my feet I gently placed the boots aside. "Please hang in there," I implored, stroking their battered sides. "I need you."

I hiked around the lake and found Debra wringing her hands together with impatience, pacing in front of their tent.

"What the hell took you so long? It's almost dark," Debra said when she spotted me.

"Actually, I stopped at the local spa and had a mud bath and the full body massage special."

"Don't you wish? Well once again we've already eaten and yours is over by the fire."

"I'll be glad to clean up."

"Good, I'm going to bed. We're beat, and Jenny's ankle isn't great. She's already sleeping."

"Is there anything I can do to help?"

"I'm trying to tape it. I told her not to play soccer the week before we came. Nothing is going to ruin this trip."

"Sleep tight. I'll sit here and watch the stars and make sure the fire goes out before I turn in. Don't worry about me. I'm used to being alone."

She entered their tent without uttering another word.

I could have watched the stars all night but knew I would need my energy for the morning. I decided to call it a night.

Dear Diary,

Whoever said the wilderness at night is quiet hasn't spent much time in it. Frog croaks explode like gunfire off the granite cliffs. The wind howls lonely ghost songs, and the water gurgles lullabies.

Moon's shadow glows and reflects in a silver-mirrored lake that's too beautiful to imagine. Hope I never forget it. Exhausted, but I'd walked ten hard mostly uphill miles. I wish Debra would quit comparing us to all those people on the trail who are hiking fifteen or even twenty miles a day. I'm not one of them. Be sad to miss out on all the stuff you don't take in when you get in a big hurry. If nothing else, I'll have visions branded in my mind.

Wonder if Debra listened to those guys from Wisconsin who said two of the five of them were quitting because they were just plain sick and tired of rushing along. They hadn't planned enough time to see anything and it wasn't worth it. They were young, in their twenties, and in good shape.

Today every time I wanted to quit I could sense something spurring me on. I'm thankful for so much…thankful to be healthy enough to be here. Thankful to BE.

Last Part of Journey: Day 10
July 25, 2004

Virginia Lake's deep blue water surrounded by hundreds of fragrant Christmas tree pines invited me to just chill. I would've loved to take a swim and lie on a giant smooth boulder in the radiant morning sun. I also wanted to take time to wash out my underwear and socks. Debra was up yanking out tent pegs and raring to go.

"I slept great." I proceeded to talk about my dream as I was packing. I couldn't help myself. "I've had food dreams during our hike before, but this was the best one yet. I dreamed of a mouthwatering, tri-tip dinner at home on a Sunday night with Smiley and my sons when they were little boys, a crackling fire in the wood stove. I could taste the salt and was salivating while chewing the meat. We had spice-scented candles glowing and classical music playing; things we always do during our Sunday dinners. We were talking and laughing and I could see their hazy faces in the candlelight as we talked about the stuff we were thankful for. Craig said he was thankful it wasn't his turn to do the dishes. Sean was thankful we only had to give compliments to each other on Sundays."

I searched around to see if I was talking to the breeze and saw that Debra had slowed down and was looking at me. It was enough encouragement for me to continue. "We said our Sunday prayer in thankfulness, and love surrounded me. An ordinary Sunday. It was awesome."

I sighed, while pulling my sleeping bag out and cleaning the tent. I realized I'd been bragging and felt kind of bad. Debra stood nearby with a smirk on her face and hands on her hips.

"Lucky you. I had a shitty night. Jenny kept moaning and bitching about her ankle, and I hardly got any sleep. Why are you able to sleep so well?"

"I didn't sleep straight through. The stuff I told you was the best part of my night. I left out the part about the jagged rocks poking me. It did teach me I need to clean under my tent better."

"No fair," Debra said. "I'll bet Jane gave you some of her *sleep good pills* and you're holding out on me. Do you have any?"

"Nope. I asked Jane not to give them to me so I wouldn't become dependent on them. The not pooping thing is really starting to bother me though. In that respect, I wish I could join you in saying I had a shitty night. Didn't you say you had some pills for constipation?"

"I have some stuff, but didn't you bring your own meds?"

"I just brought Advil."

"Jenny and I might need our pills before this trip's over. I vividly remember telling you to get any prescription drugs and over the counter pills you might need out here. Did you think there would be drugstores in the wilderness? I hope you got some antibiotics. You never know what'll happen."

"I didn't bring any. I was hoping I wouldn't need them. My doctor doesn't like to give that stuff out without symptoms, so I didn't ask."

"I told you to be proactive. You should've taken care of yourself. I have Jenny to think of."

"You're right. But I'm miserable."

"Here, take some of these. When they're gone, you're on your own," she said, unzipping a pocket in her pack and tossing me three pills.

"I should've brought my Citrucel powder. It's the only thing that helps me."

"Why didn't you?"

"It's so sweet I was afraid it would attract bears. I also thought it would've been a lot of extra weight to carry. I made a huge mistake."

"I didn't mean you should take stuff out of your pack that you really need. For example, the energy bars. You noticed I didn't ask you to leave them behind."

I tried to ignore the remark. I never ate the yucky things and she knew it. Every day I carried them I became more pissed off about it. "Boy, I'm finding you shouldn't leave anything home you might need out here. What a stupid thing to try and save weight on. I thought being in the wilderness would magically cure everything. All this fresh air seems to make some things worse."

Jenny came toward us as she was stuffing the last part of her tent into its bag. "I sure miss a bathroom."

I nodded. "I never realized how attached I was to my toilet. I don't know about you guys, but when I'm crouching in the wilderness, I'm never able to find the right angle. I thought a lot of this stuff would come more naturally. When I was younger it didn't seem to be such an issue."

"Well, that's your problem. Let's go," Debra said to Jenny.

"Would you mind taking my picture first? I love this lake. I've seen fat sassy marmots chasing each other all around the boulders. They remind me of the kids at school."

"Suit yourself. We don't have time for pictures. Come on,

Jenny," Debra lifted her backpack and cinched her waistband.

"I'll take a picture." Jenny put out her hand.

"Thanks." I handed her my camera.

Empowered by the wildness and fiercely happy in spite of my bloated feeling, I stretched my arms wide and put on a huge smile. I lifted my face to the brilliant blue heavens. I hoped the picture captured the lush trees and twinkling emerald lake behind me.

"Do you want me to take a picture of you guys?"

"We've wasted enough time. Come on, Jenny," Debra said.

I couldn't help snapping a picture of the two of them as they left, almost running down the trail. I wondered if Debra had any idea how lucky she was.

"Don't forget we have to go eleven and a half miles today, so you'd better hurry up," Debra called out as she kept walking. "Maybe we'll see you later. Plans are to stop and swim at Squaw Lake right before Silver Pass."

"Great, I'll wait to wash my underwear, and swim there. I'm a little nervous about the long hike."

"Haven't you listened to all those other people going fifteen to twenty miles a day? We really should be doing more mileage."

"I'm not all those other people. Remember I told you approximately ten miles a day was my max. It's going to be hard for me to go over Silver Pass and hike eleven and a half miles. I'll do the best I can." The map Smiley insisted I bring forewarned me the trail would zigzag up and down all day.

"We'll see you at Squaw Lake," Jenny said. "You can do it."

"Thanks." Her words meant more to me than she could've imagined.

Alone again. I was glad Debra and Jenny weren't with me, seeing me gasping for breath. Misery doesn't always love company, especially if it comes in the form of Debra. I wondered why I'd thought backpacking was fun.

For every peak, there was a valley. I had started at 10,320-ft near Virginia Lake. I'd proceeded downhill to 9,600 ft to Tully Hole. My knees were screaming at me after the numerous steep zigzags I had walked to get there. I remembered Newton's Law, *what goes up must go down.* I would have to walk straight up in order to go over Silver Pass at 10,900 ft.

Hiking that part of the trail made it painfully apparent why the JMT resembled a heart monitor chart when it was mapped. I'd gone up and down, and up and down, more times than I wanted to count. I felt like I'd been on a roller coaster without the element of speed and fun attached. My secret 100-step-suck-water routine was getting a workout.

It kept my mind off the laborious task of walking. Dirty sweat poured down my face, and I was so set on counting steps I missed the scenery—the part of the trip I'd come for. Breathing became my first consideration. Scenery be damned.

The multitudes of families and friends seemed to be tackling the trail with grace and humor. Several of them stopped and asked me why I was alone. I replied truthfully, "Because I want to be." Whenever I hiked with Debra and Jenny for any length of time, Debra would criticize my hiking prowess and try to instruct me on walking correctly. She was probably right, but it didn't make anything better.

"Don't keep taking stops. Even out your breath. You have to go farther faster," were her constant sharp remarks.

I used my inhaler three times to be able to go on. My heart pounded harder after each puff on it. A heart attack might not be a bad way to go out. I thought of my 75+ year old friends Flo and Ralph doing their cross-country bike tour. The memory of their encouragement gave me lots more help than any of Debra's snide remarks ever could. Although the inhaler made my heart race, it also gave me the lung capacity to continue uphill to Squaw Lake. The thought of a cool and cleansing swim kept me moving.

After many more zigzags on the well-marked trail and two

more puffs on my inhaler, I arrived at an upper rocky basin. I was lucky I hadn't had a bad reaction to using my inhaler too frequently. Using it too often tends to make your heart beat dangerously fast and can give you jitters. There was a trail marker with Squaw Lake written on it. This was the place Debra and Jenny said they might meet me. I didn't hold out much hope for it so I started looking around for a place to rest, have lunch and a swim, and wash out my clothes.

I'd just put down my pack and was starting to enjoy being stationery and able to breathe when I heard a loud voice. "Hey, Lori, over here."

Sunshine bounced off the granite boulders surrounding the lake. Squinting in the direction of the voice, I saw Jenny waving her arms. Hallelujah! I hurried to put my pack back on and join them. They'd found a beautiful spot right off the trail with large flat warm rocks and a shallow part of the lake just right for swimming. Debra was skinny-dipping. I was tempted to join her, but it was a bit too close to the trail for me. I'd seen lots of people, which made me uncomfortable exposing my bare ass. I did, however, take off my socks and wash them, along with my other pair of underwear. I stripped off my shorts and washed them, leaving my top and panties on. With as much enthusiasm as my weary body could muster I ran—or more like galloped—to the lake and jumped in.

The water was icy, "Yeowwww!" It felt refreshing after the long dusty trail. I whipped my stiff hair from side to side and luxuriated in the feeling of being wet all over.

"Do you want some shampoo for your hair," Debra yelled.

I noticed she was still using regular shampoo.

"No thanks, I'll just rinse it out in the water. It doesn't make any difference anyway as I always have my hair under a hat. I really might be a different person when Smiley sees me next. Dreadlocks could set in."

"We're so far out. A little shampoo isn't going to hurt anything."

It always surprised me that whatever Debra did in the wilderness that was against the rules seemed OK with her. Even though she'd been a park ranger for years, she didn't seem to think the regulations applied to her.

"I'm worried. If everyone uses shampoo, the fish and a whole lot of other wildlife might not be around when my grandkids want to hike the trail. That's if I ever get grandkids."

"Suit yourself. My hair feels great."

We had our usual lunch of gorp, dried fruit, and jerky. Resting and sunning on the smooth warm rocks I took out *The Poisonwood Bible*. I was reading it for the second time, it was that good. The plan had been for each of us to bring a novel and share them when we were finished, but Debra and Jenny had only brought one book between them.

"When do you think you'll be done? I'd like to read it." Debra looked longingly at my novel.

"I'm not sure. I'm usually too tired to read. It's a Barbara Kingsolver novel that really makes me think. Can I borrow yours when you're done?"

"Sure, but both of us need to finish it. You about ready to kick over the pass?"

"As ready as I'll ever be. About how much farther do we have to go? I feel like I've walked twenty miles today."

"Well, you've only gone about nine and a half, and we need to get off of here and down to Italy Pass Junction before any more clouds settle in. We don't want to get stuck in a storm. Speaking of storms, I can't believe we haven't had rain this whole trip except a little bit at the beginning. Maybe Smiley's right about you being the sunshine girl after all. It's good we brought you along."

I couldn't believe Debra said she was glad I was with them. It felt funny to feel happy about something so trivial. That afternoon I'd had fun with them. I decided to enjoy it.

"I'm glad I came along, too." I smiled at her. "It's been quite the journey. Hey, do you two want an extra energy bar before we go up to the pass. I don't need one. I'll just drink some Emergen-C."

"Good idea. Aren't you glad we brought the bars? They give me energy to make it over the passes."

It didn't seem to be the time to tell her again how much I hated the bitter-tasting things. I passed her two out of my pack. It had been a good day, and I didn't want to ruin it.

There was another 600-ft climb to get to the top of Silver Pass. We may have run out of luck. I noticed clouds forming, making it imperative we get going. As usual, Debra and Jenny started out ahead of me.

Sighing, I put on my enormous backpack and knee braces. Grunting, I hoisted the pack onto my back, wondering when and if walking this trail would ever get easier for me. I was exhausted before even beginning the ascent to the pass. What choice did I have?

I had to keep going. There were no taxis in this part of the world. The Emergen-C and the respite at Squaw Lake seemed to have helped. I was still doing the sucky-100-step-water thing, but I was able to look around and enjoy some of the scenery.

What a view there was when on top of Silver Pass. All around enormous mountain monoliths towered, each one appearing bigger and more formidable than its neighbor. The huge cumulus clouds surrounding and on top of some of the mountains were rimmed in silver. Silver Pass earned its name that day and marked the boundary of the Inyo and the Sierra National Forests. A wooden board declared the elevation of the pass to be 10,900 ft. I felt lightheaded but exhilarated.

Debra and Jenny were nowhere to be seen, and I realized they must have gone on. I hoped they had at least taken time to see the marvelous view of the area's many lakes shining like diamonds below me. Taking out my map, I identified Squaw, Chief, Warrior, and Papoose Lakes. I could see why the Native Americans wanted to hang around in this country. They wouldn't be at a loss for irrigation or drinking water.

Enraptured with blue hues of the lakes, the fragrant green pines, and the majestic mountains surrounding the pass, I glanced around looking for someone to take a picture of me in such a spiritual place. I'd seen more people that day than any other, but when I needed them, they were nowhere to be found. Instead, I shot pictures of the scenery. I figured the photos would probably be a lot more attractive without me in them. Still, I wanted to remember I'd been part of it. The weight of my old fashioned camera was worth it to me. It would be exciting to see the photos after they were developed.

I started on a gentle downhill slope accompanied by earthy pine scent. My asthma was in control and I filled my lungs with the freshness. I could almost taste it and was proud of the fact that my inhaler was tucked away in my pack, unused. I left the Inyo National Forest by heading south and proceeded into the Sierra National Forest. Eagles soared in front of me as beacons.

After a few miles, I came upon the flagging I was sure Jenny had put out for me. I was certainly glad, as I wasn't sure how much farther I could go. Continuing on about 200 ft, I saw where Debra and Jenny had set up camp. Both of them were lying down on thermal rest pads with hats over their faces. I felt better seeing they looked exhausted, too. I quietly took out my pad and joined them. The sun was starting to go down a bit, which meant it was about 5:00 p.m. according to my estimation. I'd reached camp a lot sooner than I'd expected, but was dog tired.

It couldn't have been more than a few minutes when someone began shaking me. I looked up and instead of seeing Smiley, who I'd been dreaming about, Debra glared into my sleepy eyes.

"Glad to see you made it. Time to get up and fix dinner. It's your turn."

"Sure. I'm kind of tired of doing the clean-up, so it'll be good to cook. What are we having?"

"Food, if you can call those freeze-dried packages that. I'm still starving after we eat. I'm glad we have servings enough for four each evening. Good thing Jenny's friend didn't come after all. At least we get to eat the extra."

Debra's metabolism was astounding. She could eat more than anyone I knew and had done so the whole trip. Most of the time she ate her share of food and some of ours, too. Maybe being mad all the time burned a lot of calories.

After dinner, we made a fire and gazed at the blazing heavens. I was amazed at how many constellations Jenny knew. She was usually quiet, but that night she lit up as she shared her knowledge of the cosmos. A couple of falling stars whizzed across the sky with the brightness of Fourth of July fireworks.

Where did they go? They appeared to get sucked up by the earth. The heavens spoke to us and welcomed us with a light show. I stood in solitude and wonder until my body finally told me it was time to call it a day.

Dear Diary,

Walked 11 miles but it seemed like 20. Feel clean tonight. Having fresh socks and underwear can do tons for a sense of well-being. Have gone a total of 85 miles. Amazed, although I know I have well over 100 more to go. I'm worried about my shoes. It looks like the sides are coming out of the soles.

Don't know what to do about it. Just have to give it to God.

The very best thing that happened today, or more like tonight, was when the others had gone to bed. I went outside under the stars and pooped. I felt so relieved, literally. Guess Debra's pills worked. I'm worried, since she'd made it perfectly clear she isn't giving me anymore.

Not going to let her make me quit. I'm the one who gets to decide that. At times, I think she's glad I'm here, but most of the time think she's just pissed off she invited me.

Smiley was right having me bring the flagging tape and maps. He also tried to get me to buy a smaller more efficient flashlight. Had to be stubborn and say the one I have is fine. Frankly I was just sick of spending umpteen dollars on gear and was trying to be frugal. Need light to read and do my journal. Need sleep. God—wish I had a bed. Even the terrible ones in the Motel 6 seem divine in my imagination. Used to be able to sleep anywhere, anytime. Used to be young.

Last Part of Journey: Day 11
July 26, 2004

I woke to the sound of Debra barking orders at Jenny. "Get the tent down, make sure and wipe all the moisture out of it, go filter water before we leave, get ready fast. We have twelve hard miles to do today and we can't be messing around."

I poked my head out of the tent, feeling once again like a sluggish turtle. I hoped Debra wouldn't see me right away and bobbed my head from side to side cautiously before getting out. I usually didn't put my tent close to theirs, as Debra had made it apparent she needed her own space. Unfortunately, there was only so much flat ground. The place we were camping made it impossible for us to be far away from each other. It soon became apparent I'd been spotted.

"Better get your ass up and moving." Debra's feet stomped the ground. "We have to go up and down Bear Ridge today. We'll be going from 7,750 to 9,980 ft. Then down about another 1,000 ft and camping at Italy Pass Junction. That's about twelve miles."

I couldn't help sighing and rolling my eyes.

"Don't look at me like that. I know it's more than the ten miles we agreed on. Jenny is already bitching at me. She's pissed off we aren't taking the trail junction to Edison Lake where we could go in and eat *real food* as she likes to call it."

"I was thinking the same thing. I'd love to go over there and eat. The last few days I've been starving," I said.

"Well, you don't look it."

I was hoping I misunderstood what she meant, but her commenting on my weight didn't surprise me.

"I think you've lost weight, Lori. Your face looks thinner to me," Jenny interjected. "I hope you don't mind my saying that. I never did think you were fat or anything."

"Thanks. I was hoping to lose some weight on this trip. I know I'm overweight and I sure wish I wasn't."

"Jenny's right. You do look skinnier." Debra bit her lip as if perhaps she felt bad for her nasty remark.

For the sake of avoiding conflict, I decided to let it go. "Thanks, I think." Why in the hell did it matter to me if Debra thought I was fat? She'd almost negated the good feeling I got from Jenny telling me I looked skinnier.

"I feel like I'm losing weight, too," Debra said. "That isn't good. I was only 110 pounds when we started. You think you feel starved, you should be me. How about handing over a few extra energy bars?"

So much for feeling bad. Everything was all about her. Always. I really was growing tired of her abuse. "You'd be doing me a favor," I told her with an annoyed shrug. "I don't want to carry them. I never eat them. Here are the ones I have left in my bear canister." I took them out and threw them at her. It was a relief to finally tell her how I felt.

"I'm not taking them all. Just a couple. They weigh a lot."

"Tell me about it," I said, ready to argue my case.

To my surprise, she took them all and put them in her pack,

then looking sternly at Jenny and me, said, "You two need to get a grip. We aren't stopping and going to Edison. We'll be at Muir Ranch in two days where our resupply was sent to. We don't need to stop both places."

Even though I hated to admit it, she was right. When we reached Muir Ranch, I hoped she'd keep her word and let us spend a layover day there, but I'd wait until then to discuss it.

Debra whipped around the campsite, tearing down their tent, starting the stove to cook oatmeal, and packing up. She moved at warped speed.

I got out of turtle mode and joined in the frenzied activity, gearing up for what would be a difficult day. The trek would be brutal on my knees and shoes. I thought about my shoes, noting their shabby appearance. I pointed to them and said, "I'm not so sure my old friends here are up to making it the whole way."

"You should have figured that out sooner," Debra said.

"If they give out on me I don't know what I'll do. They look like they're holding on for dear life with their tongues hanging out panting in desperation."

"They look pretty bad. When we get to Muir Ranch, you need to send a message out. Tell Craig to bring some shoes for you. That's if you expect to go on."

She didn't need to remind me I might not finish the trip. There were too many variables pointing to the fact I probably wouldn't. I didn't want to think about it and needed to get going. I strapped braces onto my knees tightly, finished breakfast, and helped take down camp. Once again, my body was tired before even starting to hike. Not a good sign.

Laboring up Bear Ridge was worse than I expected. The sun glared unmercifully and there were hardly any trees shading the trail. Groaning with each footstep, sweat poured down every crevice on my body. I couldn't even perform the 100-step-suck-water routine that had kept me going previously and allowed myself to reduce it to seventy-five steps. Even at that rate, I could barely go on. I added wiping my face with my bandana to my little secret activity. My bandana resembled a fly swatter working vigorously without much success. The sweat poured down from my hat to my neck and face and into my eyes stung, making it nearly impossible to see.

Unwanted salt slid into my mouth and made me even thirstier. How could anyone enjoy any part of this back-packing hell? I tried to take my mind off of the pain by talking to my mom in my head and telling her she was right. I should have chosen Hawaii.

Praying silently, I mouthed the words *please, please help me go on; I can't do it alone.* I felt my friends' prayers lift me and enable me to continue. I knew Flo Seeley, my friend in her seventies wouldn't give up. She'd finished her cross-country bike tour in her late sixties and hadn't let mean people stop her.

There was no way out of my predicament anyway. I wasn't hurt, just exhausted and out of shape. The thought kept running through my mind that I would probably be doing everybody a favor if I gave up and hiked out with Craig when he brought our resupply in at Charlotte Lake. Or, when we reached Muir Ranch in two days, if I hiked five miles, there was a boat that could transport me out to the road. It was tempting.

It became painfully apparent I needed to ration my water. There was supposed to be a creek at the bottom of Bear Ridge, but I couldn't count on it as it had been a dry year. I forced myself to go back to a hundred steps before drinking. Think happy thoughts, I told myself.

Unfortunately, I couldn't conjure up even one pleasant thought. Thirst, hunger, and an aching body became my constant companions. The only memory coming back to me was the story about the *Little Engine That Could.*

Visualizing that train making it over the mountain helped me believe in myself. The book was one of my sons' favorites and it was such fun to put our arms around each other and chant "I think I can." I realized my trail name would probably be Caboose. It matched my red hair and my place on the trail. I liked it.

Reflecting on how much I loved my family helped take my mind off my troubles. I reminded myself Debra couldn't make me less than I am. My sons had been the high point of my life. When they were little, they'd made me feel important and cherished. I clutched their invisible hands and they brought me to the top of Bear Ridge. I sent them a mommy message thanking them for giving me the strength to get to the summit.

At the top, I drank some of my magic Emergen-C. I thought about eating an energy bar but even in my famished condition couldn't bring myself to do it. Then I remembered Debra had them. Yippee!

I ate a little of the jerky I'd managed to hoard. It added some needed salt to my body after losing so much as I'd sweated up the hill. A young couple was fast approaching, and I hoped to get them to snap a photo for me. I needed proof I'd made it and the way I looked would tell the story. It had been a helluva hike.

"Would you mind taking a picture of me?" I asked the attractive twenty-something year olds, holding my camera out to them.

"No problem," said the guy, sweeping his hand through his thick brown hair. "That was a bitch part of the trail, wasn't it?"

"It sure was. I didn't think I was going to make it, but then I didn't know what to do if I couldn't," I said.

The petite girl's name was Brandy and her smiling partner was Brett. After a few minutes of conversation, I found we were fellow teachers. They lived in upstate New York and three years ago had honeymooned doing the Appalachian Trail for five months. A trail that covered over 1,000 miles. That summer their plan was to complete the 211-mile JMT.

"Does your husband like to hike with you?" Brandy asked, glancing at my ring.

I laughed, "My husband doesn't like to hike at all, even though he's often described as a mountain man. His reason is he's done too much walking as a firefighter. What made you guys decide to do it?"

"Well, being teachers, we don't make tons of money. I'm sure you can relate. I guess you could say we're adventurers looking for a cheap vacation," Brett looked at my old-school camera.

"We thought we should do stuff like this before having kids," Brandy said. "It's cool you're out here doing it at your age."

"You're smart to do it while you're young. I was a lot fitter years ago."

"Do you have kids?" Brandy asked.

"Two adult sons. When they were growing up, I got so busy with being a mom and a teacher and didn't have time to do some of the things I'd dreamed about. My family says it's my time now."

"I wish my mom would do something like that," Brett said.

"This trail must seem like a piece of cake after hiking the 1,000+ Appalachian Trail."

"Not really. The JMT is much harder. The constant uphill and downhill and the high elevation make this a lot more difficult than the Appalachian. The other trail is much longer but more civilized than the JMT. The only real trouble we had with the Appalachian was the weather." Brett held up the camera and motioned for me to pose before he snapped a photo.

"Would you take our picture, too? We need to get going." Brandy handed me their camera.

"Sure." I took my camera back from Brett so it wasn't in their picture. "Smile big, and act like you're having fun."

After they left I felt lonely. I missed Smiley. I knew he wouldn't want to do this kind of hiking but told myself I'd hound him to come out and share the wilderness with me in some fashion.

Reaching the bottom of the ridge was an enormous relief. My knees screamed in agony. I sat down by the icy cold stream and plopped my feet and knees into the water. The cold numbed the pain. I swallowed three Advil tablets for reinforcement.

I filtered some water and cleaned myself up. Lacing my beat up old shoes, I realized I hadn't developed one blister on this portion of the trip. My trusty old boots were doing their best to help me.

Time dragged and just when I thought I couldn't go another step, and certainly not another mile, I saw the flagging indicating where Debra and Jenny had gone to camp. I let out a big sigh of relief.

Approximately 200 yards off the trail, I found them.

"Where've you been? It's almost dark," Debra pursed her lips at me. She sounded worried instead of pissed off, which surprised me.

Before I could reply, Jenny chimed in, "We've only been here a half hour or so. Wasn't that a terrible hike? I thought about your knees. My ankle was killing me. Even Mom had to use the hiking pole some of today."

I was shocked she'd said so much all at one time. I loved that girl. Whenever I felt awful she said just the right thing to cheer me up. I almost forgave her mom for treating me like dirt. A daughter like Jenny gave Debra lots of points in my book.

"All I can say is I've never been so glad for a day to end," I said, throwing off my pack and lying down on top of it.

Dear Diary,

Sometimes the only thing that keeps me going is knowing I'll get to read a little at night and write in my journal. However, the best part of the day is looking at my family picture. Smiley's heart rock gives me courage every time I reach in my pocket and feel it. It's solid and comforting. Just like Smiley. He's my rock. I might have forgotten to tell him that.

Hated the hike today. Don't know how I made it. There were forty-five switchbacks. Back and forth, back and forth. Each more difficult to maneuver than the one before. Had to use my inhaler twice. Even after that, could hardly breathe and my knees felt like Jell-O. I once read that we can bear what we think is unbearable. That is certainly a true story about hiking up Bear Ridge.

I opened up the Science of Mind *paperback book Jane gave me. Randomly went to a page. Tonight, it said: I am a perfect expression of God. Every part of my body functions with the excellence of God. I am created in the image and likeness of perfection. I accept health as my divine right.*

I laughed aloud and said to myself, they must be talking about somebody else's body. Think I'll try to believe it anyway. Should be thankful for my health and the fact I'm able to be on this hike. Need to quit obsessing about weight. Remind myself once again—God is good—all the time.

I WILL SURVIVE.

Last Part of Journey: Day12
July 27, 2004

We should've given up and eaten mosquitoes for breakfast. Zillions of them buzzed around us. We'd camped by a marshy meadow, and I was sure it had contributed to the large infestation of pesky insects.

We put on our net hats and long pants first thing and covered our arms even though it was already hot. Dead mosquitoes lay all over the top of our oatmeal. As soon as I scooped some out more relatives took their places.

They looked like black pepper sprinkled on top. I stirred them in and tried not to fixate on my less-than-appetizing meal. I had read about the soccer team who got in a plane wreck in the Andes and how they had to eat their dead companions. My belly rumbled reminding me what hunger feels like, and I empathized with those guys. Their predicament made eating bugs tolerable. I needed nourishment, and insects were part of the food chain in the wilderness.

I pulled my net hat up and down like a shade, but still got

some of it caught in my mouth as I was eating. I worried about tearing a hole in it. Even a small opening would make me a target of the lowest life form on earth.

Why had God designed them? He must have needed a good laugh. Maybe they were good fish food, but that's it. I tried consoling myself with the fact that because they're filled with blood (a lot of it mine) they must be a good source of protein. I was getting sick of oatmeal anyway, so the mosquitoes didn't ruin the taste. In my other life as teacher and mom, I'd never have considered insects food. Starvation can certainly humble you. My sons would've been proud of me.

My stomach was twisted in knots, growling, and I leaned over while clutching it. I was probably losing weight. My pants were looser. I was eating maybe 1,400 calories a day and burning about 5,000. I kept telling myself this was a good thing.

I wasn't a stranger to food shortage while growing up. There was a time I was very skinny. As a child, I was called The Red Lollipop because of my big red hair and thin body. I remembered being a small child feeling the same hunger pangs.

Mom wouldn't accept welfare. She'd tell me, "It's OK. Eat slowly and it'll seem like you have more food." She'd later said she should have swallowed her pride and at least accepted food stamps.

After eating as much oatmeal as possible, I scurried around breaking down camp. Debra and Jenny joined in.

It's amazing what a swarm of mosquitoes can do to produce speed in even the slowest of hikers. I walked twice as fast. I ran down the trail with Debra and Jenny behind me.

That didn't last long. Before I knew it, Debra jogged past me with her pack slapping against her back hollering, "Who knew what a fast hiker you could be. All it took was an army of bugs chasing you."

My pack was lighter. Without the extra fifteen pounds of

food we'd eaten out of my bear canister I zoomed along.

We hadn't eaten anything fresh, salty, or sweet for days and were down to basic essentials. A light pack felt great, but a little extra food would have been better. The only good thing was Debra and Jenny had eaten all the energy bars. The only bad thing was I wished I had one to eat. I couldn't believe I was that desperate.

I hiked so fast I kept up with Jenny and Debra. Jenny and I talked through our net hats and laughed. "You look like you're from outer space, Lori."

"Well, what makes you think you look any better?" It was fun hiking with someone else. "I'm so excited we're going to have a layover day at Muir Ranch. I'm planning on swimming, reading my book, and just sleeping. I can't wait."

"I wanted to talk to you about that," Debra said. "I've been discussing it with Jenny, and I think we should not stop but go on."

"Mom told me we could get home a day earlier. I've got other things to do this summer. But if you really need to hang out there, it's fine," Jenny twirled her braid and shifted her eyes.

I wasn't surprised, but I was mad. Debra constantly changed our plans, most of the time without consulting me. I knew I'd better come up with something quick.

"I need the break. Besides, Craig, Todd, and Devon won't know we've gone on and will bring in our next resupply on the wrong day."

Her face wrinkled in thought, showing me she realized the consequences of leaving early. "Well, I guess we might have to stay. But I'm getting more fit and could do a lot more miles a day. Do you realize we're only walking seven miles today?"

"Yes, and it's a relief." I sighed. "I'm pretty good for six or seven miles but then my ass starts dragging.'"

In my mind, I could hear my mom telling me, "You're

swearing way too much, Lori dear. The F-bomb bothers me the most." It bothered me, too, but I figured she'd understand if she knew the circumstances. Mom was always one to listen to another person's side of the story. Besides, I was one of the lucky people whose mom loved them unconditionally.

"When we hike over ten miles I can hardly get going the next day. I love the short days when I can see and enjoy things. I'm so glad tomorrow's only six miles," I said to my two companions. Jenny smiled and nodded. Debra just shook her head.

Hiking along and keeping up with Debra and Jenny did something good for me. I was in better shape than when we'd started. I didn't need to stop as often, and my breath came easier. As we approached the pass, a warm glow of satisfaction came over me. I hadn't been counting steps. Jenny engaging me in conversation helped, and my guidebook had told me reaching the top would be relatively easy.

Sparkling Lake Marie appeared right before the summit. It reminded me of a diamond ring set in a green velvet box. We decided it would be a great place to stop, eat lunch, and take a dip. The granite rocks surrounding the lake sparkled, accentuating the lake's luster. Thankfully, the mosquitoes had thinned out the higher we climbed. We'd met three or four other groups and everyone going the other direction spoke about the beauty of Seldon Pass. I loved the views from on top of the passes I'd crossed and was looking forward to being on Seldon Pass with Debra and Jenny. If only it wasn't such hard work.

Debra and Jenny stayed near the front edge of the lake and swam. Since nobody was around, I found a secluded spot and decided to chance a skinny dip. The sensation of cool water against my dirt-caked skin made me shiver in delight.

My hair moved like copper-coiled ribbons in the water. I swished it slowly from side to side. My body felt light as a feather in the rippling lake. I swam in my favorite position, on my back with my face staring at the sky. Cradled in water I watched the tall cathedral pines surrounding me and the cotton candy clouds floating by. I imagined myself spreading wings and flying toward the heavens.

My thoughts were interrupted by visions of my friend Connie. I sent up a prayer for her to stay strong. Then I pictured my mom as a warrior, battling cancer, not letting it stop her from doing the things she enjoyed. She was walking slowly and deliberately with her two little King Charles Cavalier dogs, a determined set to her jaw.

I prayed to the clouds, to the Lake Gods, and to whatever power there was in the wilderness to take care of them. To keep them mighty in spirit, even if they couldn't be robust in body. These visualizations buoyed my spirit. Mom and Connie were there, wishing me well, holding me up on the trail and in the water. My body shimmered with moisture and radiant joy. Faith and hope were with me, and the lake and I became one.

Renewed in mind and body, I climbed out of the water and met my comrades. We dressed, loaded our gear, and continued the hike together. It felt good. Each pass I climbed stood out in my mind as prettier than the one before. Seldon Pass was kind to me. It offered such beauty with relatively little effort and only a few zigzags to the top.

Wings spread, an eagle soared making tight circles, then it flew back toward me seeming to lead the way. The hike was just difficult enough to make me feel challenged. I imagined trumpets playing as we reached the top. I don't know if it was because Debra and Jenny were with me, but I was able to reach the summit after stopping for water only three times.

A group of people were also going over the pass. I asked them to take pictures of us. I snapped a few shots of Jenny and Debra. I knew if I was out here with one of my sons, I would want photos. I still couldn't believe Debra hadn't brought a camera. She took light packing to the extreme.

I wrote down Craig's cell phone number and handed it over to the woman in the group. "Could you please call my son and ask him to bring my Citrucel? It'll probably embarrass him to death but tell him his mom is miserable and needs it."

The heavier set woman I'd handed the number to smiled. "I can relate, I've been out three days and can't seem to poop for the life of me. I'll be glad to give him a call. We're going home in two more days. I have to get back to work."

"Thanks so much." I grinned. "It might make the difference on whether I continue this hike or not."

"Other things might keep us from finishing. I can't believe we haven't had any bad weather yet," Debra said. "We don't have any rain flies for our tents. If we get a storm that could be a real deal breaker."

"It does seem strange there haven't been any storms since we've been out," said one of the men. "There's usually a lot of afternoon and evening showers this time of the year in the Sierra."

"Lori's the sunshine girl. Her husband says it never rains when she's around," Jenny said. "He might be right. We haven't had any rain except for a few sprinkles."

"What a beautiful lake down below. It must be Heart Lake." I tried to change the conversation. I was embarrassed about being called the sunshine girl. "Wow! It is shaped like a heart and looks so pretty nestled in the trees. I can't wait to get there."

"We can't stay around the lake gazing all day," Debra said to the other hikers who were taking time to sit down and enjoy the view. "Have a good trip."

I looked back at them with envy as we rushed off. I would have loved to linger but didn't want to get left behind again.

"Thanks a lot for calling my son," I yelled back at them. "It means the world to me."

I decided, at least for that day, I'd work extra hard to keep up with Jenny and Debra. Since there were only about two and a half miles left, I believed it was possible.

We walked by Heart Lake, and it was every bit as pretty as it had looked from the pass. Giant logs were stacked on top of each other all along the shore and granite boulders surrounded it. Several sandy beaches made me want to stop and dive in. The lake's name reminded me of the treasure I carried. I reached into my pocket and felt the cool solid heart shape of the rock Smiley gave me. It was only the size of an acorn but it was my anchor and helped me feel strong. We didn't take time to swim, but went on to Sally Keyes Lake, where we planned on spending the night.

Since it had been a short hike, we arrived at camp in the early afternoon. I wasn't exhausted for a change and was glad to get there at the same time as Debra and Jenny. My asthma inhaler had stayed in my pocket the whole day. I hadn't done the 100-step-suck-water-dance even once. A personal best on the trip.

Jenny's voice interrupted my thoughts. "After we set up camp I'm going to go catch a fish. I'm starving."

"How in the hell are you going to do that? We didn't bring a pole or any line." Debra swiped her bandana across her sweaty brow. "We don't have any way to cook it, even if you're lucky enough to snag one."

"I'm gonna jump in and catch it with my bare hands. Then I'm gonna eat it raw if I have to. I can't stand being hungry anymore," Jenny wailed.

"Let's go down to the lake and see if we can help her," I jumped up. "I could sure use some real food. Trout sounds wonderful."

Debra frowned and grumbled but followed us down to the lake. It was comical watching Jenny repeatedly dive in the water. She'd come up empty handed with her mouth full of water and shaking her wet hair. I couldn't help laughing. She reminded me of a playful otter. I had to admire her spunk. "You go girl, and if you get one I owe you a big expensive dinner when we get out of here."

The truth was, I didn't believe she'd catch anything. I doubted Debra did either. Therefore, when we heard a loud sound like a high-pitched whistle coming from Jenny, "Yeowwwwwwwww!" we both looked up surprised. We were even more astounded when we saw what Jenny had inside her shirt as she came running towards us. Cradled inside was a beautiful golden trout. Fresh fish had never looked so good. I could almost taste the firm, sweetness of it in my mouth.

"God, Jenny, I can't believe you caught one." Debra grinned while jumping up and down. "I think I have some tinfoil. We'll build a fire and cook it. It'll be so good."

Jenny held up the fish, pulling its mouth open so I could take a picture. Her smile was wider than its gaping mouth.

A horrible thought occurred to me. "Oh shit, isn't that a golden trout that is a protected species up here? I don't think we're supposed to catch them or eat them." My stomach did flip-flops. Part of me wished I'd said nothing. It had been a minor miracle Jenny had caught the thing.

We stared at the fish then at each other. It was, without a doubt, one of the endangered golden trout.

Breaking the law had never tasted so good. I was as guilty as Debra and Jenny. Nevertheless, I licked my fingers and hands when finished, enjoying every last succulent taste of that trout. Fresh food cooked over a campfire couldn't be beat. For the first time in days, I felt full. We were heading to Muir Ranch the next day, so minus the oatmeal we saved for breakfast, we ate the little bit of food we had left in our packs.

I prayed our resupply was there.

Jenny was one of my trail angels from the beginning. She was the *someone I can count on* during the trip. The food she'd provided raised her even higher in my esteem.

Going to bed with a satisfied stomach made me feel better than good. Looking at the glowing yellow moon there appeared to be a man smiling in it. I imagined it to be my husband. I clutched his heart rock in my pocket. The moon grinned wryly and winked at me. A full belly, a full heart, and my rock put me to sleep.

Dear Diary,

How lucky I am to cherish and be cherished by the same man after twenty-five years of marriage. He believes in me—and that's a gift and a burden. Need to believe in myself. My heart rock keeps me centered. That's what Smiley does for me. I miss him.

I was a good hiker today. Going only seven miles seemed like a vacation. It was almost fun.

Jenny's my hero. The food she caught made all the difference in the world. Jesus said, "Give a man a fish and you feed him for a day. Teach him to fish and you feed him for life." Need to get Jenny to teach me to fish.

Last Part of Journey: Day 13
July 28, 2004

This morning I felt a song in my heart, and I began the day singing "You Are My Sunshine." I was so happy, I almost leapt out of my sleeping bag. We were going to hike to Muir Ranch and pick up our resupply. It was only six miles, and I was good for it.

Debra and Jenny weren't up yet. Another first for me. I looked around the campsite and noticed a squirrel scampering by. It seemed to be chattering a friendly good morning. I started boiling water for breakfast and raced around pulling out tent pegs. Grabbing my sleeping bag, I stuffed it like a sausage into its casing.

A few minutes later Debra joined me. "You know we could've skipped oatmeal this morning and just eaten the gorp and dried fruit left in our canisters. It would've been nice if you'd helped with breakfast on the days we had to hike long distances."

My first thought was to tell her to screw herself. Instead, I decided to try and kill her foul mood with kindness. Jane had taught me well.

"I've noticed you always have water boiling in the morning,

and I appreciate it. I thought it might be nice if I did it for a change."

Scrunching her small brown eyes, she replied, "Well, thanks. I'll use the water for my coffee, but I don't think I'll have any oatmeal. Maybe Jenny'll want some." She dashed to their tent and woke Jenny.

Nothing could sour my mood. When we reached Muir Ranch, we would have hiked over 100 miles. We were almost halfway home. I'd never backpacked that far. I couldn't help but feel proud. The food we would be getting and the layover day we'd promised ourselves gave me much to look forward to. Life was good.

I left before the two of them; my load was easy to carry, probably only about thirty pounds. I told myself to enjoy it. When we got our food, our packs would once again be at their heaviest, and I had struggled when that happened.

Though the hike was short, the trail was hot and dusty, making my mouth dry and eyes sting. My boots kicked up loads of dirt. Looking down at them I couldn't help but notice how bedraggled they were. The only parts that appeared to show any life were the new red laces I'd bought. There were places where the soles were coming off of the leather. Having boots with holes might work on a dry trail, but what if it rained and the bottoms came apart?

We still hadn't had any storms. Debra was starting to get mad about it. A few days before, she'd looked at me and said, "We could use a little rain on this trip. All the sunshine you bring may be a bit much." She seemed to feel I was responsible for the weather—good or bad. I couldn't win for losing with her.

Walking along at a good pace, I contemplated how much I was going to enjoy resting at the ranch and swimming in the hot springs. The research I'd done had told me the second part of the John Muir trail contained the wildest sections, a succession of ever-higher passes before arriving at the foot of Continental North America's highest mountain—Mt. Whitney at 14,496 ft.

Our hope was to climb to the top of it. When we left Muir Ranch, we would be in complete wilderness. No more roads, resorts, or habitation of any kind, except for the occasional ranger's station, from Muir Ranch until the end of the trail at Whitney Portal. For me, it would be the first time I'd been in such a wide expanse of unspoiled wilderness. It would be difficult to turn back or leave the trail.

Muir Ranch is the most remote resupply on the JMT. The supplies are brought in via boat from Florence Lake. There are a few cabins and tents available for backpackers and other campers to use. I wished we were going to stay in one. In my past life, I might have thought it would be cheating, but right then, a bed seemed heavenly.

This was a definite bail out spot if needed. I could take the ferry back across the lake. I could then call Smiley to pick me up and take me home. My only other opportunity would be to walk out with Craig. In nine days, he would come over Kearsarge Pass and bring in our last food supply. It seemed like an eternity. I reminded myself I was going to hike one day at a time or sometimes 100-steps-suck-water at a time. I'd decide the next day what to do.

After eating mouthfuls of dust, I puffed on my inhaler. My lungs felt tight and wheezy, and I could hear them whistle even after using it. Like Debra, I thought a little rain wouldn't hurt us. Too much of it could be bad however and would mean the difference between finishing the trail or not. If it did storm I would need to use my poncho for a rain fly. Not the best defense.

Debra and Jenny were worse off than I was. Since they supported light gear hiking, their tent could barely survive a strong wind. I remembered my son's orthodontist, a marathon runner, telling me he and his friends had to quit the JMT. They got a few miles past Muir Ranch when severe thunderstorms hit for three consecutive days and they couldn't go on. I realized many things—including a lot of luck—made hiking this trail possible. I wondered when my luck would run out.

Zooming by, almost as if she were in a race, Debra hollered, "We'll see you there, when you make it. We don't want to waste any more time. I need to get this trail dirt off and a swim in the hot springs sounds sensational."

"I couldn't agree more. See you soon." I choked on the dust they left.

It was good to be alone. Any idea I had of keeping up with Debra and Jenny exhausted me. I continued hiking and decided to enjoy the day by once again living up to my trail name. Caboose.

The clouds puffed up like helium balloons edged in gray. One resembled a duck, and another looked like a huge whale swimming across a wave-filled heaven. Wind rustled the trees and blew the clouds around. An old cowboy song about how the clouds danced in the sky popped out of my mouth. *Mariah.* I loved the song and could even sing it on key. My second graders enjoyed joining in, and we called it one of our *pretty* songs.

A woman's voice startled me. "Hey, you don't sound too bad. I remember that old cowboy song. Mind if I sing it with you?"

"Be my guest."

A lone woman hiker strode on my heels. She sang along and made me think of Jane. She was probably in her mid-thirties, I thought upon seeing her more closely. It's hard to tell on the JMT. Most of us cover up our hair with a hat, our eyes with sunglasses, and our bodies are swathed in backpacks. She didn't have the telltale hiking poles or knee braces lots of older hikers like me used. Young ones usually did without. Even on the trail, this woman was attractive. She was slim and wore a hiking skirt that showed off her strong and muscled calves. High cheek bones showed off lips that any model would be proud of. Her voice was melodious, and we kept singing as we walked. What joy.

After finishing the song, we stopped on the trail. She stuck out her hand. I took it in a handshake, a warm and companionable feeling.

"Hi, I'm Jeanette."

"I'm Lori. Are you out here all alone?"

"Yup. I'm having an adventure."

"I guess I am, too. Theoretically, I'm hiking with two other people, but they're always way ahead of me. It's earned me the trail name Caboose. Where're you from?"

"My trail name is Boston. It's also where I'm from. I came over to do a few day hikes in the Sierra. I went into the sports shop in Yosemite Village and started hearing about everyone doing the JMT. It made me decide to try and hike some of it."

"How ambitious." Our steps fell into sync as we walked.

"I bought all my equipment there and thought for fun I'd see how much of the trail I could do. The plan was to be out for four or five days, but people have been so nice, giving me food and everything, I've now been out twelve days. I'm thinking maybe I'll try to finish the whole thing."

"What about food for the rest of the trip?"

"A guy I met had some food sent ahead to the Muir Ranch. He told me he was sick of the whole thing and was going home. He wrote me a note so I can get his food and continue. I hope they believe me." She smiled, her grey-green eyes lightening up with anticipation and delight.

"Wow, I'm impressed. We planned this trip for a year and I'm still not sure I can finish it. Do you mind my asking how old you are?"

"I'm thirty-two and feeling it."

"I'm fifty and feeling it too. I don't mean to be nosy, but it's nice to have someone to talk to. Are you married? What kind of job do you have that makes it possible for you to do this? I'm a teacher, so I get summers off."

"I'm one, too. I teach high school. I have some friends in California by the coast, but I thought I'd make a stop in Yosemite. It's been a long stop."

"So, then you aren't married?"

"Yeah, I am, and my husband was kind of pissed at me when I phoned him from Reds Meadow. He wants me to come home. I'm going to try to call him at Muir Ranch. He's a great guy, but I'm angry he's forcing me to choose between him and this trail. Are you married?"

"I've been married twenty-five years. My husband is the opposite of yours and keeps telling me I can do this damn trail. He even gave me this heart rock to keep me going." I pulled it out of my pocket. "My problem is I don't know if I want to finish. I admire your conviction. I've enjoyed the trip, but I'm not in the best shape. My shoes can tell you part of the story."

Jeanette looked down and gasped. "I don't know if you'll make it with those. Do you have any plans if they fall apart?"

"I'm hoping my son brings in my tennis shoes on our last resupply. If he doesn't, I could be in a world of hurt."

Time and miles went quickly hiking with Jeanette. We walked along and I felt good about the fact I didn't seem to be slowing her down.

"You don't have to stay with me if you don't want to," I said. "I'm used to walking alone."

"I've been hiking by myself, too; it's nice to be with someone. We can hike to Muir Ranch together if you want."

"Great. I'd love the company."

Jeanette was fun to hike with. Not only did she know when to talk, but she knew when to be quiet. In the overhead sky, a majestic bald eagle soared and circled. Its sharp beak seemed to point the way. We simultaneously stopped in our tracks and went stone silent. Jeanette sighed when it was gone and said, "That's why I'm here."

"Me too." My gaze stayed glued to the sky hoping for one last look.

For the last couple of miles my shoes and I cruised along. I felt like a real backpacker, and I had a buddy. Life was good. Without the added weight of a full load, I was a much more competent hiker. In addition, it helped there wasn't a pass to go over. I'd even collapsed my hiking poles and put them on top of my pack. My arms were happy as they swung by my sides free from the cumbersome poles.

It was a culture shock to arrive at Muir Ranch. Even on the well-traveled JMT, there were days I saw very few people. I'd been enjoying getting to know my own thoughts and conversing with myself. When we arrived, I saw little campsites all over the place. It looked like there might be more than a hundred backpackers. The loud racket from their voices offended my sharpened senses.

Jeanette looked at me with a scowl on her face. "This place is certainly congested, isn't it?"

I nodded in agreement. I didn't want to talk and add to the havoc. Lots of people waved as we went by. That was nice. Campers lay on the ground, eating, talking, and reading books. A conglomeration of clothing and gear hung in the trees, strung along rope. We kept walking until I spotted Debra and Jenny off to the side of the trail. Jenny lay on her ensolite pad, and Debra appeared deep in conversation with two attractive men. Jeanette and I walked over to them.

"Hi, Debra, this is Jeanette. We met hiking. Is there room for the two of us to camp here?" Jeanette stuck out her hand, but Debra either didn't see it or ignored it.

"Sure, just go over and find a place. These two guys work for a company that sells new improved bear canisters. They're wondering if I'd like to demo one of them," Debra said, smiling sweetly.

"That sounds interesting. I'd like to hear more about it later," I said.

We walked over to an area close to them, and Jeannette turned to me. "Are you sure it's OK if I camp with you guys? That friend of yours didn't say one word to me and wasn't happy to see me."

"Don't worry. She doesn't talk to me much either. You're more than welcome to stay."

"I think I'll rest awhile then go check to see if I can get the food that guy left. Then I'll go up on a ridge and see if I can get any cell phone reception. I need to call my husband and let him know my plans. What do you think I should do about finishing the trail? I have an idea if I continue, it may finish my marriage."

"That's a tough one. There're days I don't even want to go another step, but that's my personal problem. I've been lucky; my whole family has supported me in making this trip. Truth is, I don't imagine my husband would be happy if he thought I was on a short vacation then found out I was hiking the whole JMT."

"What do you think he'd do?"

"He'd probably feel a lot like your husband. Miffed. Smiley and I have this thing. We let each other have enough rope to not hang ourselves. As much as I want to do this, I'm glad my husband didn't make me choose between him and it. Do you think your husband will?"

"Not in so many words, but we have a lot of differences. Like, he wants kids, I don't. I see how some of the kids at the high school act and it scares the shit out of me. I feel so old next to them and it worries me. What would I do if I had a kid turn out wrong? Do you have any?"

"Two boys. I've loved having my sons. They've grown into wonderful men and are one of the greatest blessings in my life."

"Weren't you scared about how they'd turn out?"

"Sure. I wouldn't be a mom if I didn't worry. They've had

their issues, but the good times have certainly made up for the bad. I never knew fear until I became a mom. I'd advise you to not think too much about becoming a parent. Just do it if you decide to. People who reflect on it too much never have kids."

"Do you feel like I should quit the trail for my husband?"

"You have to decide that. Maybe you'll figure it out."

Debra was having a great time talking with the guys about the bear containers. I heard them laughing and her giggling. One of them hollered over at us. "Hey, you guys, come over and look at our canisters." I walked toward them while Jeanette stayed at the campsite. The canisters were clear plastic, and I could see the food inside.

"Don't you think the bears will see the food and it will look like a picnic box to them?" I asked.

"Bears can't see well, so it's no problem," one of them assured me.

I almost asked them how they knew what a bear could see, but kept my mouth shut. The dark black bear containers we'd brought were opened with a penny or the end of a knife by twisting a little screw on the top. It took a short amount of time and little energy. The clear ones were supposed to pop open when you unscrewed them a certain way. Jenny was sitting up by now and both she and Debra tried to pry the top off the canister. They grunted as they tugged, twisted, and turned it. No matter how hard they tried, they couldn't get it off. Several failed attempts later one of the guys took it from them and opened it after a short battle. I noticed it took both of them to do it.

"Well, what do you think?" the big guy asked. I was glad Debra answered before me. These guys reminded me of the tailors in *The Emperor's New Clothes*. Frauds.

"It would take some getting used to, but I think it's doable," Debra said. "Will we get paid for using them?"

"We don't have any extra, but we could take your names and numbers and you can try them out on your next hike. You being girls and all, we'd only charge a small fee for you to use them," the smaller man said. Debra looked surprised that they wanted us to pay them. "Would you be interested, too?" he asked me.

It seemed absurd that there were salesmen on the JMT, and I was insulted they offered us a discount because we were *girls*. "I'm happy with the one I'm using," I said. "I believe bears are smart animals. If they see the food inside it would make them curious. I like the black plastic one I'm using, and I can open it by myself. I don't always have someone around to help." Debra shot me one of her looks. "I guess I'll go take a rest and let you guys discuss it." I went back to my gear under a tree and laid down. I was ready for a nap. Jeanette was there and resting, too. I could still hear voices.

Jeanette looked over at me and said, "Does your friend always flirt like that with the guys on the trail?"

"I don't know. I'm not with her much. Though it's kind of nice to see her in a good mood."

I was able to sleep in spite of all the activity around me. When I woke, Jeannette wasn't there. I assumed she'd gone to try and contact her husband.

Jenny came over. "Mom wants to know if you're ready to go to the ranger's hut and pick up our food?"

"Sure," I said, standing up and walking toward her.

We started along the trail to the hut. When we arrived, I saw little cabins scattered all around. Once again, the civilized part of me wished I'd been smart enough to arrange to stay in one. I spotted a man and his young son sitting on a nearby tree stump. We stopped to chat. I noticed that Jeanette was right; Debra perked right up around attractive men.

With his rugged jawline and thick black hair, even I thought the guy was good looking. Most of the time those kinds of things escaped me. He was an exception. His sparkling blue eyes were accentuated by a Crest toothpaste smile that would make any dentist proud. His physique put many movie stars to shame, and he had an easygoing friendly way about him that made me like him.

"How far are you three going?" he asked.

"To Whitney Portal, then climbing Mt. Whitney," Debra replied.

"Isn't Whitney the highest peak in the lower forty-eight states?"

"Yeah," Debra wrapped a strand of her brown hair around her index finger.

"How tall is it?" the man asked.

"14,496 feet," Debra replied.

"Wow, that's really high. Where'd you start?" asked his son, a boy I guesstimated to be around eight years old.

"In Yosemite," Jenny said.

"Isn't it a really long way?" asked the boy.

"Too long," Jenny answered.

"I read somewhere it's over 200 miles. Is it?" the man rubbed his thumb along his stubbled chin.

"Two-hundred eleven and when you add Whitney it is 233 to be exact. At this point we're almost half way there," Debra said. "We're going to pick up the resupply we sent to the little store here."

"We're headed there, too. Mind if we hike along? My name's Tom," he said.

"No, that'd be great," Debra batted her eyelashes.

We trekked through a dense wooded path until we came to a small building. A sign out front said the ranger would return shortly. We sat down and began to chat.

"I can't believe you guys are hiking all that way. No offense," Tom said. "I took the ferry over from Florence Lake with my son. We're staying in a cabin and then going on a three-day backpack. I thought that was something."

"Every person has their own journey," I said. "I remember taking my two sons backpacking when they were small. It's nice you're out here with each other. It'll make for some good memories."

"This is certainly a beautiful country," he commented, gesturing around with his arms. "We're from Southern California, and this is like a different planet."

We noticed a plump, elderly woman approaching.

"Hey, are you the one who's supposed to be working here?" Debra asked in a not-nice voice. "We've been waiting for over an hour for our supplies."

The woman glared at her. "You'll be waiting a lot longer with that attitude. In fact, I'm not quite ready to open yet." She stepped inside the cabin and shut the door firmly behind her. Debra had met her match.

Tom and his son got up to leave. "Good luck," they said, almost in unison as they walked away.

"I think I'll need it," I mumbled.

Debra couldn't believe we had to wait. She kept commenting on it loudly outside the cabin. "You go knock on the door and tell her we need our supplies. I'm sick of being the one to always have to take charge," Debra said.

I wasn't sure how the woman would respond to my pounding on the door, but I didn't feel like arguing with Debra. I went over and knocked. A gray head poked out. "What da ya want?"

"First off, I'm sorry to bother you. We had our food sent here and were wondering if we could get it? Also, I was wondering if you sold anything here for well ummmmmm..." I couldn't finish.

Maybe she could tell by my face I was desperate. Her tone

softened. "Well what is it you want besides your supplies? We do sell some stuff here. She looked out the door and hollered, "You two wait out there for a minute," she said to Debra and Jenny. She pulled me inside.

"Something's wrong, honey. What is it?" she asked, reaching out and enveloping me in her soft ample bosom. Like a child who sees her mother after her first long day of school, I felt safe, that feeling of relief I could finally let down my guard all the way down. To my utter surprise, I began sobbing.

She held me tight and patted my back tenderly. I cried so long and so hard, I started hiccupping. A thought occurred to me that maybe I should feel embarrassed, but I didn't. It was wonderful to let it out and be comforted.

When I felt like a well run dry, I stepped back, wiping my eyes and nose on my shirtsleeve. "I can't thank you enough. You'll never know how I needed that."

"My name's Susie. Sit down here and tell me what's wrong."

"My friend's going to be really mad at me if we don't let her in soon. I'm so sorry to involve you."

"Don't worry about it. I'll take care of her." Susie went outside, then came back in a few minutes and sat next to me.

It was nice to talk to someone. I jabbered on and on and couldn't shut up. "I'm taking this trip with Debra, the woman outside, and her daughter. Debra hates me. I've hiked most of the time alone, which I've found I actually like. Honestly, I shouldn't be doing it. I'm out of shape. My boots are falling apart. I hate mosquitoes and they love me. I'm hungry all the time. I'm overweight. I have asthma and have to use my inhaler a lot. I miss my husband, sons, and dogs. I even miss sex when I'm not too exhausted to think about it. I can't believe I'm telling you all this. I'm an idiot and I can't read maps very well. I get lost. Right now, the worst thing of all is I can't poop. I try, I try, and I'm always constipated and bloated. I'll never make it. I don't know what to do."

When I finally came up for air, Susie looked at me with the kindest eyes. They were aged and foggy with the wisdom of life. She patted me on the back again. "Well, some of that stuff I can help you with and some I can't. I have to wonder if the woman outside is really your friend. But first let's work on the constipation problem. I have some prunes, but I don't think that'll be enough. So, I can give you about ten laxative pills. I work here all summer and keep a small supply."

"That'd be wonderful."

"I also can probably help you make your shoes last longer. Come to my trailer later, I have some Shoe Goo. We can try it. I also have some duct tape we can wrap around them. Even the astronauts use it. Then I'll lasso some rope over the tape to help the goo set. What else do you need?"

I stared at her, speechless. She didn't look a thing like my mom but I felt a kinship. They were women who solved problems. She looked angelic, her silvery hair surrounding her head like a halo. God had sent me many angels along this trip. Her overwhelming kindness helped me realize she was one of them. Small miracles kept occurring daily. "I need my son to bring in my tennis shoes when he meets me on the trail in nine days in case my boots bust. Thanks for offering to help patch them up. I also need him to bring in Citrucel. I think I can make your pills last until then."

"I'll be going home to Coarsegold for a week's break. I'll contact your son and talk to him or leave him all kinds of messages. 'Save your mom,' I'll tell him."

"I don't know how to thank you."

"Then don't. First off, do you really want to continue this hike? Listening to your alleged friend out there and the way she treats people doesn't seem very appealing to me."

"I have to try. I don't see me finding the time or energy to do it ever again. I absolutely love the country. It fills my soul and brings back the sense of wonder I'd almost lost. I'm certain you can relate."

"I sure can."

"I've felt stronger and have gotten to know myself better out here than I have for years. I've had time to think about what makes me happy and learned to rely on myself. It's changed me. Debra can be a real tyrant, but she's honest. I never could've done the trail without her. She managed all the logistics. I didn't even know about sending food. She took care of the details. In that respect she's been great."

"Well then," she said, handing me some prunes, "let's see about getting your supplies. You stay here while I have a little pow-wow outside."

She must have been very convincing. Debra was a changed woman when she was allowed inside. Susie found the two boxes we'd mailed ahead and gave them to us. "You kids go ahead and get some rest. Lori, come to my cabin tonight for the Shoe Goo. If that doesn't work, aint nothin' gonna do it."

We took the boxes outside the store. It felt better than Christmas. There was a paperback book for me, toilet paper, which made Jenny ecstatic, and some batteries for my headlamp so I could continue writing in my journal and reading my *Science of Mind* at night. There was more of my magic Emergen-C powder, tons of gorp, dried fruit, my favorite jerky and enough freeze-dried food to last us nine days. We dived into the baggies of gorp, shoving it into our mouths as fast as we could.

What began as a bonding time for us soon became a battlefield of differing opinions. Debra said, "We have too much stuff here. We only need enough for seven days 'til we meet the guys at Charlotte Lake."

"I'm sure we'll require more food than that. I've been keeping a daily journal and I'm certain it's nine days until we meet them," I said as I continued stuffing my face with gorp.

"I'm not packing anything more than I have to. I'm exhausted, so we need to give some of the food away when we leave here," Debra said. "Let's see what we can eat here and get our gear down to being as light as possible."

"You're always saying you're starving, and we've given you extra rations," I said. "How do you think you'll feel if we don't have enough food?"

"Well, I'm not fat, so it won't bother me. Besides I know I'm right."

I could feel my blood pressure rising. I hoped she was correct, but I knew she wasn't and I had to stand up to her.

Dear Diary,

So excited about tomorrow. Get a whole day to just BE. Going to go to the hot springs again and take a looooooooooong bath. It was blissful to do that today. Going to read, filter, and drink as much water as I want, clean my clothes and my hair, eat and eat some more of the food Debra wants to leave, and just enjoy being in the woods. I believe we should carry it all, but don't know how to convince Debra.

Think Jeanette is going home. She hiked a long way and was able to talk to her husband on her cell phone. She came back saying the trail isn't worth her marriage and maybe I was right about kids after all. She said if I could still hike after having kids then maybe she could too. I told her I thought she'd made the right choice. The mountains will be here waiting for her. They aren't going anywhere. That's what Susie, the ranger at the store, told me. She said a mountain's life is way longer than mine is and I can come back if I don't finish. She reminded me there is no shame in trying.

I'm certain Susie will contact Craig. She's kind. A person of substance, like my mom. That's what I'd like to be when I get old: a woman of kindness and substance.

Last Part of Journey: Day 14
July 29, 2004

Dear Diary,

This was the best day of the trip. I love the wilderness, but don't love killing myself hiking. Swam for two hours in a large pond beyond the hot springs. Hair and body feel clean. Group of about fifteen senior citizens swam with me. One guy told me they were all over seventy and meet up in the wilderness every summer. They gave me hope that even in the aging process there are things to look forward to. Met lots of amazing people here at the layover camp. I read a hundred pages of a novel, relaxed, took pictures. Debra was in a good mood.

Jeanette is hiking out today. I'm lucky; I've been there, done that, been newly married and had my kids. My men, Smiley, Sean, and Craig are here with me in my mind and heart. All I have to do is take out my rock—makes me feel they're nearby. My family's the foundation of my life, the rock-solid core of my existence. Walking this trail without guilt is a gift they gave me. I'm grateful.

Hope I can get the energy to leave this place tomorrow. A little bit of civilization makes you soft. Saw bats all over the sky tonight doing their nightly clean-up of mosquitoes. Jenny said a bear came into camp in the early morning. I slept through the whole thing. It probably doesn't speak well for my character, but it does help me realize how tired I am.

A bear ate up Debra's sports balm that we need for Jenny's ankle and tore up the garbage. Hope it doesn't come back. Wasn't able to convince Debra to hang on to all our food. Doesn't speak well for my character either. I could have packed the extra food myself, but instead ate a ton. We did keep some extra gorp, but we gave away two freeze dried dinners and some oatmeal. Hope it doesn't come back to haunt us.

Last Part of Journey: Day 15
July 30, 2004

"Don't forget, you can get a boat out of here and be back to civilization within a few days," Debra reminded me, an annoying smile pasted across her face.

We were packing up camp and getting ready to leave. Her not-so-friendly piece of information didn't do much for my ego. I wondered if my quitting would be the best-case scenario for us all. Everything I read about the trail said the hardest parts were still coming.

"I'm thinking I'll be going on with you guys. My boots seem to be holding up. I took off the rope Susie had wrapped around them and they're pretty snug."

"Are you sure?" Debra continued stuffing her sleeping bag in its case.

"Susie told me she'd get a message to Craig to bring me my tennis shoes so I have them in case my boots fall apart."

"Good thinking. I'll help you carry your shoes," Debra said to my great surprise. "You don't want to miss going over Forester.

That's the kick-ass pass everyone says is way worse than Whitney."

I was beginning to think maybe Debra was somewhat enjoying my company. She continued on. "Besides you have the only camera to get a picture of us on top of it."

"I'll help you carry your shoes, too," Jenny looked down at my old ones.

"Thanks."

"That Emergen-C powder drink you shared gives me a lot of energy," Jenny said. "We have super power goop in the tubes for when we go over Forester, but it looks yucky. I wonder how it tastes and if it really works."

I was still surprised Debra had offered to help carry my tennis shoes. I am always so worried about being pokey that I forgot I might have something to "add to the party" as my mom liked to say. My camera seemed to be my ticket.

We finished packing and headed along the trail. "I need to drop this off and say goodbye to Susie." I twirled the rope in the air.

"I have no desire to see her ever again. She wasn't nice to me, so Jenny and I will just be going ahead. Plans are to hike about ten miles and camp at McClure Lake. We'll flag it for you." She tugged her shoulder-length brown hair into a small ponytail.

"Thanks, I think." They scurried off without even letting the dust settle.

I decided to follow their example and head for the trail. Before doing so, I stopped at the store to see Susie. Knocking on the door, I heard a muffled, "Come in if you can find your way." I looked inside and saw the store loaded with boxes and canisters holding JMT hiker's resupplies. Amidst it all, Susie's cropped silvery halo of hair.

I held out the rope that had kept my boots together. With a life of their own, my legs rushed my body over, and I threw my arms around her. I started to sob. Something about Susie let me know it was OK to cry around her.

"There, there, honey," she said, hugging me tightly. "There's nothin' that can't be fixed. What's wrong?"

"I'm so scared, Susie. You must think I'm a crybaby. I don't cry much, but it seems like you bring the tears out."

She took the rope from my hands. "Does this mean you're goin' on?"

"I think it does. Look, my shoes are sticking together. I did what you told me to and put some duct tape over the Shoe Goo, and it's amazing. I can't thank you enough."

"Don't thank me 'til they hold up for you. I still have my doubts. So, you want me to tell that son of yours to bring your tennis shoes and some Citrucel, right?"

"That'd be great, Susie. You are most definitely my trail angel. This might sound strange, but for some reason I know God wants me to do this trip."

"I believe you may be right. But, remember there's no shame in tryin' and not succeeding. Success isn't always about finishin', it's about the doin'. And you, gal, have been doin' your best."

"Please tell my family that I'm trying my hardest. Tell them I love them and miss them."

She handed me a big bag of prunes with a smile on her mountain weathered, wrinkled face. I realized she was one of the most beautiful women I'd ever seen. She gave me another quick hug and sent me out the door with a friendly shove. "Now you git goin', gal. We both have work to do."

I took several steps, then turned around and shouted, "Don't forget. We're the only Tierneys in Mariposa, so if you lose my phone number you can still contact Craig."

"I won't forget. I'm your trail angel, aren't I?"

I entered another national park: Kings Canyon. I'd never been to this part of the Sierra before. Butterflies fluttered in my stomach in anticipation and worry about the next part. Still, the trail was relatively easy, so I used the extra oxygen to sing as I walked.

John Denver songs were high on my list of favorites, and I sang the two songs my friend had sung at our wedding, "Annie's Song" and "You Fill Up my Senses." I found myself remembering that day twenty-five years ago with delight. A day when head-over-heels in love young Lori and Smiley married in the woods where they met. Many thought we were foolhardy for tying the knot after knowing each other only five months. Somehow, I'd known it was the right thing to do. Reaching into my pocket, I caressed my heart rock. It was smooth and steady, like my man.

Thinking of my life with Smiley made time pass quickly. I've always angered quickly. But I forgave easily, too. I'd had a hard time with a man who simmered and didn't know how to say sorry.

A few times I checked into a hotel just to escape his silence and so I didn't have to count the beers he drank. He kept his drinking to a minimum when the boys were small but as they grew older, he got bolder, and it bothered me.

He called me a control freak and said that just because I didn't like beer I shouldn't limit him. He was charming and funny when he'd had two beers, but he wasn't a man I liked very much after three. We needed to talk about that when I returned home.

Talking wasn't easy for him, but his excessive drinking wasn't easy for me. There in the mountains, I was finding the piece of me who wasn't afraid to say what I thought.

I knew I'd been hiking well when I came upon Debra and Jenny sitting by the side of the trail eating lunch.

"Wow, Lori, we just got here. You're really moving. Come eat with us," Jenny said.

"Yeah, we need some water and could use your filter. We

might even have time to rinse off in the river," Debra added.

"Sounds great." I dropped my pack with a loud thud beside theirs. "What do you guys do when I'm not around for water?"

"I already told you. We look for rushing water from streams and drink it. It's probably cleaner than what we get at home. I'm not sure the giardia scare is real anyway, and I'm glad we didn't pack the extra weight of a filter."

"I have a problem. I think my filter is starting to clog, and I didn't bring an extra insert. I didn't realize you were serious when you said you weren't bringing one."

"No use worrying about it now." Debra took my filter over to the river to get water and pump.

It wouldn't do any good to argue since they didn't have a filter and I did.

After eating, we decided to rinse off in the river. We didn't take off our clothes, just dove in. The icy river sent delicious chills over my body. I rinsed water through my hair, and the three of us splashed each other. Jenny, acting like the teenager she was, scooped up large handfuls and flung them. We tossed some back, laughing and shrieking. In the midst of our fun, we heard noisy shuffling. An approaching figure hollered, "Coming through."

It was a commanding voice, and all of us, Debra included, scooted over to the bank to see who it was. Running into the middle of the river lifting up hatsful of water and pouring it on himself was a very unusual older man. Several small packages hung on his back and he wore flowered shorts.

I waited for Debra or Jenny to say something, but when they didn't my curiosity took over. I started firing questions at him. My husband always said I could get anybody to tell me their life story, and I really wanted to know this guy's.

"Hi, could you tell us who you are and what part of the JMT you're hiking? You don't look like you have a lot of gear so I'm assuming it's a short distance."

He looked over at me with a sly grin on his sun-browned face and said, "Well then you'd be thinking wrong honey. I'm hiking the JMT. All of it."

"For real? Where do you get your supplies and food?" Jenny wore a bewildered look.

"I have 'em with me," he said, still splashing water over himself and filling up the four-plastic water bottles he had hanging from him.

"Where do you keep all your stuff? How long's it going to take you anyway?" Debra asked.

"Well, I'm hoping less than five days. That's my record—five days—and I'm looking to beat it," he replied.

"That's more than forty miles a day," Debra said. "You must run it or something."

"I do run a lot of it and don't get much sleep. I can't take much time here. I need to readjust my stuff, eat a handful of gorp, and move on."

"Do you mind if I keep being nosy and grilling you while you're saddling up to go?" I asked.

"Fire away, but you'd better hurry. I'll probably be here ten minutes tops," he continued his creek bath while removing his shoes.

"What do you eat?" I asked, always concerned about food and how people did without it.

"I have vitamins, oatmeal, lots of gorp, dried fruit, jerky, and that's about it. I sleep when I can but only for a very short time and I only use a little blanket. If it rains I keep running."

By now, he was starting to put on his shoes, so we knew if we had any more questions we better ask them quick. Jenny took the initiative. She asked the ones on all of our minds. "How old are you? What's your name?"

"I'm Reinhold Metzer. Sixty-three years old and proud of it."

"Wow, didn't it take you like forever to train for something like this?" Jenny asked.

"What did you do to get ready?" Debra asked.

Mr. Metzer finishing putting on his shoes and in less than the ten minutes he had said it would take him, he was ready to go. He turned around, looked at us with a twinkle in his eye and saluted. "You gals have a good trip now. I'll tell you my training secret. It makes my wife happy." We could just make out what he was saying as he took off, laughing, up the trail. "Sex my friends. Sex is my secret. Three times a day."

We looked at each other and started laughing. "You know, I thought the best thing about this trip was going to be the scenery, but I have to say the people are right up there. I don't think I'll ever forget all the characters we're meeting," I said.

"Me neither," Debra said. "People like him make me realize how slow we're going and how I could've done this trail so much faster. Let's get going before we grow roots."

The camaraderie I'd been feeling disappeared. Once again, Debra had reminded me I was slowing her down, and she sucked the joy right out of me. "You guys go ahead. I'll meet you at McClure Meadow."

"Sounds good." Debra cinched the belt on her pack. "See you there."

I spent the rest of the day immersed in thought and trying to let myself become part of the fluidity and grace of the mountains. My sense of well-being increased with every step. I didn't hurt, I wasn't afraid, I just *was*.

Jenny saw me as I arrived at camp well before sunset. "Gosh, I'm proud of you. You almost beat us," she said. It seemed silly to feel so good about a teenager saying she was proud of me, but Jenny's opinion mattered. I didn't care anymore what Debra thought.

"Thanks, Jenny. Where's your mom? I'll cook tonight."

"We met some judge and his wife and she's over at their

campsite talking to them. I didn't want to go."

I busied myself putting up my tent and setting up camp.

"Did Jenny tell you about the people we met?" Debra walked up behind me.

"Only that you were visiting with a judge and his wife."

"I was. They're hiking the whole JMT, too. Their packs weigh only twenty-five pounds and they have special equipment, including a one-pound tent made specifically for them. Horses pack in their food every five days and bring in filet mignon, wine, fresh veggies, and fruit. They only carry extra clothes, special packs of vitamins, and fishing gear. The only thing weird is they're taking thirty days to do the trail. I could go so much faster with all that good stuff," Debra said.

Taking time on the trail is what I found most appealing. I didn't bother to mention it to Debra. Going slower, they'd get a chance to really see the scenery and enjoy it. At this point, the filets and fresh fruit sounded grand, too. Just as if they knew we'd been talking about them the two new people came strolling into our campsite.

"Hi," said the woman. "I'm Jill, and he's Dave. We wanted to meet you. Debra told us all about you."

"I'm Lori." I didn't doubt at all the part about Debra talking about me. "She told me about you guys, too. Sounds like you're doing the trail in style. I have to admit the lightweight pack part sounds great."

"We probably sound like real Yuppies doing it this way," said Jill. "But Dave is sixty-four and has a heart condition and I'm in my fifties. We could've done the Europe thing again but wanted to try something new. We're loving it out here, aren't we, Dave?"

"Yes. It's great to know when Jill married an old geezer like me she still thought I could do exciting things."

I couldn't help but admire them. I hadn't been around rich people a lot, but these two seemed like they'd be fun to know.

After an interesting conversation and sharing some hot chocolate, Jill and Dave left to go eat their steak and drink wine.

"Maybe if we get to know them they'll share some of their food with us," Debra said.

"I wouldn't count on it." I replied. "I didn't see them rushing to invite us over for wine and cheese or anything. Besides, if they shared with every camper they met, they wouldn't have any food left."

Debra and Jenny took me up on my offer to cook. We had my favorite freeze-dried meal, lasagna. I went to bed with a full tummy and no aches and pains even after a 9.7-mile hike. I felt fit.

Dear Diary,

Just when I thought the evening was over and was reading a new novel, I heard a lot of commotion. I realized we'd left our dishes outside and maybe even some cups with cocoa in them. Was wondering why Jenny and Debra were throwing things around out there when it occurred to me they probably weren't.

Poking my head out of my tent, I saw the one thing I'd hoped not to see. A huge, maybe eight foot, several hundred-pound brown bear picking things up and throwing them. It stopped and turned its head toward me. It did not have on a friendly papa bear look. I know it saw me, which didn't make me feel any better.

Smiley says that sometimes I don't have any sense. He might be right. I jumped out of the tent and started hollering at the bear. I took a spoon and pan from near the campfire and banged them together. A few seconds later I noticed Debra get out of her tent and start throwing rocks. We both made as much racket as possible and I could hear Jenny in her tent screaming for the bear to go away. It seemed like forever, but it was probably only five minutes or so before the damn bear finally left our campground.

Debra came over and gave me a big hug. I hugged her back. "This time

I needed to help you scare it off. Maybe instead of Caboose, we'll give you a Native American name. Bear Chaser."

I couldn't believe how much the hug meant to me. The fact she'd helped scare the bear off made me feel supported and not alone.

Maybe I'm not as bad off as I think. Did well today. No inhaler, no 100-suck-step-water dance. Proud of Jenny, and yeah, Debra, too. Proud of me. Maybe we're a team after all. I like my new name: BEAR CHASER.

Last Part of Journey: Day 16
July 31, 2004

It seemed like we all got up on the wrong side of the sleeping bag. Before breakfast was over Debra and I were arguing about what day it was. Debra kept insisting it was at least Sunday, August 1, and I assured her it was Saturday, July 31. I tried to show her the mileage chart and dated journal I kept, but she didn't want to see it.

"Mom, you promised we'd be home in time for me to start volleyball practice," Jenny said. "I have to be back. The team's counting on me."

"Don't worry, we'll make it. I'm sure Lori's wrong."

"I'm not wrong. I write in my journal daily and track mileage. I tried to tell you we shouldn't give food away at Muir Ranch. Light packing is one thing. Starving to death is another."

"Well, you don't look like you're starving. If it's Saturday today and not Sunday or Monday, we're going to have to start begging for food from people on the trail," Debra said.

I hoped I'd heard her wrong. I'd done a lot of stuff on this trip that hadn't thrilled me, like wearing mosquito netting for a hat, eating horrid tasting energy bars and mosquitoes in my oatmeal, not sleeping more than three hours at a stretch, and burning up used toilet paper. None of those things seemed nearly as humiliating as begging for food.

When I was a kid, there were times my mom, my siblings, and I had nothing more to eat than a single loaf of bread and a quart of milk. It had to last for three days and there were four of us. I'd worked hard to not have the same situation occur in my household.

At home, I had a pantry full of food that would probably take a year to eat. I was proud my sons had never gone hungry. My mother hadn't begged for food when she was trying to feed us all on a waitress's salary. When tips were good and leftovers at the restaurant abundant, we ate well; otherwise a grumbling stomach had been my constant companion.

Jenny barricaded herself in their tent. I'm sure she was trying to not think about our situation. Wringing my hands, I glared at Debra. "I was taught to take care of myself and not ask anybody for extra favors. I think we'll just have to go hungry."

"No way."

"It's our own fault. We miscalculated the days. It'd be easy for me to blame you, Debra, but I should've made you listen when I said we were two days behind where you thought we were. Believe it or not, sometimes I know what I'm talking about."

"If you're right, we can't finish with the food we have."

"I don't think I have it in me to beg."

"Well, what in the hell do you think we should do? We don't have enough to make it until Todd and Craig bring in our next resupply. Do you have a better idea?"

I couldn't come up with one.

"Going hungry is something that won't hurt you, but Jenny and I burn more calories than we take in and we don't have any extra fat to burn."

Trying to ignore her insulting remark, I proceeded to come up with a solution. "Let's stretch our food out since we know we're short. We could save part of our packets from dinner and cook them the next day. Technically the meals are supposed to feed four people."

"You've got to be kidding. I'm always hungry as it is, even with my extra ration at night. I can't sleep, and even though I've asked you repeatedly, you won't give me any of the pills Jane gave you. I thought we were supposed to be a team," Debra said.

"I've told you over and over, I don't have any pills. I asked her not to give me any. I didn't want to depend on them."

"Well that's fine for you. You sleep all night, take your time hiking and living up to your name Caboose and don't have to worry about anybody but yourself. Must be nice."

I started in on one of the long lectures my sons hated. "It isn't always nice for me. I haven't slept through the night since I started this trip. I hate those damn energy bars I've packed, and I miss my family terribly. I'm continually hungry, thirsty, exhausted, and I never know if I'm going to be able to make it over the next pass. I'm trying my best to make this trip work. Talk about teams. I feel like the lone ranger out here. Let's just get over the Muir Pass today, take inventory tonight, and talk about what we should do. I haven't got a clue how to beg for food."

"It's an acquired skill. Practice makes perfect. We don't have much choice. You ask everybody you meet if they have any extra to share. Do you see any supermarkets?"

"No, but I haven't met many people with a lot of extra stuff. Most of the time they just pack what's needed. Nobody wants extra weight, so sometimes, like us, people pack less than they need." Unable to stop myself, I added, "I'm sure you can relate since you're so hot on light gear packing. That's why we don't have enough food."

"Jill and Dave could help us." Jenny peeked out of the tent. She was referring to the judge and his wife whom her mom had made friends with the previous night. "They have lots of food. Maybe you could ask them, Mom. They like you."

"Maybe I will." Debra turned and marched toward Jill and Dave's campsite.

I tried to hurry and clean up our site while she was gone. Jenny extracted herself from their miniscule tent to help me.

"I can see why your volleyball teammates would miss you," I said. "You're a hard worker and a team player."

Kicking dirt and pebbles, Debra came back to the campsite. I could tell by her face she was not a happy camper. "Can you believe it? They told me they need all their food and vitamins. They've calculated their equipment and grocery supply precisely. Damn Yuppies."

"It doesn't surprise me," I mumbled.

"Unbelievably, they also said they'd teach Jenny how to fish with a line, lure, and bait, then we could catch our own. They think that would work out best for everyone. I can't believe they're so selfish."

"It sounds like they're looking out for themselves," I said.

"I'm going over and asking them to show me how to do it." Jenny scurried out of camp. She probably couldn't wait to get away from the arguing.

"Maybe you could ask them if they have anything extra to eat, Jenny," Debra hollered at her. "I bet they'd give you something. We can take turns. I asked someone for food, now Jenny is asking. It's your turn next, Lori."

I didn't answer. It was no use arguing with Debra. I was tired and the day hadn't even started. I put aside a little of my dried fruit from breakfast to save for one of the miscalculated days. By the time Jenny returned, I was ready to leave.

"They gave me this fishing line and some bait." Jenny smiled and swung it from side to side. "I think it'll be easier than trying to catch a fish in my hands. I hope the lake we're camping by tonight has fish in it."

"Did they give you anything to eat?" Debra had a starved look in her eyes.

Jenny looked at the dirt. "I didn't ask. They already told you they didn't have any extra."

"Forget it. We'll ask people on the trail. Let's get going," Debra said.

In spite of it all, I was looking forward to the day. I'd seen pictures of Muir Pass and knew the Sierra Club had built the only manmade structure on the entire trail on top of the pass. They'd built the small stone building resembling a beehive for emergency use. The pass and the structure were named after my wilderness hero, John Muir. I could only imagine how he must have felt hiking solitary with hardly any other hikers on the trail. I related to him during the times I hiked alone and didn't see anybody for several hours. I wondered if, like me, he had the feeling of trail angels hiking along with him.

Debra and Jenny strode ahead. I was glad. There was a secret I didn't tell anybody. Debra and Jenny might think I was alone, but I knew better. I'd hike along and hear voices talking and urging me on. My mom's came to me clearly. It was always gentle and kind, enveloping me in her unconditional love. I could hear her saying, "My crazy, fun, big-hearted daughter, you're amazing."

My friend Connie suffering from cancer, "Do the trail for both of us."

My prayer partner Trisha, "I'm praying for you and helping water your yard. Your plants are fine."

My sister Rhonda's, "You're my big sister. You can do anything."

I felt my dogs running and romping beside me, free from fences and talking to me in their own special language. "We're here with you, in your dream space, on the loose in the wilderness."

I heard the Methodist women's prayers surrounding me, "God be with you," and lifting me over the rocky parts of the trail. Ralph and Flo's wise, lined faces smiled and urged me on.

Smiley's wry grin so often in my mind. "Have you found your lost pieces? My heart is with you. Feel it in your pocket."

My sons, Sean and Craig, were all ages as I walked. I could smell their baby breath and feel them in my arms as I rocked them. They marched beside me as young boys, laughing and throwing rocks on the trail as we traveled through time. I heard Sean asking, "Is this another nature hike to hell, Mamma?" Their fresh, handsome, young men faces came to me and I could almost touch them. They seemed to be laughing and saying to me in unison, "Keep going, Mamma. You can do it. Remember the story of the little engine. Keep hiking, Mamma. We love you."

"You go, girl. It's all good." Jane's long wavy brown hair billowed behind her as she rode her horse in the clouds.

My Dad's voice, "I wasn't always there for you, but perhaps it helped make you strong. I'm sorry."

En route to the pass, the trail traversed a series of mountain shelves. Several lakes with crystal clear waters reflected the high mountains surrounding me. A majestic barren world void of trees and most other vegetation transformed the place into a moonscape. I was an astronaut stepping on the surface of an alien world. Instead of a space suit, I wore a backpack. Huge granite slabs lined the trail, and the sharp biting wind, unfettered by trees, danced like a gypsy in a swirling skirt. Some of the finest views I'd seen on the trip surrounded me.

Continuing on, my mother's voice returned, ringing the clearest. "I love you, my darling daughter. You're strong. You're beautiful. You're smart and good. I'm with you always."

I came upon another group of hikers before reaching the hut. The building itself could be seen from quite a distance, alone on top of an isolated and barren pass. It rose like a lighthouse amidst ocean waves of granite. My steps grew lighter, and I saw several people in the distance. Getting closer, I recognized Debra and Jenny sitting on the ledge of an open window in the hut. Jenny grinned from ear to ear. She shouted down to me, "Hey, hurry. The view up here is awesome."

She was right. When I got to the top, I felt exhilarated. The sharp, icy wind made me more aware of the stark beauty surrounding us. Jenny scooted over. Plopping my pack down, I joined them on the ledge. We bathed ourselves in reverent silence.

Dear Diary,

Hiked 11.6 miles today!

Debra informed me it's my turn to beg for food tomorrow. Never believed I'd be fifty and have to ask for handouts. Instead of begging, maybe I can think of it as asking for a favor.

So many people and memories were with me today. Know I'm not crazy but keep seeing dead people walking alongside me. Guess it helps me realize people don't die as long as someone remembers them. Living people were with me today, too. Even if their bodies were somewhere else. Probably home doing real stuff. Maybe eating real food. When you love somebody, they're always with you. I stepped out of my tent tonight and it was BRRRRRRRRRRRR *cold. The shining stars reminded me of diamonds. Maybe they twinkle for each life going on in the heavens. Thoughts of my trail angels warm me. I'm not crazy. I'm blessed.*

Last Part of Journey: Day 17
August 1, 2004

Plans were to hike eleven miles and camp at Palisades Creek. At 8,800 ft, it was about 3,000 ft lower than the night before. I looked forward to being warmer and realized I might be grateful to Smiley for making me pack the space blanket.

It looked like an enormous piece of tin foil. He used it when he was on fire assignments camping at high elevations. He'd told me to wrap myself in it like a baked potato. Debra had said I needed to take it out of my pack, but I'd hidden it from her. Good for me. We still had the hardest and highest passes to cross. The thought of Forester Pass at over 13,000 ft made me shiver. I reminded myself that people say if you can get over Forester, you'll make Whitney for sure.

The different scenery along the trail enticed me on. Often tired but I was never bored. Our minds are the part of us we have the most control over. The constant thumping and beating of my heart cheered me. Godlike mountains always fill me with wonder.

I'd done a lot of praying on this trail, and it'd paid off. I inhaled the strong pungent smell of the earth, and my lungs felt good in the clean mountain air. This would be the last time I'd walk the whole JMT continuously during my life on earth. I'd never set foot in most of this majestic wilderness again. Closing my eyes and inhaling deeply I infused the sights and smells into the emulsion sheets of my mind.

My plan was to stop and filter water at the next stream. I approached it and saw Debra and Jenny standing there. They were talking to a young man and woman wearing forest service uniforms.

"Hey, Lori," Debra called out. "These guys are studying the endangered yellow-legged frogs and know a lake where there are thousands of them." She motioned to a man with a bright red bandana around his head and a young woman with no hat and very spiky blonde hair. "They're willing to take us there. Do you want to go?"

I couldn't imagine going even one extra step but didn't want to state it outright so I asked, "How far off the trail is it?"

"Only about a mile or so, and you won't be sorry you did it," the woman replied with a big grin on her face.

I looked over at Debra. The smile lighting her face and her open body language radiated excitement. She said, "I can't believe there are that many frogs in one place. It shows hope for the survival of the ecosystem. I can't wait!" She jumped around like a leprechaun who has found the pot of gold at the end of the rainbow.

Anything making Debra so positive warranted a look. I told myself to suck up the pain in my feet and agreed to go the extra mile. "Sounds great. Can we hide our packs here?"

"Good idea," said the lanky guy with round Ben Franklin glasses. He introduced himself as Mike.

The girl who had several piercings in each ear extended her hand and I took it. "I'm Jessica, and I take it you're the Lori I've been hearing about?"

"I am, and please don't believe any of what they told you if it's bad but believe it all if it's good," I grinned.

"Actually, they told me you're the good sport who came with them on the JMT and that you hike a bit slower than they do. But they thought you'd want to see the frogs, too."

"Hurry up. Let's go." Debra stepped behind some trees and threw her pack on the ground.

Their enthusiasm was contagious. I placed my gear near Debra's and followed them. It was wonderful to be hiking without my turtle shell backpack. Freedom.

It seemed like we'd gone a lot farther than a mile as Mike and Jessica led us cross-country. I tried to think of hiking off the trail as an adventure. We were heading to a place we'd probably be the only people around. A few hundred feet farther, we came upon a small lake.

"Oh my God," said Debra, running ahead of us. "Just look around. There are hundreds, no thousands, of yellow-legged frogs here. It's a miracle!" She skipped across rocks and exclaimed over each frog. She smiled from ear to ear. I'd never seen her so excited.

I loved looking into the lake. It was a sight for sore eyes and a natural salve. Much better than drugs, it made me forget all about my aches and pains. "This is amazing. I'm so glad I came. Thanks for bringing us," I said to Mike and Jessica.

"It's nice to see other people so excited," Jessica hopped across a log.

"You guys sure have a great job," Debra said, "What else do you do for the forest service?"

"We're scientists studying the frogs all summer," Mike said.

Flowers in full bloom surrounded the lake, and the entire area looked like a Monet painting. We scampered around for an hour or so while Mike and Jessica eagerly shared their knowledge. The fact the frogs were making a comeback from the endangered list was hopeful. Everything in the woods is related to everything else and losing a species weakens the entire ecosystem.

Debra had already asked Mike and Jessica for food. Unfortunately, they were leaving the next morning for a three-day respite and only had oatmeal left to share. I was glad I wasn't there when she'd asked. Jenny told me about it as she stayed behind and walked part of the trail with me. "It was so embarrassing when mom asked those two for food. Maybe we don't even need it," Jenny said.

"I think we do. Your mom and I went over my notes and figured we'll have two days without any food. As much as I hate to admit it, I think she may be right about asking people. We can only stretch things so far."

We hiked about a mile and spied Debra ahead waiting for us like a rattler ready to strike. "There are a couple of hikers coming this way. You need to ask them for food. It's your turn." She looked at me with narrowed eyes.

I wasn't quite sure how to go about it. I'd never had to do that kind of thing before so I didn't have much skill in begging. I thought to be polite I needed to start a conversation.

The two middle-aged men approached us as we waved to greet them. "What're you up to? We've been trying to walk the John Muir Trail. It's been a bitch coming from Whitney," the taller of the two bearded men said.

"We're hiking it, too, but I figured it'd be best if we started in Yosemite and worked our way to Whitney at the end," Debra tilted her head to the side flirtatiously and smiled.

"Good idea," said the other hiker. "I'm not sure I want to finish it. This everyday backpacking isn't what I thought it'd be. Instead of a vacation, it's more like work. Hard work."

I sensed the golden opportunity to ask for food. This was it. I had to do it. Looking down at my boots I stammered, "You wouldn't happen to have any extra food, would you? We're going to run out before my son and our friends bring us more. We'd really appreciate anything you could spare." I felt heat radiate up my neck, my face burning in shame.

I had a sick taste in my mouth like rotten eggs. I felt even worse when I looked up and saw their faces. The big burly one blushed. It was hard to imagine him finding the trail difficult to hike. "I'm sorry. We packed just enough to make it to our next food supply. We have only one drop, so we have to carry a lot. I wish we had some extra to help you out."

"There're some boy scouts trailing us by about a day. I bet they have extra grub. They seemed to be eating well and having a big celebration last night," said the other hiker.

"We need to get going," said the burly guy. He shuffled around and it was clear he was uncomfortable as he looked over at skinny Debra and Jenny. He probably thought I was eating most of the food. I was beyond humiliated.

"Thanks anyway." I was happy to see them leave. "Happy trails."

"Now was that really so hard?" Debra placed her hands on her hips.

"Yes." I walked away, then turned to face her. "Don't expect me to do it again. It was even worse than I thought. We made those guys feel awful. It isn't other people's fault we screwed up."

I stomped away, getting as far from Debra as possible. Inside, I seethed. I couldn't believe she'd talked me into getting rid of the food we needed at Muir Ranch. We were in a terrible position, and begging was the new thing I hated most about the trip.

It wasn't long before they passed me. In about an hour, I reached Palisades Creek and was happy to see they had a fire going. We arrived later than usual at camp because of our Yellowbellied Frog adventure. However, it had been worth it. I was delighted to carry the vision of Debra hopping around amidst them. It helped a little with the hostility I was feeling concerning our lack of food.

We were at a nice campground and it was so much warmer than the night before. I'd expected tons of mosquitoes because of the flowers, water, and green grass, but they weren't nearly as bad as those earlier on our trek. Either they were getting sick of the flavor of my blood, or the sweat and dirt I wore as my daily perfume wasn't appealing to them. Whatever the reason, they left me alone, and I was grateful.

After dinner, we sat around a peaceful campfire. It was one of those deeply silent and inky nights. We were startled when we heard something rustling through the trees. It didn't sound like the bears we'd heard previously but there was crunching twigs and heavy breathing. The clumping of approaching footsteps made my heart rise up to my throat. I consciously told myself not to scream.

"I knew I shouldn't have let you talk me out of bringing my gun." Debra jumped off the stump she was sitting on. "Now what're we supposed to do if we get attacked?"

I soon realized it wasn't a bear or an attacker either. A man dripping sweat and panting heavily came running toward us.

"I need your help. Please, please." He waved his hands in the air. It was apparent he wasn't from the United States, as he had a heavy accent and spoke broken English. "My brother he has broken place by his head. Right here," he pointed at his collarbone. "You have phone I use?"

"We don't have a phone. Even if we did, I don't think it'd work here," Debra stood up. "Do you need food and water?"

"Yes, water, food no. I have not the time. I need run for help." He gulped down two canteens of water and another with a package of the Emergent-C I gave him. Debra and Jenny had taken to using it, too, and I was concerned I would be running out soon.

"Do you want us to go stay with your brother? How far away is he?" I asked.

"He far. Six maybe miles. Some people stay with him. I run for help. Thank you much." He gasped for air and continued. "I from Czech Republic. How you lucky to live in America. Beautiful, beautiful. I go now. Thank you." He waved and bounded off into the woods.

Dear Diary,

I feel warm, not starving. Hopefully the man with the hurt brother got some help. I don't remember when I last felt full. Not easy to go to sleep when you're hungry and cold. Glad it's warmer tonight. I put my heart rock under my pillow after reading Science of Mind *pamphlet, said prayers, kissed the pictures of my sons and Smiley good night. I will pray for the man and his brother. Prayer is powerful. He was right. America, beautiful, beautiful. This place is beautiful beyond words.*

Last Part of Journey: Day 18
August 2, 2004

Food was always on my mind. Trying to go to the bathroom was always on my mind. I wasn't sure how much longer I could stand the constant bloat.

To top it off, the next day was my birthday. I'd be fifty-one years old. At home, Smiley would have taken me out to eat anywhere I wanted, or we might have gone to the coast.

Instead, I hiked. Mileage wise it should have been an easy seven miles. As soon as I got started that morning, I realized it wasn't. In fact, it was God-awful. Mid-morning two hikers who looked to be in their twenties approached from the opposite direction.

"An Irish girl on the trail is it, for sure might just be seein' a silkie," one of them exclaimed.

"You aren't goin' ahead on this trail, yes? The next seven miles are the worst of it," said the taller of the two in a splendid brogue. His curly brown hair and ruddy cheeks reminded me of Smiley's nephew, Tommy.

This information was not comforting, but I chuckled at their accents. Smiley's heritage was Irish, and he was more than a little proud. He'd been to Ireland two times without me—a bone of contention with us. I never stopped reminding him of it and the two men made me homesick for him.

"Out here all by yer lonesome, is it, missus?"

If I'd been in the city that question might have put me on alert. But in the wilderness, I felt safe. "Alone is pretty much how I'm hiking the whole trail," I replied. "You might've seen my friend and her daughter ahead of me. I can't keep up with them, so I follow behind like a little red caboose."

"With yer red hair ya could be from County Mayo. See 'em, I think we did. The woman was in a big hurry, yes, but did ask us fer some food," said the shorter one who also had bright red hair. "Wish we'd a had some ta give her. The two wankers what was with us, took off with any extry we had."

Without another word, we laid down our packs and sat on some tree stumps.

"What part of Ireland are you guys from?"

"We live in County Clare. Here fer holiday we are. Michael is me name, and whom might you be?"

"Nice to meet you. My name's Lori. How much of the trail are you hiking?"

For some reason this seemed to amuse them. I felt bad because I thought they were laughing at me.

"Hike fer a week we reckoned, but with the wee bit a food we have left we'll have ta find a place to get ta the road as soon as we can," said the other one.

For some twisted reason it made me happy to know we weren't the only idiots who didn't have enough food. "Didn't you plan correctly? What happened?"

"We reckoned well enough, but the other two blokes with us thought backpackin' would be a piece a cake. We've hiked all over our country together, but I guess we forgot to realize hiking at 2,000 to 4,000 meters in the Sierra is a lot different than climbin' St. Patrick's Peak, the highest mountain in Ireland. It is at about 1,000 meters, yes," said Michael.

"Where are the other two guys?"

"Wouldn't we just like ta know," said the redheaded one swinging his arms around. "We woke up and their tent was down, their gear was gone, and like I said, most of our food was gone too."

"I can't believe we didn't hear 'em They'd been complainin' about the hike the last couple of days and sayin' they didn't want ta go on, but I didn't believe they'd just leave us and not even let us know where they were goin'." Michael rubbed his head with a bandana.

"That's awful. I thought I had it bad. My friend leaves me every day, but she lets me know where to meet up with her at night."

Michael reached in his pocket and handed me a crumpled-piece of paper. "This is all they left us. It was under a rock where their tent had been."

I took the paper and looked at the words, *Hell No We Won't Go!*

"So, it seems like we need ta get out of these feckin—excuse the French but we're Irish—woods as soon as we can. I be needn' a Guinness in the worst way."

"My husband loves his beer, but I prefer an ice-cold Coke. I've been hiking for ten days straight and lots of days I'd like to quit. In spite of it all I'm hoping to finish the whole 211 miles of trail just so long as my knees don't give out and my boots make it."

The redhead looked down and whistled. "That's no Blarney. Those boots look like they've seen the thick of it. How many more miles are ya needn' ta go now?"

"I have three more days until my son's coming to meet us and bring in our resupply. I hope he's got my tennis shoes as backup. I had such horrible blisters from the new boots on our trial hikes I gave up and just put my faith in these old ones. I'm doing a lot of praying they make it."

"Well me thinks it might take more'n St. Patrick himself to see those things through. What's that stuff all over 'em that looks like glue?" Michael asked.

"Shoe Goo. If these shoes make it I'm going to buy stock in that company."

"Brilliant," said the redhead, who pulled out a map and surveyed the trails.

"Well, we better get going. I'm sure not looking forward to the uphill you were telling me about."

"It's asail," said Michael.

"What does that mean?" I asked.

"In your country I guess it means the shit," he said. "Don't believe anybody when they tell you it's a marvel of engineering and a golden staircase like some of the guidebooks say. Believe me when I tell you it's asail."

I gathered my gear and got ready to go. "Good luck finding your friends. I'll have to tell my Irish husband I met some of his kin on the JMT and I'm waiting for him to take me to Ireland someday."

"Regretting it you won't, missus," Michael said. "The land is flat, the beer the best, and the men the handsomest. Good luck ta ya, too. You'll need it."

"Happy trails." I waved and smiled while heading off.

They weren't kidding when they said the trail was *asail.* I was definitely on a 100-step-suck-water routine. The rock staircase that must have been a bitch to build seemed a never ending uphill. Once again, I could barely breathe. I wondered if each step might be my last. I stopped and leaned over trying to take some weight off my knees.

A group of Boy Scouts approached me from the rear and one of their three leaders looked like I felt. Sweat made dirty racetracks down his pale cheeks, and his shirt was bathed in perspiration. He wiped a bandana over his face and walked barely ten steps before he had to rest. Even the boys huffed and puffed. It appeared they'd stopped for a break. "Hi, how're you doing?" I mumbled.

One of the smaller freckle-faced boys looked at me as if I had snakes coming out of my head and said, "Awful. This is the worst day of my life. I'm never hikin' again."

"Me neither," said his friend with the skinned-up knees.

"Now boys, let's not be negative." The leader, who looked like Rick Moranis in *Honey I Shrunk the Kids*, clapped his hands. I could tell by his tone he was trying very hard to sound chipper. "I'm sure this woman doesn't want to hear our problems."

"Actually, I do. It kind of takes my mind off my own."

The boy who said it was the worst day of his life began his tirade about the rock staircase we were climbing. "I don't even like regular stairs, but these awful rock ones are gross. They just keep going straight up, and I can feel them through my boots. Just when I think I've got to be done another set appears. I hate 'em."

The leaders looked too tired to comment, and I somehow got encased in their convoy on the never-ending staircase going to the top of the mountain. I continued hiking with them. Misery loves company. The pale-cheeked leader lagged behind with me.

"I can't help noticing you've used that inhaler thing several times," he said as he puffed up some steep steps. "Does it help?"

"I'm not sure I could do without it. That, my water bladder, and stopping every hundred steps are what keep me going. What keeps you going?" I asked, incredulous I'd shared my 100-step-suck-water secret with him. We both plopped down on the trail to rest.

"The thought of getting home to a bed and a Coors," he

replied. "I never should've done this hike. I'm out of shape, and we have three more days. We packed way too much shit."

I looked at him puzzled.

"I know scout leaders aren't supposed to swear. But I feel like I'm in hell," he said.

If there ever was a time to mention the necessity of needing some extra food this seemed to be it. He said they had extra, so it wouldn't be begging. Maybe I could mention our situation and he'd figure out our predicament.

"You're lucky your group brought a lot of food. I'm hiking with a woman and her daughter, and we figure we're about two days short. Not sure we can make it to our next resupply. We don't know what to do about it."

The guy might have been exhausted but could take a hint. "I'm sure we could give you some of ours. Let's keep going, and when we reach the rest of the group we'll figure out what there is to spare."

This bit of hope gave me the energy to move. "That would be sooooo great." I held out a hand to help him stand. "Anything you have would be much appreciated."

"If you'd let me try your inhaler, that might give me some relief," he replied.

I knew I shouldn't, but desperate situations call for desperate measures, so I handed it over and instructed him on how to use it. He sucked it into his lungs and seemed to breathe easier. I hoped he didn't have a heart problem. The medicine in the inhaler tended to make your heart beat fast and hard.

It was often said *the scenery on the Golden Staircase is awesome,* but I never had a chance to enjoy it. I was too busy sweating, drinking water, puffing on my inhaler, and counting steps to care. The steps were even worse than the boy scout had described.

My knees popped and my legs screamed in pain at each rough and narrow stair I pulled myself over. My new bedraggled, plump, scruffy-faced scoutmaster friend and I took turns painstakingly passing each other on the trail. Neither of us had enough energy to say a word. We didn't pass anybody else, however, a whole stream of scouts and other people went by us.

Some of them didn't look too happy but seemed to be hiking the stairway to heaven or hell (or at least to Palisade Lake, five miles away) with a lot more vigor than us. The fact I'd been promised food was my greatest motivator. Maybe when I brought it to Debra she'd leave me alone about the begging issue for a while.

We came upon a trail crew of five young men hanging from huge rock extensions, pounding iron pegs into the boulders. The mom part of me clicked in. I approached them and hollered, "Hey, you guys need to be careful. The work you're doing looks incredibly dangerous."

"That's why we do it." One worker laughed.

I looked enviously at their lean strong bodies. "Have fun and take care." I tried not to wheeze as I trudged on.

At one point, the scout leader and I almost crawled up the hill. Our hands reached down and pulled our bodies along. Now not only did my feet hurt, but my hands were torn and bloody. It was not something I'd want to write home about. When we reached the top, we looked at each other and collapsed.

A few minutes later, a couple of the scouts came back and told us the group was waiting for the man, who by then I knew as Steve. My body screamed at me to stay and rest, but common sense told me the best course of action would be to proceed on with him. The food he'd promised seemed to be in the boys' packs.

When we reached the group, he introduced me and said, "This is Lori. She and a couple of her friends are running out of food. We should give them some of ours. We brought plenty." He was my new best friend.

"Sure, why not? We have extra. The Boy Scout motto is *Be Prepared*," the Rick Moranis guy replied in a chipper voice that made me wince.

The other boys agreed, except for one who looked like he belonged in Charlie's Chocolate Factory instead of being on the JMT. I heard him mumble, "How come we have to be prepared and they don't?"

Perhaps nobody else heard it, but I agreed with the kid. We should've been better equipped. They pulled food out of a stuff bag, and I had to contain myself from drooling. My buddy Steve came over and gave me a bag filled with three bagels, a container of soup, some crackers and, best of all, a freeze-dried peach cobbler.

"The peach cobbler is for your birthday tomorrow. We heard you telling one of the trail crew workers you couldn't believe you chose to be out here instead of at a fancy restaurant for your birthday. Hope it's happy."

Lowering my head so nobody could see, tears streamed down my face. I couldn't believe how much it meant to me that they'd given me something to look forward to. I desperately missed my family, and it'd been hard not to feel sorry for myself. "Going up that Golden Staircase was worth it after all. You guys giving me peach cobbler is like a little piece of heaven. I'll never forget your kindness." I reached out and took the bag.

I hugged each of the ten boys and the three scoutmasters as best I could enveloped in my pack. "Thanks for helping me up the Golden Staircase," I whispered to Steve, holding him in a friendly embrace. "You might have saved my life, or at least my sanity. Good luck."

"I'll need it," he sighed, rubbing his bearded chin. "Same to you."

I headed in the direction of Palisades Lake, where Debra and Jenny would be. They planned on camping there.

Everything that could hurt did during the last mile or so to Palisades Lake. The thought of bagels, soup, and crackers spurred me on. I planned on saving the cobbler for the next day as a birthday treat. I held the bag tightly in front of me, not even wanting to put it in my pack. No bear or anything else was going to get my new provisions.

Approaching the lake, I had passed by a few groups. Maybe I'd missed the campsite. A few hundred yards later, Jenny's yellow flagging led me to their campground. *I'm so lucky,* I thought. The note that said, *Hell no we won't go,* kept running around in my head, and I wondered how the Irish men were doing and if they made it out to the road. I sent a prayer to the heavens to keep them safe on their journey.

When I came to the campground, I noticed Debra and Jenny sitting around a campfire with Jill and Dave. I approached slowly.

"Hello," yelled Jill, "We were starting to worry about you."

"Do you need any help?" Jenny asked, as she walked over to me. I handed her the bag of food and put a finger up to my mouth. She looked inside and grinned but didn't say a word.

Arriving at the campfire, I heard Dave say, "Well it's about time for dinner. What are we having tonight, Jill?"

"I think it's stew and biscuits. I can't wait 'til our steaks and wine are delivered at Charlotte Lake. Yum," she answered.

It was hard for me to believe they were talking so cavalierly about food when they knew how little we had. Maybe while I'd been gone they'd given some to Debra and Jenny.

"Come on over after you've finished eating and we can sit around and talk," Debra said as they left.

I waited to see if she would tell me they had given her some food. She didn't say anything, so I asked, "Did they invite us for dinner?"

"No, but I'm hoping they bring something to share afterwards," Debra said. "I'm starved."

"Look what Lori brought us." Jenny passed the bag to her mom.

Debra looked inside. It took a minute to register the bag contained food, and good food at that. "Where did you get this?" She turned toward me. "It's about time you did something to help out. Who gave it to you?"

"The Boy Scouts I walked up the godawful Golden Staircase with. One of their leaders and I nearly perished on the way. He asked the boys if they'd share some of their food with us after I told him we were short."

"I asked one of those guys, too, and they didn't offer me any food," Debra said. "Why'd they give it to you?"

"Guess they changed their minds. I'm sure glad. We now have something for dinner besides oatmeal."

"We can make this cobbler for dessert. We'll share it with Dave and Jill. Maybe then they'll feel more like helping us out," said Debra.

"They gave it to me for my birthday tomorrow." I snatched the bag back and put it in my pack.

"We could celebrate early," Debra said.

"No thanks, I'd rather save it."

The bagels were delicious, and the soup and crackers hit the spot. I brought out the last four energy bars and offered them to Debra and Jenny.

Debra reached over and took one, handing the other three to Jenny. "Put them away. We'll save the rest for tomorrow."

Relief spread through my body. I was rid of them. It would be nice to not have them in my pack anymore. If Craig brought some in with our resupply, I would refuse to carry them. Debra and Jenny could have the nasty things with my blessing.

Jill and Dave trotted back over after dinner, empty-handed.

A fire always makes for camaraderie. We all found a place to sit to share its warmth. A man and a woman approached our campsite, interrupting Dave's funny story about a woman in court who was trying to gain custody of her kids while wearing a shirt that read, TODAY IS NOT MY DAY TO CARE.

"Hi, neighbors," the man waved. "My wife and I are camped here with our five adult kids. We've been coming since they were little. I don't know if you're aware of the *No fire over 10,000 feet rule* in this area. It's to protect the environment."

"The rule is 11,200 ft." Jill looked at them and pursed her lips in disgust. "I know because I researched this whole trip."

"It used to be, but they've changed it in the last five years," the man's wife replied. "We come every year. I'm sure you wouldn't want to break the law. We'd appreciate it if you'd put out your fire."

"We'd appreciate your leaving us alone," said Dave. "I'm a judge. I should know the law."

"I hope so," said the man. "It would be nice if you followed it."

"I'm a ranger, and I think it's fine as long as there's not a problem," Debra said. She was aware of the wilderness rules, but I was starting to believe she chose to do what she wanted in spite of them.

"I'm so sorry. We should put out the fire. I think you're right," I said. "We need to check our permit."

"You guys should leave so we can enjoy our fire," Dave said in his loud court voice. "Seems like there are an awful lot of laws and things out here in the wilderness, some of which don't make much sense. There isn't much vegetation around here, so what're we going to burn up? Rocks? What's the problem?"

"That's the problem. There isn't much vegetation, and you're burning up the little amount of fuel there is. We thought maybe you didn't know about the rule, but it seems like you do and you're deliberately choosing to ignore it. We'll leave you alone," said the man.

"Good idea," Dave sarcastically muttered. "We'll be fine without you."

"Thanks for being so understanding," I jumped up to shake his hand. "I really am sorry." They turned around and headed back to their campsite.

"Who do they think they are telling us what to do?" Jill asked. "What does it matter if we have a fire or not?"

"It does matter. I'm exhausted. The trail wore me out today, so I'm going to bed early." I turned to go into my tent. "Good night."

Dear Diary,

Sometimes people who have the most, share the least. Jill and Dave aren't people I'd want for friends. They think it's OK to be selfish, rude, and not obey rules because they have money. Those people were right about the campfire rule and Debra knows it. Not a good example to set for her daughter.

The Boy Scouts saved me today. Still, what was I thinking when I gave myself this hike for my birthday? Will I leave with Craig when he brings in the resupply? Don't know.

I do know it hasn't rained this whole trip. Everyone says that's kind of a miracle in itself. So much divine help. Steve, the Boy Scouts, the Irish guys, Sally who fixed my boots, Jenny, who doesn't even know what a trail angel is, even though she is one for sure. Feeling old. Fifty-one-years young tomorrow. A new beginning.

Last Part of Journey: Day 19
August 3, 2004

Happy Birthday to you, Happy Birthday to you, Happy Birthday dear Lori, Happy Birthday to you. Opening my eyes, I thought maybe I was still asleep. I'd been dreaming about being home with a big chocolate cake in front of me, and Smiley, Sean, and Craig singing to me. I could almost taste it as I turned over in my sleeping bag.

Before I opened my eyes, my mind leapt back in time.

The previous summer after coming home from our local rural grocery store while unloading bags, Smiley had started in on a super long narrative. I remembered him saying, "Hey Lori, I met up with Debra and she said she wants to hike the John Muir Trail. I told her she should talk to you. I know you've always dreamed of walking the damn thing, and you don't have any excuses now that the boys are grown. She wondered if we'd both be interested. I told her to count me out."

My eyes had widened in disbelief. "Wow. Do you really think I could do it?"

"Sure, if you wanted to," he'd said, walking away.

All the stuff you need or think you need to run a house seemed to strangle me at times. The laundry, the bills, the never-ending food preparation. We'd talked about downsizing.

That said, as I lay there in my tent trying to go back to sleep in the early morn, it occurred to me that maybe I didn't want to do this hike after all. Especially on my birthday. Perhaps I had taken my plan to escape my daily routine a step too far with this backpacking trip.

The sound continued, people singing happy birthday. I opened my eyes. Maybe it was real. I woke up salivating and licking my lips from the imagined chocolate. With newfound vigor, I jumped out of my bag and pulled on pants. Popping my head out of the tent door, I saw a group of maybe eight backpackers standing on a rock outcropping above our camp. Jenny and Debra's heads poked out of their tent too.

I recognized the man and woman I had met last night—the ones who had told us our campfire was illegal. I crawled out of my tent as they finished the song. "Wow, thanks so much. I was dreaming about my birthday at home. It's great to hear real voices singing to me."

The woman with wavy silver-gray hair and wrinkles lacing her face came over and handed me a bag of oatmeal and some gorp. "Heard you talking about being short on food, so here's a little something. Jenny told us it's your birthday, so happy birthday."

"These are our grown-up kids," said the bald man who stood at least six feet tall, gesturing at the people behind him. "We hike together every year."

"You're so lucky your kids like to hike. I had to beg my son Craig to bring in my resupply. He and Sean are always telling me I took them on too many nature-hikes-to-hell when they were kids."

"We never liked it much in our teens either," one of the youngest men piped up. "Now that we're older it's lots better."

"Could one of you take a picture for me?" I asked, reaching

into my tent for my camera.

"Sure," said the young woman with luscious caramel skin and a rainbow visor on. Since Debra and Jenny were still in their tent, I didn't bother to include them in the photo. Perhaps Debra had the decency to feel a little embarrassed about the campfire scene the previous night. It amazed me to think that instead of holding a grudge, those people came over to celebrate my birthday.

"Could the rest of you get in the picture?" I asked. They rushed over and we crowded together for the shot. The only thing brighter than the Sierra morning sun was our smiles. I thought about how much I'd enjoy having this photo to remember the day.

A few minutes after the family group left, Debra and Jenny joined me for breakfast. Debra picked up the bag of oatmeal and shook it. "Well, this stuff is useless. It's not instant, and we don't have enough fuel to cook it. You might as well scatter it for the squirrels. At least the gorp'll taste good," she took a handful and shoved it in her mouth.

We packed up quickly. Jenny looked over at me and said, "Happy birthday, Lori."

"Thanks." I picked up my backpack, strapped my knee braces tight, and headed downhill. I wanted to start out strong. On my first day of being fifty-one I made it out on the trail I had dreamed about for so long. In my mind I could hear the refrain, *be careful what you wish for.* I sensed Debra and Jenny on my tail.

"It's going to be a long day. You better keep up," Debra said as she approached me. "We're going to Marjorie Lake, about eleven miles from here. We'll be hiking over Mather Pass and it's better to make it before afternoon in case a storm settles in. I still can't believe we haven't had any rain." She kept on talking as she left me in the dust.

"Lori's the sunshine girl," Jenny said as she passed me.

"See you at Marjorie Lake, if not before," Debra called, turning around and facing me. "We'll celebrate your birthday tonight."

My heart skipped a beat. I wondered what we would do to celebrate. When I was a child, Mom always made our birthdays special. On the day I'd turned eight, I was so excited thinking maybe somehow she'd found money to buy me the Shirley Temple doll I craved. When I was just about to open my present, my six-year-old brother Kevin could hardly contain his excitement. "Oh Lori, it's a Shirley Temple doll. I know it is for sure," he blurted out. "I saw Mom take it off the shelf and put it in her purse." Somehow, the doll lost its importance. I wasn't sure who I was the maddest at, Kevin for telling me what I got or Mom for stealing it.

Too many sacrifices had to be made for birthdays at our home. Birthdays became bittersweet after that. I tried to compensate by going overboard buying frivolous things for my kids. Not always a good thing.

The path rose above the northern shore of Palisade Lake. Gigantic rock slabs shone like metal in the sun. I climbed above another lake and Mather Pass jutted into view. Once again I was doing my 100-step-suck-water thing and used my inhaler twice. My raspy breath whistled in my ears and I could hear a catlike asthmatic wheezing in my lungs. A helluva way to spend a birthday.

The route stayed extremely rocky and austere as it zigzagged upwards. Debra and Jenny had climbed far above me, and I felt sick to my stomach. I was barely able to nod at the groups coming down the pass. One guy looked at me and said, "It's worth the view. You aren't far from the top." These little acts of kindness and encouraging words from other hikers buoyed me. *Another trail angel.*

After what seemed like never ending uphill, the path started to level. I could see the marker saying I'd reached the top of Mather Pass at 12,100 feet. Debra and Jenny were nowhere to be seen. Once again, they'd left me behind. Only this time, I resented the solitude.

Voices and laughter interrupted my thoughts. Looking around for a spot to admire the view and have lunch (gorp from the birthday singing hikers) I spied a group of young men about fifty yards away. I chuckled at the unusual hats they donned. A stuffed moose stuck out in front of one hat, a small striped umbrella sat perched on another man's head, while a third hiker found protection under a lady's cloth sun hat sporting a wild flower design. One member of this intriguing group waved at me. "Hey, come on over and join us."

I approached them and noticed they had a large assortment of food arranged on the rocks, including cheese and jerky. Trying not to look, I could almost taste it and began to salivate. I didn't want to embarrass myself by asking for a bite.

"Would you like some?" one of the guys offered, pointing at the food.

I was sure they'd noticed me staring at it.

"If you have enough, that'd be wonderful," I tried to not sound desperate.

"We've got plenty. We're at the end of a week-long backpack. We get together every year and celebrate our birthdays by hiking," the guy with the moose hat said.

Trying not to shove it in my mouth too quickly I asked, "Did you happen to see a woman and a teenage girl go by?"

"Yeah, we did. They were almost running down the trail, which I thought was dangerous. I said howdy, but neither of them responded. Are they in a race or something?" the guy in the lady's sun hat asked.

"I'm supposed to be with them, and no we're not in a race. It's been kind of like one though. I'm always way behind. My trail name is Caboose. It's my birthday today, and I thought maybe they'd wait for me. We're almost out of food, so I'm kind of surprised they didn't ask you for any."

"Well, happy birthday, Caboose. Let's celebrate together. My birthday's tomorrow. How old are you anyway?" added the one in the umbrella hat.

"Fifty-one and feeling it," I replied.

"That's cool. I wish my mom would do something like coming out here. All she does is read and play bridge," the moose hat guy said.

"That sounds kind of nice right now. I'm out of my comfort zone. Hiking the whole John Muir trail is probably a lot easier for people your age. How old are you anyway?"

"We're all twenty-two and went to high school together," umbrella-head said.

"You're about my son Sean's age. I cocked my head. "What's with the hats?"

"Well, I'm always saying we're gonna hike in Montana and see moose. That's why I wear mine," moose-head said.

"I get so sunburned," the redheaded guy with the umbrella hat remarked. "My girlfriend got me this as a gag gift, but it actually works."

"This is my grandma's." The other guy tenderly stroked his hat. "She listened to my stories about my hikes and said she wished she could come with me. She wanted to see all the amazing things I told her about. I brought part of her with me."

"I want to be that kind of grandma. One that wears wild and crazy hats, listening to my grandkids stories."

"When she died, I took this. She wore it gardening. I remember how beautiful she was and how important she made me feel."

"I love it." I jumped to my feet. "Thanks for sharing your lunch. Let me give you a hug from your moms. Boy, do I miss my sons."

They stood and hugged me in turn. Closing my eyes, I

imagined they were my sons and their human contact warmed me.

I headed down the pass, my belly nearly full and my heart swelling with gratitude. The desert landscape featured several small tarns dotting the dry barren plain to the south. I was moon walking again. Hearing something behind me, I turned.

My new young friends were waving their hats and singing *Happy Birthday*. Smiling broadly, I took off my hiking hat, and waved back. My feet seemed to dance down the trail.

A zigzagging path dropped me steeply toward the basin. Without trying, I began to pick up speed. I could see why Debra and Jenny appeared to be running when my hat buddies had seen them. Gravity was pulling at me.

Perhaps I wasn't thinking or I got overconfident, but without looking carefully, I jumped over a pile of rocks, landing on my ankle. Standing up and dusting myself off, I slipped and winced in pain. A voice in my head chastised me for not being more careful, especially since I was all alone. I sat down, took out an ace bandage, and wrapped my ankle tightly. Opening my map, I studied the trail and realized I'd have to walk several more miles before arriving at camp. I had to take it easy.

My ankle throbbed with each movement. I was almost sure I hadn't broken it, but it really hurt. My hope was that it wasn't sprained as there are no medical services in the wilderness. My old boots weren't giving me much ankle support, but that couldn't be helped. They were making it possible for me to continue the hike without blisters. The tradeoff was worth it.

Looking at my boots I wondered how much longer the Shoe Goo would last. Once again, trail angel Susie came into my mind. She seemed to say, "The mountain will always be there. Do what you can."

With each twist in the trail I hoped and prayed to see the turn off to Marjorie Lake. The sun began to set and thoughts raced in my mind. What could I do to help myself.

The most impressive suspension bridge I'd ever seen appeared in the hazy sunset. Feeling like my heart had jumped into my throat, I forced myself to take the first step. The bridge swayed and groaned like a squeaky old door as I maneuvered forward on tiptoe. Sucking in my breath and holding it, I teetered over the roaring water. Below me, white, sudsy whirlpools whirled in Woods Creek.

Gasping, my heart beating rapidly, I finished crossing the bridge and sat down to think. I tightened my knee braces and adjusted my hiking poles, trying to calm myself by gazing around and breathing deeply. The alpenglow wandered over the treetops. The sky aflame with red, purple, and pink ribbons shooting across the horizon. A bluebird chirped somewhere to the side of me and the pine trees rose above like spires. I took a minute to drink in the high mountain air.

Worry is like a bad prayer, so I forced myself to change my mindset. "Please God, let me finish this hike. I know I'm not worthy enough to do it, but it would mean a lot to me if you could help me out. Please let my ankle be OK and guide me to camp soon. I'm scared and alone. Please be with me." I realized I was saying the words aloud and I didn't feel funny. Nobody else was around but everyone who mattered most was there. Peace settled into me, and I was no longer afraid. I searched inside myself for the faith I lived on and felt it lifting and guiding me on.

Testing my ankle, it felt better, making walking doable. Bone tired, I looked hopefully at the approaching trail marker about 100 yards away. A person stood by it. Debra without her pack.

She had reason to be angry. Instead, she looked at me and said, "Hey, it's late, we got worried, it being your birthday and all. Let me take your pack for you. Jenny's waiting at the campground. She's making dinner and we saved you some blueberry cobbler. That's why we wanted to eat the peach cobbler last night. We already had your favorite blueberry set aside for tonight."

I shimmied off my pack and handed it to her. There was a lump in my throat and I felt mean inside for not letting her cook the peach cobbler the night before and share it with Jill and Dave. "Thanks so much," was all I could manage. We continued hiking, and she kept to my slow pace.

The meal Jenny had cooked was one of the most satisfying of my life. We shared our last container of freeze-dried dinner—lasagna, my favorite. The cobbler was sweet, gooey, and satisfying. We decided we'd eat the second half of the pie for breakfast the next morning. I told them about my hat buddies and the gorp they'd given me for us to eat the next day. My ankle didn't hurt at all as we ate. Life was good.

After they went to bed, I took three Advil and lay down on the soft ground outside my tent, gazing up at a treasure chest full of sparkling lights. Earth opened its arms and poured a huge array of shooting stars across the sky. It lit up the campsite like a sparkler display on the Fourth of July. I tried to think of something to wish for as the heavens poured stardust. Before another star could fall, I whispered softly, "Please, please, let me finish this hike. Help me believe in myself."

Dear Diary,

It was one of the best and worst birthdays I've ever had. Feel old and young at the exact same time. God is everywhere. God is good.

Last Part of Journey: Day 20
August 4, 2004

In the morning I ate my remaining portion of the peach cobbler in two bites. I wondered what it would feel like to be able to eat as much as I wanted. "That was a real treat last night. Thanks so much for the great birthday celebration," I said to Debra as she buzzed around cleaning up.

She nodded as she shoved her dirty shorts and a tank top into her pack. "We better get going. We have Pinchot Pass to go over today."

"According to my guide book, it's a fairly minor climb after yesterday's epic pass and the two monster ones coming up, Glen and Forester."

Jenny made herself busy putting their stove away. "Good thing we kept that Goo stuff to eat."

"I hope it does what it's supposed to and gives me some energy to help kick over Forester. It's hard to think about." I stuffed my sleeping bag tightly into its case. "Love the views from the passes, but I'm getting sick of so many of them. I could use a no pass day."

"That's exactly why we did this hike from Tuolumne instead of starting at Lone Pine. Can you imagine doing all this uphill at the beginning of our trip instead of the end? At least now we're acclimated." Debra continued packing.

"I wouldn't have made it," I said truthfully. "According to my map and book we've gone over 170 miles. I can't wait to see Craig in a couple of days. After that, there's only about forty miles. I hope he remembers my Citrucel and tenny runners."

Debra gave me a funny look as I was packing my gear. "I hope I haven't lost as much weight as you have. I'll bet you're at least fifteen pounds lighter than when we started. It looks good off you but wouldn't off me."

"Thanks, I think." My pants were fitting a lot looser.

"We need some more food today. It's going to take a lot of energy to get over the top and hike eleven miles to our campsite. Do you have any more Emergen-C? We could use some," Debra said.

I had four packets left, and I could've used them all. Some days drinking one was the only way I was able to continue. I remembered yesterday and the lasagna and cobbler they'd saved for my birthday and pulled two packets out of my bear canister. "Here you go," I tossed them to her. "I put some more in the resupply Craig'll be bringing. I'm going to drink mine now since it'll help me do the climb. Shouldn't we be there soon?"

"It's about a mile and a half. Can we use your filter?" Debra asked.

"Sure. What have you guys been doing about filtering when I'm not around? Have you found people to borrow one from?"

"I told you we've been drinking running water from streams or off rocks. I'm sure we'll be fine. I've only known one person who has ever had giardia and saving the weight in our packs is worth it to me. We'll just keep borrowing yours when we're together." Debra reached for my filter and went down to the creek.

I hadn't wanted to spoil the good feelings I was having toward Debra but her asking to use my filter reminded me of all the things she'd discarded to pack light. I still couldn't believe she hadn't brought a camera to get pictures of Jenny and her. I took some when I was around, but mostly I wasn't with them on the best parts of the journey, like the passes. Her loss.

I was getting angry about sharing my filter. I didn't want to seem greedy but I had packed it knowing clean water was a priority to me. The filter wasn't working properly anymore; running slower and clogging up. It would've probably been fine for all three of us on a shorter journey, but it might not last the whole 233 miles. We didn't have another one coming with the resupply goods. Perhaps Debra could ask her boyfriend Todd, who was coming in with Craig, if she could use his for the last forty miles. Maybe I'd ask him for her. I'd think about it tomorrow.

We drank our Emergen-C, then Debra and Jenny started at their usual hare speed. I followed at my standard tortoise pace. Hiking alone didn't bother me nearly as much as it used to. Sometimes I looked forward to seeing them leave so I could do what I needed to make my journey work for me. As soon as they left, I put fresh water in my bladder and adjusted it to my pack. I made sure the tube was hanging out by my shoulder so I could easily reach it and do my 100-step-suck thing. I had a feeling I was going to need it.

After taking my preventative asthma pill, I reached in my pocket to make sure my inhaler and my heart rock were there. I wasn't sure which one I needed most, but I wasn't about to take any chances with either of them. Both were snug against my hip, giving me a warm feeling. Smiley was there beside me. It increased my comfort thinking about how steady and reliable he is. I could also hear him saying, "I'm glad it's you and not me going up that mountain. Hope you find a missing piece of yourself."

The Emergen-C kicked in. I did the 100-step-suck-water thing but found I was able to extend the steps to 150 before needing another sip. It occurred to me I might be in better shape than I thought. The 12,000-foot elevation didn't seem to bother me and I was grateful.

It helped me think that maybe I'd be able to do Forester Pass after all, even though it towered at 14,000+ feet. I'd been giving some serious thought to hiking out with Craig, Todd, and Devan when they came in. It amazed me that I was now giving some serious thought to finishing the entire hike.

Humming and walking at a steady pace brought me closer to the top of Pinchot Pass, which is the column between Mount Wynne (13,179 ft) to the east, and Crater Mountain (12,874 ft) to the southwest. It was an easy back and forth hike to the top and I found myself looking ahead instead of at my feet. A couple of fat marmots scampered around playing tag making me think of my little doggies at home.

The wind blew gently as I took off my hat and tilted my face toward the welcoming breeze. I lifted my poles skyward. My stomach rumbled, pleading for a snack, but it would have to settle for a long drink of water. Life is full of compromises. Absorbing the magnificent alpine scene that greeted me and marveling at the lush surrounding greenery, I felt my senses on alert. The monolith mountains reached up like European cathedrals and the trees were my altar. I was at The Church of the High Sierra where I found peace and harmony in abundance.

Descending down the steep zigzags I monitored my footing. The hiking poles were stabilizing me, and I didn't want to take the chance of ruining my knees this late in the hike. My ankle seemed to be holding up too. I'd laughed when wrapping it, thinking about what a sight I must be swathed in gauze, kneepads, hiking poles, and a water bladder attached to me like an astronaut's oxygen tank. I'd explored wilderness frontiers that were higher in space or altitude than I'd ever expected to be in this life.

I reached an upper basin in the path and saw Jenny, Debra, and a young man. They waved at me with wide smiles, jumping up and down so I couldn't help but wonder what was going on. Walking rapidly downhill, my foot slid on some talus. My ankle steadied itself and I reminded myself to be careful.

"Hey, Lori, this is Jim. He's a ranger up here."

"Nice to meet you." I extended my hand and shook his. "What a great job you have. You must love it. I was a wilderness ranger in my life before kids."

"I do love it. Debra and Jenny told me you guys are running out of food. I'm on the last day of my ten-day rotation, so if you follow me to camp I'll give you most of the provisions I have left. There's not a lot, but I don't need much to hike out tomorrow."

"He said he has some carrots and some peanut butter and bagels." Jenny had the biggest smile I'd seen the whole trip. It seemed funny to see a teenager so excited about carrots.

"I'm about a mile or so off the trail but at least we're going the same direction," Jim said.

He must have seen the look of exhaustion in my eyes, or maybe noticed I looked a lot more tired and older than the other two. "I only have my day pack. I'd be happy to swap with you and take your backpack."

I couldn't believe my good luck. It would take more than all my fingers and toes to count how many times on this trip I wished I could get rid of my tortoise shell backpack. It didn't take but three seconds for me to respond. "Sure, that'd be great."

Jim and I swapped packs. A good twenty-five pounds lighter than my load, wearing his small daypack put a spring in my step, making me stand up straighter.

We hiked together, and for the very first time I was able to keep up without a lot of effort. I maintained a conversation with Jim while walking. I told him a little bit about my husband and kids.

"Your sons must be proud of you. I wish my mom would do something besides shop and go to lunch," said Jim. "She's about your age or a little older."

"How old is she?"

"She's forty-nine."

"Thanks for the compliment, but I turned fifty-one out here on the trail. This backpack trip was a gift my family gave me for my birthday. I think my sons are proud of me. My hope is to finish it and maybe even climb Whitney."

"I don't see why not. You're close now. What would stop you? Debra said you're getting a resupply in a few days. Forester is worse than Whitney. It's the kickass pass of them all, but the view's worth it. When you get to the top of it you'll have it made in the shade."

I couldn't help but notice he'd said *when* I made it and not *if*. We kept walking, and Debra and Jenny marched ahead. As I started to limp and lag behind, Jim held himself back. He whistled and hummed as we hiked.

"Your parents must be proud of you. Are you going home on your days off?"

"I'm meeting some friends and heading to the beach for a few days. I love the mountains, but a change of scenery'll be nice."

Debra was waiting for us. "Aren't you the lucky one? You do know the part of the trail you're hiking wearing Jim's daypack, doesn't count, don't you?"

"What makes you say that? It looks like she's walking the trail to me," Jim said.

"Maybe it doesn't count to you, Debra, but it does to me. I don't care how I hike this trail. The fact is I'm walking it, and to be honest it's a lot more fun doing it without a big pack on."

Even without my backpack, I was getting tired. We'd already hiked eleven miles and adding the extra mile to get to Jim's camp was difficult. It was worth it though when we arrived. The limp carrots and quarter jar of peanut butter we put on stale bagels, was a king's feast to the three of us. We could have passed as street people as we shoved the food into our mouths. After finishing, we uttered heartfelt thanks.

"I sure wish I had something else I could give you," Jim said.

"That hit the spot. I think I can make it until the guys show up in two days with our food. You sure are another of my trail angels, Jim." I gave him a big hug.

"We better get going before it gets any darker," Debra said. "Thanks, Jim. I'm counting you as a trail angel, too. It's amazing not to be hungry."

"Thanks," Jenny said, leading us away from Jim's camp. I saw her turn around and smile and wave at him.

It dawned on me that maybe Jenny had been attracted to him. He was probably only five or six years her senior and just because I was old enough to be his mother, she wasn't. As we hiked I thought about Jenny and realized she probably missed being with kids her own age. I wasn't the only lonely person out there.

We all walked together the last two miles or so until we reached the place we decided to make camp. It wasn't much of a site, just the side of the trail. When we noticed a campfire ring, we all dropped our backpacks at the same time. I could see Debra and Jenny were tired, too.

It was beginning to get dark so we put our tents up quickly. Since we had eaten at Jim's camp, we decided to save the one freeze-dried meal we had left for the next night. We usually had two a night, which was supposed to feed four people, though Debra was still ravenous when we ate them. I wondered if she had a tape worm inside her. I'd started wanting less food as the hike progressed. Even though I was still hungry, I didn't feel terrible.

I foolishly commented on this to Debra. "That carrot and bagel with peanut butter really hit the spot. I think I'll be able to sleep well tonight."

"Well, aren't you the lucky one. I haven't slept this whole damn trip and doubt I'll be sleeping tonight. I'm starved and exhausted. But, I carried my own pack and so did Jenny. It sure must've been nice having someone carry yours."

I stared at her. I was tired, but not beat. I was hungry, but not starved. In addition, she was right about at least one thing. It had been great to not carry that damn pack for a few miles. I didn't even comment. I went to bed with a smile on my face.

Dear Diary,

Not making excuses to Debra anymore for why I'm so happy. My life and family aren't perfect. We've had our share of misfortunes. My brother became a heroin addict at twenty and got murdered when he was twenty-seven. It changed my mom's core being. She walks with a sadness that can't be reached. Craig and Sean have given me cause for alarm. We've been broke, and I constantly worry about Smiley's safety. He has a short fuse and doesn't like to help me with complicated computer stuff or figuring out T.V. remotes. When I say I'm technically challenged he heartily agrees. He must know how dumb it makes me feel and doesn't seem to care. Truth is I get up every morning and talk to myself about getting happy. It doesn't just happen. It's a conscious choice. I'm not perfect and don't expect my family to be.

For some reason I have the gift of faith. Going to quit trying to pretend my glass is half empty around Debra. I'm one of the people who choose to see their glass as half full. Lots of times mine is overflowing. A waterfall. Today was one of those days. Jim carrying my pack gave me a new lease on life.

Can hardly wait to see Craig. Jim reminded me of him. Love my sons, my husband, my dogs, my friends, my family, my life and every trail angel I've met. Waterfalls, waterfalls, all around. Whoooosh….

Last Part of Journey: Day 21
August 5, 2004

Dear Diary,

For the first time I'm writing my journal outside in the daylight. It wasn't a long hike today, only seven miles, but we're all tired. Made camp at Upper Rae Lake at the base of Glenn Pass. Another pass! Still awful at uphill hiking but love the view when we get to the top. Only one more pass—Forester—after Glenn Pass. The Kick Ass Pass. Most people say if you get over it, you can do Whitney for sure. Honestly feeling there's a chance I might finish the JMT. Proud!

Think I'll plant flowers in my boots when get home and put them on front porch. They deserve a good resting spot. They're my old dependable friends. Gotta love them.

Last Part of Journey: Day 22
August 6, 2004

When I woke in the morning, it felt like Christmas, New Years, and my birthday all rolled into one. Craig, Devan, and Todd would be meeting us at Charlotte Lake later in the day. I jumped out of my sleeping bag and put on the ragged pink T-shirt I'd washed the night before in the lake. I even took time to comb my hair instead of just shoving it under my hat.

I was the first one up and hurried to start the stove. The little bit of oatmeal we had left should tide us over 'til the guys brought food. I could already taste the Snickers bar Craig would bring. The creamy smooth chocolate taste punctuated with nuts and caramel surfaced in my memory. I salivated with the thought of it.

Even though I loved food, there was something more important to me. As thrilled as I was to be getting stuff to eat, I was at least ten times more excited to see Craig and hear news from home. I imagined him giving me his trademark bear hug with a wide smile lighting his face, and long bangs swept to the side with his head cocked. Perhaps he wore his hair that way to make up for all the years he'd had an old-fashioned crew cut when he played basketball in school.

I wondered how Sean was doing at his station and if he'd been to a lot of fires. He loved the thrill and excitement of his job and was happiest when busy. Smiley had been studying for his pilot's license and was going to take the certification test this summer. His dream to own a small plane and not just be the co-pilot on fires for the forest service might have become a reality.

Maybe he paid for his half of the little Cessna 150 he's been piloting. He finally had the money to buy into a partnership after his parents died and left him a small inheritance. Would I muster the courage to fly in his little putt putt? Even big planes scared me. I figured there were lots of things I'd missed out on and couldn't wait to hear about them.

Perhaps the plane would make up for the fact that Smiley had no memory of either of his parents saying they loved him. It would be an impossible task to try to count the times my mom told me she loved and adored me. She made sure to tell Smiley she loved him, too.

He often commented on it. Whenever I visited her he sent us flowers with a card saying *To the women I love.* I wondered how he could be the dad and husband he was after his upbringing. He'd also been a sniper in the Vietnam War, a whole separate issue. Many times, I had to force him to say, *I love you.* It had been worth it.

The meadows were drying out because it was late in the summer and that meant fewer mosquitoes which made it a lot easier to cook. I liked not having to wear my net hat. It made me feel like a beekeeper without the plus of honey. I heard Debra and Jenny rustling around.

"Hey guys, up and at 'em. I've got some breakfast for you. I'm heading out real soon," I hollered, shoving the oatmeal down in two bites. I scurried over to my tent to start taking it down.

Debra poked her head out of her tent. "Aren't you a bundle of energy this morning?"

"I am. I can't wait to see Craig. I've sure missed my family."

"I can't wait to get some real food." Jenny came out of the tent and stretched her arms high over her head as she yawned. "I hope they remembered to bring some cheese and chocolate."

"We only have to hike about five and a half miles, so you don't need to rush," said Debra. "How're your boots holding up? Have you thought about walking out with the guys and going home?"

It hit me hard. Mentioning that maybe I should be walking out and going home made me feel like a second-class hiker. I didn't need to look down at my feet to answer her. "My boots are about shot. I'm lucky they made it this far."

"Isn't Craig supposed to bring in your tennis shoes?" Debra asked.

"I hope so, but if he doesn't, I'm not sure what I'll do. I'm not looking forward to the added weight of packing extra shoes. If he brings them, my plan is to carry them as a backup in case my boots blow out. You said you'd help me with them, didn't you, Debra?"

"I can't handle the extra weight. Sorry, but you'll have to carry them yourself."

Jenny looked at me. My face must have said it all. I didn't know why I was surprised at Debra backing out of her promise, but I was.

Turning toward me, Jenny said, "Don't worry, I'll help." I twisted my head and let the tears run down my cheeks. I didn't want Debra to see me. I wasn't sure if I was crying because I was hurt that Debra said she wouldn't help, or because Jenny said she would.

I had some thinking to do on the trail. I knew if I left with Craig it would be easier on all of us. I just didn't think it was always best to choose the easy way out. What would it tell my sons about me? What would it show Jenny, who didn't want to be on this trip but had no other choice?

While heading out of the campsite I heard Debra and Jenny cleaning up. If I could've run the next five and a half miles, I would have. Instead, my plan was to keep trudging along steadily. After being on the trail for almost three weeks, I was sure I could pace myself for such a short distance. The biggest problem would be getting over Glenn Pass.

The hiking wasn't hard, but I wasn't getting where I wanted fast enough. I hadn't seen anyone for the mile or so I'd walked. I made several turns on the trail. Standing beside a giant pine stood a middle-aged woman with a big scowl on her face. She was trying to rearrange her backpack, and I could tell things weren't going well.

"Hi, can I help you?" I asked quietly, trying to get her attention without frightening her.

She turned toward me and seemed startled. "I was just getting a snack out of my pack, and now I'm having a hard time putting my bear canister back in. I hate the damn thing."

"Join the crowd. I hate 'em, too, but they seem to keep the bears away. I'm Lori. Would you like some help?"

"I'm Kathy. Be my guest. If you can get the canister inside I'll owe you."

I delved into her backpack and took out a few articles of clothing. I proceeded to pack the canister in her upper compartment and helped her put her clothes around it. Together we did a mediocre but passable job. When finished we started hiking toward Glenn Pass. Walking at a determined clip and trying to stay abreast with another hiker helped take my mind off the elevation gain.

"What part of the JMT are you hiking?" she adjusted her glasses while talking.

"I'm trying the whole thing, believe it or not. We started from Yosemite and have done it in sections. This last time we've been out almost three weeks. How about you?"

"I'm hiking the whole thing, too. I guess you aren't alone since you said we. I think I remember seeing you at Muir Ranch when I was getting a resupply. I remember your red hair."

"It's hard to hide anywhere with this hair, that's for sure. Mostly it's up in my hat. Yesterday the mosquitoes got a little better so I didn't have to do the bug hat thing. Who are you hiking with?"

"It's just me. I started out with a friend, but her knee got messed up in Tuolumne so I decided to just keep going without her. It's been kind of hard."

"I'll bet. I'm impressed. I'm with two people, a woman, and her sixteen-year-old daughter. Mostly I hike alone, but I do have someone to meet up with at night. Have you been scared?"

"Not really, but I think it would've been more fun doing it with someone else. Where are you heading today?"

"Off the beaten track to meet my son and a couple of other guys who are bringing in our resupply. What about you?"

"I'm hiking up to Kearsarge Pass to meet my son, who is bringing me the rest of the stuff I need."

"What a coincidence. That's the pass my son is coming over. Maybe they'll meet. Is your son hiking any of the trail?"

"I wish. He has to get back to work so he's just meeting me on the road. I have to go out of my way about ten miles to get it. Like I'm not already exhausted."

"I'm a teacher in my other life. What do you do?" I asked, as we hiked along at a good steady pace that was making me feel rather smug.

"I'm a pediatrician. I've been planning this trip for six years since I was fifty. I just couldn't give up and go home. It's tough getting the time off."

I knew what she meant. This was my once in a lifetime chance to hike the JMT. I doubted I'd ever find the time or money to try it again.

"Wow, I'm fifty-one, and having a hard time. Here you are all by yourself and you're fifty-six. How awesome is that. It looks like you're doing OK."

"Sometimes it seems like I'm hanging on by a thread. I really want to finish the trail. I'm a bit concerned about Forester Pass. I hear it's awful."

I tried to talk without wheezing. I'd forgotten to take my asthma pill. "I've heard that, too. I think we should be acclimated pretty well coming from Tuolumne. Are you planning on climbing Whitney?"

"I hope so. Isn't it something how it hasn't rained at all the last three weeks? I think that has to be a record up here. There are almost always afternoon storms in the Sierra." We both looked up at the blue sky with only a few white clouds billowing in the distance.

"My husband calls me the sunshine girl and says I bring sunshine wherever I go. That's one of the nicer things he says about me. Even the woman I'm with, who doesn't think I add much to the party, seems to believe I might be partly responsible for the good weather."

"Well if you are, thanks, it's been a blessing not to deal with the rain. I know two very fit men doctors who got chased off the JMT because of weather. They couldn't take it."

"I'm pretty sure none of us have a say in the condition of the skies, but I'm not above taking some credit even if it isn't warranted. Keeping the weather sunny is about the only thing the woman I'm with thinks I've done right this trip. And, of course, that's a joke. Nobody controls the weather. "

"That's for sure," she replied.

I reached into my pocket, stepped back, took a deep puff on

my inhaler. I was surprised I did it in front of her. "It's been a lot easier getting up this pass while talking with you. Usually I have to stop every 100 steps and do this suck water thing. I have asthma and the uphill takes a toll. Thanks for taking my mind off of it." We continued hiking, the top of Glenn Pass peeking in the horizon. It was a steep climb but looked like the view would be worth it.

Her poles swung evenly as we walked. "Maybe you're doing better than you think. You haven't seemed to have much problem going up the pass. We've been hiking evenly."

"It's nice to be with someone."

"Wow, it's great you're doing the trail with asthma. I treat a lot of kids who have it and trying to convince some of their parents that it's better if they stay healthy and exercise is sometimes a chore."

"I've had it since I was a child. My mom's the one who made sure I stayed fit. A couple of doctors told her I should be as inactive as possible. She'd looked them in the eye and said I'd dance, skate, and be a normal kid."

"Good for her."

"She also paid for me to get antigen shots since I was allergic to almost everything. We didn't have any insurance and that was tough for a single mom."

"I bet it was. She was right, and those doctors were wrong. Just doing what you're doing now proves it."

"We made it!" I hollered, as we reached the top of the pass. I raised my hiking poles high. Pulling my arms out of my pack dropping it the ground, I spun in circles taking in the magnificent 360-degree view. The feeling of being on the moon once again assailed me. I looked over the tops of mountains above timberline. Below me, the gray peaks and turquoise lake without any visible signs of vegetation surrounding them were stark reminders of the almost 12,000 ft elevation.

Kathy also took off her pack. We slapped our hands in a high five, then silence settled over us as we kept turning and looking. A feeling of peace enveloped me. I glanced at Kathy, realizing she was another trail angel. I said a silent prayer of thanksgiving. I once heard that if the only prayer you ever said was thank you it would be enough.

"Those might be your friends coming up now," Kathy said.

"I turned around and saw Debra and Jenny approaching rapidly. Debra, as always, zoomed at a determined pace. It only took a few minutes before they joined us.

"What a view," Debra said. "The passes are my favorite part of the hike."

"Not mine," Jenny said coming up behind her and plopping her pack down.

"You beat us, Lori, that's a first," Debra said.

I almost commented on the fact that it wasn't a race we were running but kept quiet and tried to enjoy the compliment.

I turned toward Kathy. "It made it easier to hike when I had someone to talk to. These are my friends, Debra and Jenny."

"Nice to meet you," she raised her hand.

"You, too," Debra replied.

We spent some time on top of Glenn Pass eating some cheddar cheese and Ritz crackers Kathy gave us as we took in the view. I'd told her about our food predicament, and it was nice of her to share. Debra had moved over and sat by herself on a rock outcropping. The only attempt she made to join in our conversation was to say, "Lori might be going home with her son after Charlotte Lake. She's had a hard time hiking and her boots are worn out." Even though both of those things were true it still stung my pride.

"We've been here precisely fifteen minutes, and it's time to go," Debra said, jumping to her feet. "See you later, Lori. The guys should meet us at Charlotte Lake this afternoon. Maybe we'll see you around." Debra extended her hand to Kathy.

A few minutes after they left, Kathy and I prepared to take off. "I don't mean to pry, but it doesn't seem like you and Debra are best buds or anything. What made you take this trip with her?" Kathy asked as we started hiking, watching our feet carefully as we traversed down the pass.

"To make a long story short, it's been a dream of mine to hike the JMT, she asked me to come, and I said yes. None of my close friends were either willing or able to do it. Debra needed someone to share the cost. She's a park ranger and knew the ins and outs of planning the trip. I couldn't have done it without her."

"Well, good for you."

"Thanks for the vote of confidence."

Walking down the pass, I felt my right knee popping, and I stopped for a minute to adjust my braces. I looked over at Kathy, who had hiking poles and knee braces, too. She was also adjusting hers. We started laughing and simultaneously lifted up our poles in a toast. I liked to do that when I had something to celebrate. She seemed to enjoy doing it as well.

"Here's to life in the fast lane and trying to be young in our fifties," I said loudly, poles raised high.

"Here's to being able to be out here in our fifties," Kathy said.

We soon reached the trail signs indicating where Kathy needed to go.

"I hope we meet again," she said. "It'd be fun to go up Whitney with a buddy."

"I'd like that, but I'm not sure I'll make it up Whitney. Like Debra said, I have the option of going out with my son."

"Why would you do that? You're within forty-miles of

finishing the trail, and you're doing great. You should be proud."

I threw my shoulders back and did feel proud, and a lot of it had to do with Kathy and the camaraderie we'd shared. "Thanks. Hope to see you again."

Heading toward Charlotte Lake, my feet sprouted wings. I saw Jenny's red hat telling me which direction to go, picked it up and turned on the fork of the trail. I was sure I'd never hiked harder or faster the whole trip. Some of it might have had to do with the fact I had absolutely no food in my bear canister as we'd eaten it all, and my pack was so light. Even though Kathy had shared her snack food with us, I could hear my belly growling. Hunger is a big motivator. I wondered how soon the guys would show up at the lake.

The trail veered off the official JMT when I headed toward Charlotte Lake. My excitement increased with every step. It wasn't long before the lake came into view, sparkling like a gem in the woods. Surrounding it were towering green trees and gigantic granite boulders. It took only a moment to notice a group of men camped near it. Before I could wonder whom they might be, one of the youngest of the men with a big floppy hat and a wide grin came running toward me. He shouted, "Mamma, Mamma, Mamma, you made it!"

While I struggled to catch my breath, he wrapped me in a warm bear hug. The familiar curve of my 6'4" son's shoulder cradled me. I laid my head on his shoulder and rested in his tight embrace. I was filled with awe and wonder that this gangly man/child was mine.

I finally let go of Craig and stepped back. He unclipped my backpack, took it from me, and put it on. "You're skinnier. Come on over to the campsite, Mamma, and see what we brought you," he took my hand and walked toward the rest of the guys.

"I'm so glad to see you, son," I murmured, holding on tightly.

Three other men (with Debra and Jenny) sat on some

boulders. They talked and laughed while Debra and Jenny ate juicy oranges. I couldn't wait to join them.

As we approached, I recognized all but one. Craig and I joined the others. "Steve, this is my awesome mom." Craig said to a small, compact man I didn't recognize.

"Great to meet you," Steve said. He was full of muscles, had shoulder length dark hair, and a smile that lit up his face. "I've been hearing a lot about you from your son. He's sure proud of you."

"I'm proud of him," I reached for one of the oranges sitting on a tree stump. "We've been so hungry I wasn't sure what we'd do if you guys didn't show up. It's wonderful you're here early. We didn't expect you 'til later on tonight."

I peeled the orange and shoved a whole quarter section into my mouth as we talked. The tangy, sweet liquid spilled over my lips and I sucked the juice off my fingers. I had passed up the Snickers bars sitting there and went straight for the orange. Fresh fruit and vegetables had become such a luxury. I took advantage of them, reaching for a handful of carrots on my next food swipe.

"Craig's quite the hiker. He carried about seventy pounds of stuff. His buddy Devan got altitude sickness and wasn't able to carry a thing. I'm surprised Devan made it at all," Todd said, with his arm dangling around Debra who smiled with joy as she laid her head on his shoulder.

I looked at Devan, who hadn't said a word. His head was cradled in his hands and I felt horrible for him. This was not a good first backpack experience. He'd taken off work and had been the one to convince Craig to come. Devan told Craig if his fifty-one-year-old mom was hiking the John Muir Trail they could at least bring supplies in for her. I knew Devan had a lot of pride. It was probably hard for him to let Craig and the others carry his stuff.

I went over and put my arm around him. I loved Devan. He

was like another son to me. He'd slept on our couch more times than I could count, usually after a basketball game, or a night out with Craig.

"Devan, I'm so sorry you got sick. I've had altitude sickness before and it's not fun. I'm proud of you for hiking in here. It must've been really hard."

"I feel like an idiot. The guys had to carry all my stuff. I can't believe I got so sick."

"It doesn't matter how fit you are," said Steve. "I'm on a trail crew, and once in a while even one of the seasoned guys gets altitude sickness. Don't sweat it."

"Yeah, we brought Steve as an extra guy so it wasn't a problem," Craig said. "Besides I know you wanted to see how much I could carry and if I'd wuss out," he punched Devan in the shoulder.

The rest of the day was heaven. We had all the food we could want: cheese, vegetables, potato chips, Snickers bars, jerky, fruit, and a bottle of wine for dinner. We spent time exploring, washing out our clothes, and swimming in the lake.

Craig had brought me a whole gallon zip lock bag of Citrucel, and my old tennis shoes. He also gave me a bunch of belated birthday cards and a present from Smiley. I felt rich.

We sat on a rock so I could open the cards and presents. Devan and Jenny napped, while Todd and Debra took off to do whatever couples do when they haven't seen each other in almost three weeks. Steve left to explore. He was still raring to go after a twelve-mile hike with a loaded seventy-pound pack. I had to agree with Craig that Steve was *an animal.* Craig had said this with the utmost admiration.

"So, Mamma, you ready to hike out with me?" Craig asked. "From all the phone calls I got from your trail angels, as you like to call them, I'm assuming things aren't great. I'm impressed you got this far."

"Who did you talk to? What did they say?" I asked.

"Susie, the lady who runs the Muir Ranch store, phoned to tell me how mean Debra was to you and said I should try and talk you into coming home if Debra hadn't started treating you better. She was wondering if the Shoe Goo she gave you worked and said Debra was a real bitch to her at the store. Two other people called, I forget their names, reminding me to bring your Citrucel and tennis shoes."

"You're a great son. I really do need the Citrucel. I'm not sure if my hiking boots will make it. Susie's Shoe Goo is starting to come off." I pointed down at my boots.

"Yeah, they don't look so good, and I think everyone in the Central Valley and Mariposa knows that you're constipated on the John Muir Trail. If I embarrassed easily it would've been bad."

"Good thing you don't." I hugged him even tighter.

"We're supposed to stay here tomorrow for a layover day with you guys and walk out the next day. I thought you'd look a lot worse than you do. Actually, you look great. I still think you should plan on leaving with us, though. I'd feel a lot better if you did."

"Let me think about it, Craig. I've come so far. I hate to give up."

"Nobody would blame you, Mamma. It doesn't seem like it's been much fun."

"Life isn't always fun, son. But I've had some good times here and learned important things about myself," I said, opening the card from Smiley.

Happy Birthday and just keep on walking. In the box is a frog necklace for your trip. Remember how they are always all over our property at this time of year? Maybe you've seen some on your trip. The socks are to help your feet the last part of the journey. You need them more than you need me right now. I'll see you in a week or so. Stay strong. Hold on to my heart rock, and of course, I love you 3xs more. I believe in you. Always, Smiley

Inside a wrapped gift I found two pairs of wick drying, cushy, expensive hiking socks that would make it much easier to finish the trail. I laid them against my cheek and felt fibers that were strong and solid, like my husband.

I wondered how Smiley knew I needed them. After twenty-five years, some things didn't even need to be said. Somehow, I believed he magically knew about the amazing golden frogs we'd seen and how much their coming back from near extinction in the wilderness meant to me. I put the necklace around my neck and felt the solidness of the metal. I told myself I would leave it there 'til I saw him again.

The sun would rise tomorrow, and my son would be with me enjoying a day in the Sierra Wilderness.

Dear Diary,

Smiley's card made me cry. I've been lucky to have had a crazy love with him all these years. He believes in me, and that means a lot. I believe in him, too. I'd feel awful giving up on this hike. He'd be disappointed in me just as I'd be in myself. I need to decide tomorrow if I stay or go on. More than letting myself down I'm wondering how I can let down all those people who believe in me. Frog necklace lies heavy on my chest, reminding me of the decision I have to make. So tired and miss Smiley's arms around me. Even the necklace isn't enough to make me quit missing him.

Last Part of Journey: Day 23
August 7, 2004

Dear Diary,

The best days are like rainbows, coming after a long storm. Although it hasn't rained at all on this hike, I feel like I've weathered many storms. Craig's my rainbow today.

A deep-throated pulsing sound that we heard last night waking us all up, came from a bear. I couldn't help but start screaming. Debra and Jenny joined in and soon the guys were outside ready to go. Flashlights in hand they converged and took off on a hunt. I had to question their sanity. I was just glad the thing was gone or at least not right in camp. They seemed to think they needed to make sure it was far far away.

There's almost nothing in the world that appeals to a boy's heart more than a dangerous adventure. Chasing the bear out of our campsite gave the guys plenty of time to show off and prove how brave and fearless they are.

Debra, Jenny, and I had got up and were sitting around the burning red embers of our campfire hearing hoots and yells off in the distance. It felt weird to let those guys take care of us after we'd hiked by ourselves without benefit of men for seventeen days. It also felt kind of good to let someone else be in charge.

Seemed like forever, but they finally returned and Steve said what good bear hunters they were. They stood around and bragged for an hour or so and we heard their exaggerated stories of being the great white hunters. The truth was, we never did hear anymore from that bear even though we were all awake the better part of the night.

Fun to get up this morning and not have to pack up and get ready to move again. Seeing Craig and Devan's smiling faces in the morning was another refreshing sight. Hearing them banter about who was the strongest and bravest after the bear hunt made me laugh.

I'm sure Craig and Devan will have some big stories to tell their friends and most of them will be factual. This morning Craig told me it was one of the most exciting things he'd ever done in his life and he'd never forget it. Devan agreed. Wonder how many parents waste money on Disneyland-type experiences when what most boys really want is a chance to live an adventure.

The area surrounding Charlotte Lake boasts many tall peaks with a lot of talus and enticing views. This morning Craig, Steve, and Devan went off to climb one. Devan said he couldn't believe he was doing it but since this was his first and last backpack he might as well make the most of it. Craig told me he was having a lot more fun than he'd expected. He asked me if it was OK for him to leave me for a while to go climbing. Where in the world did I get such a nice kid? It made my heart happy to see them take off, almost running, to sidle up a rocky peak. As they went higher and higher, Craig would turn and wave, and soon they looked like nothing more than a small regiment of ants.

Two men on horseback came in, and I asked them what brought them to this neck of the woods. The one wearing a big sombrero told me he was bringing in steak and wine for Jill and Dave. I remembered how they wouldn't share their food but had given Jenny a fishhook instead. Guess being rich does have its advantages, steak and wine on the JMT being one of them.

While I'm writing this, I'm thinking maybe I'm one of the richest people

I know. My son has hiked in to bring me fresh food, my family is taking care of things at home, and I have many people rooting and praying for me.

Craig was a little surprised when we were sitting by the lake in the afternoon and I told him I'd be continuing. He asked me why I wanted to do it and told me I didn't need to finish for him. Was honest and said the journey I'm on isn't about him, or his brother, or his dad. It's about me.

Last Part of Journey: Day 24
August 8, 2004

"I guess you'll be heading out with the guys today?" Debra asked while our group sat gathered in a circle reminiscing.

I stood up, wiping the dust off my pants. "As a matter of fact, I've decided to finish. My Citrucel worked, and the good food and amazing company has spurred me on."

"What about your boots? I don't think they'll last. Then what will you do?" Debra asked.

"Craig brought in my old tennies. I can carry one of them, and didn't you say you'd help carry the other?" I knew she'd backed out of it, but the mean part of me wanted the others to hear it, too.

The guys were packing up quietly, and I could tell by the way they moved slow and tilted their heads they were all listening.

"I already told you I can't handle any more weight," Debra replied, glaring at me.

"I'll take both of them. Mom and I have lots less weight to pack than you do," Jenny said.

"Wow, that'd really help me. Are you sure?"

"I'd rather you didn't pack anymore stuff, Jenny. We still have Forester Pass to get over before climbing Whitney," Debra walked over to her pack.

Jenny grabbed my old tennis shoes from the ground and tied them to her backpack. She didn't say anything, just stared at her mom. Everybody else looked at Debra, too. She kept her mouth shut. There was an awkward silence amidst our formerly jovial group.

"Mamma, why don't you come home with me? You've gone far enough," Craig broke the silence and put his arm around me. "We miss you."

"Thanks, Craig, but with Jenny packing my shoes, I'm sure I can make it. I really am. There's only forty-miles or so left, and I'm not ready to quit." I leaned my head against his shoulder.

"There's no reason you can't make it since you've come this far," Steve said. "Wish I could finish with you, but we need to get going."

We spent the better part of an hour taking down tents, arranging food in our canisters, and giving the guys just enough food to make it back to the truck. I finally made a stand about the energy bars they'd brought.

"I'm not carrying any of these. I don't eat them. I only need my Emergen-C packets. If you want them take them." I handed the bars to Debra.

"You might need them to get over Forester, then you'll be sorry."

"Nope, I won't. Just give me two of those GOO things we brought and I'll be fine."

I noticed Debra took only five of the ten bars and handed the others to Todd.

"Would you guys like a couple of Emergen-C packets, Jenny? I know you said they helped you." I handed her four packets.

Debra said nothing.

"My mom's climbin' Whitney, my mom's climbin' Whitney," Craig sang, dancing around in his silly floppy hat taking my hands and twirling me around. He stopped and put me down and gave me a hug then lifted my now fully loaded pack and helped me put it on. "You rock, Mamma, carrying this. I'm so proud of you. Let's walk up to the turn off together."

He took hold of my hand and held it tight. I remembered his tiny fingers in mine when I was teaching him to walk. His hand had grown so much bigger and stronger than mine. Something huge was happening between us. Giving him my blessing when he left home had been hard but had helped him grow. The shift that had just occurred helped me understand he would be there when I needed him. He was letting me go, so I could grow strong, too.

Debra and Todd walked behind us on the trail. This was a first for Debra, who was always the lead dog except for when Jane had been with us. I was impressed Todd could get her to hang back at the end of the group. When they reached the turnoff, I could tell by Debra's narrowed eyes and frowning face the time they'd spent together hadn't been good.

Devan was raring to go and feeling much better. "Good luck. I'm amazed you're continuing. I sure wouldn't." He gave me a hug, which was difficult with a backpack on.

Craig took off his pack, and so did I. Staring at him, I tried to etch his image in my mind. His big arms engulfed me, and I wasn't sure I'd be able to continue hiking. He felt solid and homey. I tried to keep from crying. Letting Craig leave was the hardest thing I'd done so far on my journey.

Debra, however, wrung her hands together and kicked at the dirt with impatience. "Time's a wasting. See you at dinner." She gave a swift wave.

Jenny followed her after saying goodbye to the guys. It dawned on me she might be the one who would like to quit. What would I do without her?

"Mamma, how often does she leave you behind?" Craig asked, after they left.

"Every day. It's OK. I've found I don't mind hiking alone and I almost always see someone on the trail."

"How do you know when to stop or where you'll be camping?"

"Oh, Jenny always marks the trail with the flagging tape your father sent along and leaves her red hat at the turnoff."

"Last chance. Come with us now. We need to get going," Steve said, looking at me.

"I love you, Craigy, go on. They're waiting." I pushed him away from me. "I'm never alone. I always have my memories, God and—"

"Your trail angels." He grinned and waved as he walked away.

I blew kisses in the wind.

I missed him the moment he left. I started walking and talking in my head, which happened when I was afraid or unsure. Today I talked to people who had helped me on my journey. Their spirits surrounded me.

"I've got the socks on you sent me, Smiley. They feel so good. The only thing that would be better is if you were rubbing my feet. I know you hate to do that but do it anyway because I like it. Maybe I'll start getting pedicures when I come home so you can't say I have troll feet. Sometimes you say the worst things but do the best stuff. You are a weird and complicated man. But you are my weird and complicated man."

"You've lost that weight I told you to, Mamma. You can finish the trail. I know you can." Sean urged me on.

Susie, who gave me the magic Shoe Goo kept popping into my consciousness. I sent Smiley, Craig, and Sean big hugs. Maybe today would be easier than I thought.

The JMT doesn't stay flat for long. That's part of its beauty.

Zigzagging up and down, if viewed from an airplane, it would resemble a roller coaster. Now closer to Forester, my heart raced with excitement. It would take a lot of strength and determination to go over that pass the next day, but I felt up for it. I'd never hiked or climbed at over 13,000-feet. The seventeen days we'd spent acclimating made me feel like I was fit enough to summit. And if I trudged up Forester, Whitney could happen.

A few miles into my venture, I came upon another lone hiker. Approaching her, I realized it was Kathy, the pediatrician I'd met a few days before. We chatted for a while as we hiked.

"How are you doing hiking alone?" she asked.

Once again, I realized while I'd planned on hiking the JMT for the scenery, the people had kept me going. "I'm fine today. We just got the resupply from my son and some of his pals and had a layover day. It was great. How about you?"

"I saw my son, too, so that helped. I guess I'm good. If you guys come out of the trail about the same time as me, I have a ride to Lone Pine if you want one."

"That'd be wonderful. I'm going to meet with Debra and Jenny a mile or so before Forester Pass so we can be ready to go up it tomorrow. Want to camp with us?"

"Maybe another time. I'm gonna stop soon. I've had a long day."

It was fun to hike with Kathy. She led a fascinating life. Hiked a lot. Traveled a bunch. She served as a Girl Scout leader, helping at their camps, and she also worked with Doctors without Borders. Debra said she thought Kathy was grumpy and that's why she was hiking alone. I chuckled, thinking about Debra calling someone else grumpy. I knew the real reason she appeared a little irritable. There was no one to hike with, so she'd mustered enough courage to continue on her own after her buddy had been hurt early on. Kathy wasn't a grouch. She was stalwart.

After making a steep descent, Kathy decided to stay behind and set up camp by a stream. I was sorry to lose her company. It wasn't long, however, before I came upon a couple of old guys sitting on a log and whistling.

"Hi, what are you up to?" the one with a *Life is Good* T-shirt asked me.

"Plans are to meet with my two hiking partners later. Did you see a woman and a young teenage girl go by?" I scanned the area.

"We did, tried to say howdy, but they seemed in a big hurry. They didn't stop to talk or even say hi," said the one with the funny army hat. There were lots of interesting hats on the trail and even more interesting people under them.

"Where you heading?" I asked.

"Trying to finish the JMT. We plan on going up Whitney in a few days, if all goes well," said the older looking one. "My partner here, Jim, is sixty-three, and I'm seventy, so if we are ever gonna do it, we better do it now. There might not be a later." He chuckled.

"Wow, good for you. Do you think the weather will hold? I can't believe it hasn't rained, can you?"

"Nope, we've been out twenty days and only a few little drops."

"Well, my husband calls me the sunshine girl. He said it wouldn't rain on my parade. Good luck. Maybe I'll see you at Whitney."

"I hope your hubby's right about you. Some people told us it might storm in a couple of days, which means we won't make it up Whitney," Jim said.

"That's one thing my friends and I agreed on," I nodded, "we wouldn't chance going to the top in a thunder storm. It isn't worth risking your life."

"Let's hope for the best." Jim checked out the sky.

I'd only hiked a mile or so when I met another lone woman. When I tried to engage her in conversation, she looked at me with pained blue eyes. Her cropped silver hair dripped with sweat. "Hope you don't think I'm rude, but I'm in a hurry. I'm trying to hike twenty miles or so a day and need to finish this trail in ten days. I've already done Whitney, so there's not much else to conquer."

She stood at least 6 feet tall, fit, thin, and all business. "I have to get going. Lots of miles to travel and so little time to do them." She hustled in the opposite direction.

"Have fun," I said to her back.

She turned around, "That's not what I'm here for. I'm here to finish the trail."

A little while later I met a man and a woman. They told me they were in their mid- thirties and were hiking the trail with all their gear. They had no resupply and had made it this far. "It hasn't been easy, but we've had fun," the man touched his partner's shoulder with affection.

"That's nice to hear. The last lady I met told me she wasn't on the trail for fun, just to finish it. It's nice to be young. I couldn't have done this trail without a resupply."

"Well, our intent is to get to the end but in the meantime, have fun. Don't you think we've had a good time, Virginia?"

She used her bandana to wipe a dirt trail off his face. "It's been great, and now we can get married. I know we'll be OK." She grinned.

"I'll take that as a yes then." He zoomed over, got down on one knee, and kissed her hand.

"Was that an answer to a proposal?" I asked.

"I hope so," he said. "I've been waiting to ask her the whole trip."

"Now I've heard it all. Good luck, you two. You should have

no trouble weathering married life if you've done this whole hike without a resupply. I can't wait to tell my family about you."

"How long have you've been married?" the woman asked.

"Twenty-five years."

"Hasn't it been hard?" She lifted up her sunglasses and rubbed her eyes. "You actually give me some hope. I don't think we know anyone who's been happily married for over twenty years. Any advice?"

"It's a lot like this hike. Lots of ups and downs and some long plateaus. We aren't happy all of the time. We realize if we're patient and kind to each other, happiness will come back. If you're willing to work as hard at marriage as you have on this hike, you'll make it."

As I left them I started thinking about my marriage and what life would be like if I were single. It was hard to imagine. Smiley was my friend, as well as my lover. One of the best things about our marriage was Smiley's understanding that I'm my own person, both of us accepting we don't have exclusive rights to each other's lives. We trusted one another. My hike was a testament to that. While he didn't like to backpack, he supported me in my dreams. I'd tried to do the same for him.

I put my hand in my pocket, touching my heart rock, and reached up to feel the silver frog dangling from my neck. Smiley believed in me. The new socks he'd somehow known I needed reminded me our marriage was made up of two whole people who accentuated each other. Having warm dry feet can do a lot to give you courage and make you feel loved.

The trail became rougher, it hadn't been cleared and rubble just continued up up up. The loose rocks made my feet slip. I started using my water bladder and counting my steps again. I had to stop and use my asthma inhaler but reminded myself how I used to have to do the suck water thing the whole day. Now I could last a long time without doing it, even on a hard ten-mile day. Still, I knew every part of my body would be relieved when I made it to camp.

Jenny's flagging finally became visible after I spotted her hat. I followed it for about 100 yards and saw where she and Debra had set up camp. A short Asian man sat by their campfire. As soon as I arrived, he stood. "Hello, my name Jun, and you Lori, yes?"

"Yes, I am. Nice to meet you. Are you hiking the JMT, too?"

"I do hike. I from Japan. Nikon Company sponsor me. I one lucky guy."

"Boy, that's a really big pack. What do you have in it?"

"Camera equipment, food."

"Where did you get your resupply?" I asked.

"No resupply. Pack seventy pounds. Carry all food, film, and stuff."

"That's amazing." Jenny inserted. "My mom didn't even want to carry a camera because of the weight."

Jun's English was a bit broken, but it was fascinating to hear his tale. "My uncle he dies, leave me $5,000. Told me do something worthy with money. Something for to make me sing inside." He touched his heart and smiled from ear to ear.

Jun had seen a *National Geographic* special on hiking the John Muir Trail and then contacted Nikon. The company agreed to defray some of the costs if he would take pictures with his Nikon camera for them to use in advertising. Knowing nothing about backpacking, except what he'd read and seen on the special, Jun purchased supplies and set off for a foreign land to do this *worthy thing.*

Dear Diary,

The people I met today blew me away. I feel humbled. So many stories, so much courage. Jun is amazing. He sat outside long after we went to bed and meditated. Told us he's never been anywhere so sacred and he is honored to be here. His happiness is contagious. He is so excited about climbing Whitney and said maybe we could do it together. Even Debra seems in awe of him.

I won't ever forget the lessons I'm learning from this JMT hike and the people I've met.

Tomorrow is Forester. The mountains speak to me and they sigh in the dark. Wonder if they hear me sighing back? Ahhhhhhh!

Last Part of Journey: Day 25
August 9, 2004

"Well I'm ready to conquer Forester today. What about you guys?" Debra asked as we packed up to leave our campsite. Jun was already gone.

"I don't know about conquering mountains. I'll be happy if Forester lets me pass over it in one piece. Mountains are constant, we're fleeting. We're like flies to them," I replied.

"Well you better hang tough, 'cuz I hear this one is the mother of all passes." Debra picked up her backpack.

"Mom, maybe we can hike together today. Looks like we're all ready to go," Jenny suggested, strapping my tennis shoes to her pack. "What if Lori needs these shoes?"

"Then she should pack them herself. We have to get going. She seems to have been OK on her own so far."

It was weird being talked about like I wasn't there, but I realized she was right. "I'm fine Jenny, and I'm sure my boots will last through today. Thanks for thinking of me and for packing my shoes. Are you sure you can take them both? I could carry one."

"No problem. I hardly feel them."

"Do you have some Emergen-C?" I asked Jenny.

"Yes," she replied. "Do you have the GOO that's supposed to get us over the pass?"

"Yup, and I'm going to use it and just believe it works. Mind over matter. For some reason I'm not feeling great today. Maybe I have morning sickness, without benefit of pregnancy." My hand reached for my queasy stomach.

"Good luck," Debra said. "You might need it."

"I make my own luck," I said under my breath as they headed off.

I started a few minutes after they left. I needed to remember the main objective of the day, *Get over Forester Pass.* It would be no small feat. To reach the pass, I needed to make a 4,000-foot elevation gain and we would have to hike approximately 13.5 miles to our next campsite. After shooting over Forester we'd agreed on meeting at a small lake located above Guitar Lake. Then we'd get up about four a.m. in order to tackle Whitney.

I shivered. Ominous black fluffy cumulus clouds clustered overhead, filling the sky. I reminded myself it was the journey of hiking the trail, not the thought of climbing Whitney that had gotten me to where I was. I kept going and tried to enjoy the scenery.

In two more days I'd be off the JMT. It seemed impossible I'd hiked this far.

Forester marks the boundary between two national parks, Kings Canyon and Sequoia. It'd been fun hiking in areas I'd never known existed. With the exception of Trail Crest Pass on the other side of Mt. Whitney, Forester Pass at 13,180 ft is the highest point reached on both the John Muir Trail and the much longer Pacific Crest Trail. Mt. Whitney is technically not part of the JMT but is right off the trail and is the highest mountain in the Continental U.S. Most hikers hiking the whole 211 miles try to climb Whitney as a culmination of the trip. *The Icing on the Cake.*

Not only is Forester the highest pass on the JMT, but it's considered by most people to be the finest. Hiking toward it I could see why. To the east is one of the most impressive mountains in the whole region. Junction Peak (at 13,888ft.) is a massive tower of steel gray rock that dominated my vision while trekking up the talus of the steep pass. For every ten steps forward, I seemed to slip at least one step back.

My feet made crunchy noises as I stepped on the sharp rock and limped along. I'd gone approximately six miles and hadn't seen any animals, birds, or another living soul. The still air and magnificent silence gave me goosebumps.

A lightness in my head and my short raspy breaths made me aware of the steady increase in altitude. Fear and loneliness settled into my bones. I wished I'd had someone to share the natural high of the altitude shift with.

Where was Jun? Where was Kathy? I reminded my fearful heart that if Kathy could hike alone at fifty-six, I could do it at fifty-one. The cloud formations grew bigger and blacker. I had enough sense to know I must get over Forester before the storm. I had no desire to be a lightning rod on top of the pass.

The trail grew steeper. I kept doing my 100-step-suck-water thing. I felt lucky to go that far without gasping for air. I had used my inhaler for the fourth time, and it made my heart pound harder. I tried not to think about what would happen if I had a severe asthma attack or, worse a heart attack. I wasn't supposed to use my inhaler as often and as close together as I already had. I tried to not fixate on it.

I wondered why each day's hiking was still so hard. I should've been in better shape after coming so far. The path should've be easier.

Seeing the empty trail, hiking its sacred dirt all on my own, served as a profound reminder this was indeed a difficult hike. Maybe I was doing better than I thought.

I felt exhilarated and lightheaded. I prayed fervently not to get altitude sickness after all the time we'd spent acclimating. So far, I didn't have a headache.

Still, I had a stinging, burning sensation and stomach cramps each time I peed. I hoped with all my heart it was a mild yeast infection, if anything, and not a bladder infection. I should have heeded Debra's advice about bringing antibiotics, which I would need if it was a UTI. If that was the case all hope of doing Whitney would be gone, even if the weather cooperated. I'd have to forgo climbing it and get off the mountain as quickly as possible. A bladder infection wasn't something to be taken lightly. The infection could spread to my kidneys and destroy them.

I'd had to stop five times to pee and was getting concerned. Up until now, my body had used up most of the water I drank. One good thing about not seeing anybody on this fully exposed ascent was that I didn't have to go far off trail to take care of business. Even after all this time on the hike, seeing people's exposed butts or exposing mine to others had little appeal, and I avoided it.

After yet another bathroom break (one that let me know I probably had gotten a UTI) I sat down to rest. The clouds were breaking up. I marveled once again at my good fortune concerning the weather. My stomach growled with pain. I took out my daily allotment of gorp, some jerky, and the GOO stuff that would hopefully help me get over the pass. Once again, meals had become something to look forward to. Food was plentiful since the guys had resupplied us. I was thankful for that.

I swallowed the GOO, which tasted like chalk. I chased it down with my ever-faithful Emergen-C drink. Water had become burdensome to filter, so I'd been going without. That was probably part of the reason I was developing a bladder infection. I chastised myself for being so stupid. Unlike Debra, I was unwilling to drink unfiltered water. I had to go back and teach school and didn't want to risk giardia.

Noise down the trail drew my attention. A group of four people slowly approached. I decided to stay and see who they were as I felt the need for some human contact. Two young men, a young woman, and another who appeared older than me, chatted as they neared.

"Hi," the older woman said. "What're you doing out here all alone? You're a long way from anything."

"I'm hiking the JMT and the rest of my group's ahead of me as usual. I'm slower than them."

"I'm slow, too," the woman said, "but I see a lot that way. I'm Betty and these are my sons Brett and John, and John's wife, Sue."

"How cool you got your kids to come with you. My son brought me in a resupply, but I'm not sure he'll ever backpack again. I took my boys out when they were little, and I think the novelty wore off."

"You might be surprised. When we were six and eight, Mom and Dad brought my brother and me. We hiked the whole JMT. Now we're twenty-six and twenty-eight. I wasn't sure I'd want to do it ever again," Brett said, "but here I am."

"I've never done it, so it's been quite an experience." Sue pulled out her water tube to take a drink. "I'm glad John and his mom convinced me to come."

"Where's your husband, Betty?" I asked.

"Probably the same place as yours. He says he's too old and hurts too much to backpack anymore."

"Yeah. Sounds like Smiley. He isn't here but encouraged me to come." I pulled my heart rock out of my pocket and showed it to them. "He told me he'd be here in spirit and to carry this rock as a reminder. It does seem to help me hike better."

"This has been the best trip. We've given ourselves five weeks and it's been so nice to enjoy everything," Betty said. "I don't imagine I'll be doing it again, so I want to get as much out of it as I can."

"It's good to hear you say that. I've felt wimpy because we're taking four weeks total. I can't begin to tell you the number of people I've seen running the trail or hiking twenty or more miles a day."

"I'm glad we've taken our time. It's been great," Brett said.

We plunked ourselves down, and I could hear the sighs as we escaped the bondage of our packs. We visited and passed around snacks. I looked up and saw a park ranger heading our way.

"How are you all on this marvelous day?" he asked.

"Fine, how about you?" Brett asked.

"With a job like mine, how could I not be good?" He accepted some of the jerky and cheese we offered him.

"You know it's really odd," I told him. "Nobody has asked us for a wilderness permit this whole trip. We've seen probably four or five rangers and not a one has asked us for it."

"I guess we just figure anybody who is this far out would have one," he replied. "Would you like to show it to me?"

I felt stupid for bringing up the wilderness permit, realizing it was with Debra. "Sorry to say, I don't have it. It's in the possession of my friends who are way ahead of me."

"That's another reason we don't often ask. Groups start out one way and end up another. Have a good rest of the trip, thanks for the grub." He headed down the hill. "You're almost up Forester and you're going to love the view."

Pulling myself up and brushing dirt and crumbs off, I said, "Thanks for the company, cheese, and jerky. I'd better get going." In exchange, I'd given them one of the Snickers bars that hadn't been confiscated by Debra.

"Maybe we'll see you at the top," Betty readjusted her hat.

"I hope so. I'd love to have someone snap a picture of me up there."

Outstanding mountain vistas surrounded the final approach to the pass. The view from the summit was second to no other I'd seen on the whole hike. It was rocky, stark, and impressive. The pass cut into the Kings Kern Divide, a high ridge that runs from Junction Peak, to Mt. Stanford (13,973 ft) Mt. Ericsson (13,608 ft), Mt. Geneva (13,059 ft), Mt. Jordan (13,344 ft) and Thunder Mountain (13, 588 ft). I knew this because I pulled out the maps Smiley had wisely made me bring.

I basked in heaven, feeling sorry for those below me. Looking down on giant pine trees and continuous jagged mountains wasn't something I did in my other life. Holding my arms out wide, I twirled doing a spin dance. Happiness!

I sang "Climb Every Mountain" from *The Sound of Music.* I laughed, thinking how hokey my boys would think it was. The sky caressed my face, and instead of my inhaler medicine filling my lungs, pure alpine air expanded my chest.

Forester, the monster mountain, welcomed me, making me laugh like a wild nymph. The wind whistled, blowing my hat off, exposing my matted and wild copper hair. I could feel it spin in circles, coils springing, released from bondage. Kicking my legs, twirling my arms, and shaking my head, I danced for only me.

I put on my pack and was ready to head down the pass when the family I'd visited earlier arrived. They reached the top and for the first few minutes, nobody spoke. I wanted them to have an opportunity to experience the magic I'd felt. I didn't speak until after Betty did. "God, this is even better than I remembered. What a sight."

"Would you mind taking my picture? I want to prove I was here." I handed Brett the camera. I was higher than when I sat passenger in my husband's small airplane and felt like a bird as I looked down upon a miniature world.

"You couldn't smile any wider if you tried." Brett snapped a couple of pictures.

I did the same for them with their camera. Their interruption made leaving harder than I thought. I loved being so high. But my midsection burned and ached worse than before.

"It's time for me to get going. It was great meeting you again." They took turns giving me hugs, which kept me warm and happy as I headed down the trail. It had been good to spend time with others, but the part of me enjoying my own company was ready to go on.

Forester was my friend, no longer a foe to be dreaded.

Looking down the trail's steep descent made me dizzy, though heights didn't usually affect me. Later I noted in my guidebook that the most sensational part of the JMT is going down Forester. I looked below, and a feeling of anticipation and dread filled me. It was the steepest, narrowest, zigzagging, talus mountainside trail I'd ever seen. I marveled at the fact that horses could walk it. It was about three feet wide. I was overjoyed to be walking down, not riding a horse. It would be important to be a steady hiker.

My knees screamed at me when I put pressure on them. The extreme angle was torturous. Once again, I was grateful I'd brought hiking poles. I hadn't seen many people who looked over forty on the trail without them. The person who invented them deserved to be a millionaire.

I finally reached the bottom. It had been nice to not use my inhaler. My bladder seared with pain. I bent over like an old rocking chair. There hadn't been a place to pee without the fear of being very exposed. The vast starkness made me gasp. This same feeling always assailed me above timberline. I forced myself to walk farther, reached a valley, and found a place to relieve myself behind some short trees.

The pain in my abdomen didn't subside after I peed and

wearing my pack around my middle would be torturous. I couldn't bear to cinch up my waistband, so I let my pack hang. The weight dragged at my shoulders.

I knew I was in trouble and took a Diflucan pill in hopes that maybe it was a yeast infection. At least I'd brought pills for that. I would have to hike steadily in spite of any pain in order to reach the campsite. Taking extra time to climb Whitney the next day would be out of the question. I'd come this far, and it was enough.

I'd save my energy to finish the hike to Lone Pine. I started to pray as I walked on. "Please give me strength," I repeated over and over, "Please give me healing energy."

Climbing agonizingly slow, I felt like the old turtle I'd so often compared myself to. I barely noticed Guitar Lake as I hobbled by. Any possibility that I had a yeast instead of a bladder infection was gone. This was the worst UTI I'd ever had.

I hoped I'd at least be able to hike out. Turning around, I made myself look at the lake. It sparkled like a diamond in the shape of a large guitar. I forced myself to keep noting the beauty of the rest of the scenery as I reached our campsite. My time in the wilderness was close to an end. I could see a tent pitched up ahead and assumed it was Debra and Jenny's.

When I finally arrived, it was almost dark. Two other tents were pitched not far from ours. I flung my backpack to the ground and sat bent over on the nearest rock. I couldn't stop myself from groaning. I wasn't sure what hurt more, the knife edged pain or the fact I'd made it so far and couldn't climb Whitney. I put my head in my hands and wept. It was humiliating and embarrassing. I'd cried too much on my trip.

Jenny came over. "What's wrong? You don't look so good." Debra stood over by the stove fixing dinner and didn't say anything.

"I'm pretty sure I have a bladder infection. I feel horrible."

Debra heard my lament and immediately responded, "What

about taking some antibiotics?"

"I wasn't able to get any from my doctor."

"Why?" She looked at me coldly.

"Like I said, I didn't ask him for any. Do you have some I could use?" I forced myself to ask.

She didn't answer me immediately, and I held my breath.

"I do, but I'm not comfortable giving them to you. I told you to get some from your doctor. Jenny and I might need ours."

"Mom, we're almost done with the hike. I'm sure I won't need any," Jenny said.

She was my steadfast hero. Without her, I'm sure Debra and I would've had a major blowout. I waited, and my whole body tensed preparing for Debra's answer. I prayed she would find it in her bitter heart to share their meds.

"I know I was stupid not to get any, but I really need them, Debra. Could you please share? I only need a couple, so I can get out of here." It felt awful to beg.

"I'm sorry, but I can't. I just wouldn't feel good about it."

Humiliating myself further, I started crying again. Leaning over my stomach, I crossed my arms, rocking back and forth. It did little to ease the searing pain. I felt bad for Jenny, who was pacing. Certainly, I did not feel bad for Debra. She just kept on cooking.

Suddenly I realized that maybe I hated her, and for sure, she must hate me. Part of me was sorry I'd ever come on with her. She'd tried in so many ways to let me know I wasn't welcome. I'd stupidly thought maybe things would improve and we would somehow achieve some type of camaraderie.

I felt weak. I felt angry. I felt betrayed. I tried to stop crying but hurt too badly.

Angels come in all forms and stepping out of the little blue tent set up not far from ours, I saw a figure approaching in the shadows. I felt an arm go around my shoulders and I looked up to see the face of my friend Kathy.

"I heard somebody crying, I came over to see what's wrong." She patted my back like the good pediatrician she obviously was.

"I'm so stupid I didn't bring antibiotics, and I'm sure I have a bladder infection." I sniffled. "I'm sorry to be such a baby. I'm sure I can't go up Whitney, and I'm not even sure I can get out to the trailhead in two days."

"No problem," Kathy said. "Did you forget I'm a doctor?" I have plenty of antibiotics. We'll get you some and double up on them. You'll be good as new before you know it."

I looked at her in wonder. I loved the woman. I could have kissed her. I could hardly believe my luck.

"Oh, I was just about to offer her some of ours," Debra said.

I don't know if Debra could see my face in the dark but if she did, I'm sure it showed all the disgust I felt for her.

"I've got plenty. I'll be right back." Kathy rushed off.

As good as her word, Kathy brought over a supply of antibiotics. I didn't even ask her what they were. I didn't care.

She handed them to me. "You need to eat something with them or they'll upset your stomach."

Debra carried some food over. I couldn't bring myself to thank her.

"Jun is in the tent above mine, and in the morning, we plan to go up Whitney together," Kathy rubbed my back. "Looks like the weather may hold. Wouldn't it be lucky if we could get to the top before the storm comes?"

I didn't want to tell her I might have used up all the luck I had, so I just nodded.

"Thanks Kathy. You'll never know what your kindness has meant to me."

Dear Diary,

This is one of the most stark and beautiful places in the world. The dark forbidding shape of Whitney looks like a giant monolith.

The universe has surrounded me with amazing people and because of them I'm here. Kathy was sent by God. A lot of people search for a higher power in churches, I just needed to visit the wilderness.

The antibiotics are already working. I don't believe for a minute Debra would have given me hers. Why would anybody be so mean? Mostly I feel sorry for her. She must feel awful inside.

It's me again, Diary. After going to bed, couldn't sleep. Something told me I needed to be outside. I found Jun and Kathy standing in the starlight. I crept over and stood by them. We silently clasped hands while raising our faces, gazing at the sparkling sky. If I'd never felt the presence of God before, I felt it then, surrounded by love, peace, and a sense that anything was possible. Even Whitney.

The three of us prayed, each in our own way.

"We do Whitney tomorrow." Jun looked at me and squeezed my hand. "Will see you there."

"Yes, I think you will see me there," I whispered. And I meant it. God is good all the time.

Last Part of Journey: Day 26
August 10, 2004

Climbing out of my sleeping bag at four a.m., it must have been twenty or more degrees colder than it'd been the whole trip. I brought out the tin foil pup tent Smiley had given me and was happy I hadn't left it behind. I could hear his raspy, sometimes gruff, but loving voice. "I had to use one in the army. It saved my ass. I haven't asked you to do anything else, so take it for me. You'll thank me some day."

That night proved he was right as I shivered and my teeth chattered like chopsticks. I needed to sleep if I wanted to attempt Whitney. I reached over and pulled the foil tent toward me, wrapping it around my down sleeping bag. I felt like a giant baked potato. Every time I moved, it crackled. It was good I was the only one in the tent. It would have been impossible for anyone else to sleep through the racket. Yet the noise was strangely comforting. I imagined Smiley's arms wrapped around me like a security blanket. It wouldn't be long before I was home in our bed, safe and warm.

It seemed nearly impossible, but I was going to try to climb Whitney the next day. I felt like a kid on Christmas Eve waiting for Santa to come down the chimney. My heart beat rapidly, and this time it wasn't from my inhaler.

I finally slept. Upon waking, I jumped out of my tinfoil wrapper and scrambled from my tent. My inner alarm clock hadn't let me down.

In the inky black sky, the stars twinkled and dozens of headlamps sparkled as hikers headed up the barren switchbacks toward Whitney. I'd watched many movies about people climbing Everest and other large mountains. My stomach churned like a Fourth of July fireworks extravaganza. Was this how it felt when hikers attempting the big climb woke in a base camp where many people had gathered to tackle the summit?

Laughing softly, I reminded myself Whitney was certainly not Everest, still the fireworks continued bursting in my stomach. I looked toward the place Debra's tent should have been. It wasn't there. She and Jenny were already up and putting it inside their backpacks. I don't know why I was surprised, but some of the excitement died, replaced by a cold shudder.

It was strangely quiet at camp even with all the headlamps going by. The hikers moved silent as monks on the way to early morning mass. Jun and Kathy dismantled their tents.

Debra and Jenny approached. Jenny was limping. She'd been having a hard time with her ankle, and even though she was excited to be going to the top of Whitney, I knew she'd be glad to go home.

Debra's voice broke the silence. "We're going ahead. I guess we'll meet you below at Trail Camp. It's about twelve miles. It'll be easy to get there if you decide you don't want to climb Whitney. If you want to try it, you'd better hustle. We need to get going. A storm is supposed to be coming, and even with you being the sunshine girl it might be hard to beat it."

I'd thought nothing else Debra did could surprise me, but abandoning me on this last leg of our journey did. I looked at her incredulously and stammered, "I thought we'd be climbing Whitney together. It's amazing the weather has held out for us, and besides I have the camera. Don't you want a picture?"

"I'm sure we can talk somebody into taking our picture and sending it to us. Besides, you may not make it."

There'd been many times on the trip I wondered if I'd make it up Whitney, but hearing her derogatory comments made me certain that, no matter what, I was going to get to the top. It had been a minor miracle I'd come that far. I wasn't about to quit at the end. Nothing short of a broken bone or a major thunderstorm was going to stop me.

"Hurry up, Jenny. We'd better leave so we can go conquer the mountain. See you at Trail Crest, Lori."

"I'm not planning to conquer any mountain," I said more loudly than I'd intended, "but I'd sure like to make friends with Whitney. You might beat me to the top, but I'll get there," I responded to their departing backs.

Jenny turned around and waved. "Good luck."

"You too, Jenny." I couldn't bring myself to wish Debra luck. Kathy and Jun came walking toward me, their packs on their backs.

"What's her problem?" Kathy shook her head. "Did you have an argument or something?"

"Actually, it's been like this pretty much the whole trip. She goes ahead, and I follow. Kinda like the tortoise and the hare."

"I thought she was mad at me last night and couldn't figure out why," Kathy said, "What a bitch."

"We go up Whitney," Jun said, smiling wide and changing the subject. "We wait for you get ready."

I looked at my two fellow hikers, and as fond as I was of them, I realized what I was about to say wasn't a lie. "I've kind of gotten used to hiking on my own and hate feeling like I hold people back. I'd rather you go ahead. I'm OK and looking forward to this part of my journey. I want to finish it by myself, at my own pace."

"Are you sure?" Kathy asked. "I don't mind waiting."

"Positive. However, I'll never forget you asked. Look for me at Trail Crest Camp or sooner. I'll be fine."

"I not happy leave you," Jun said. "You my friend, and friends help."

"You certainly are a good friend and have helped me more than you'll ever know. Just head out. I'll be right behind you. We're wasting the day."

We clasped hands and raised them high. Jun began to whistle as they turned and headed up the trail. I continued packing. The excitement inside my stomach tickled me from the inside out. It was amazing to not have any bladder pain. Another miracle.

I hitched up my backpack and stood straight and proud, ready to go. My back didn't hurt, my breathing was strong and even, and the faces of my friends and family kept creeping into my mind. I'd never been alone on any part of my trip.

The stars and the moon were glowing in the heavens. I was glowing in my heart. I was ready. The majority of people who climb Whitney start from Whitney Portal, have a 6,000 ft elevation gain, and try to climb Whitney as a day hike. That gives them no time to get used to the elevation. I'd been out almost three weeks.

I kept reminding myself I was one of the hikers who had acclimated and it would make all the difference. The beam from my headlight shone on the massive rectangular dark and foreboding shape of Whitney as I started my hike upward in the still darkness. Debra had made a good call when she insisted we start hiking the JMT from the north. If I did make it to the top of Whitney, part of the reason would be because of her excellent planning.

As I continued moving slowly along, I thought about the times it would've been so easy to give up and go home. Just the fact that it hadn't rained more than a few drops in nineteen days made me know God had been watching over and carrying me. My friends and family believed in me and had walked all of the 200+ miles in my heart and head. It didn't matter what Debra thought. I had walked the JMT and intended to make it up Whitney.

It seemed I was the tail end of a group of hikers starting up Whitney in the early morn. I didn't hear any noise from above. Each time I began a new switchback I felt my right knee buckling. I had climbed 26 of them. The day was dawning, and I found myself having a hard time facing the next 70 switchbacks. It didn't matter how I got to the top or when. Just getting there would be enough.

I'd hoped I wouldn't have to resort to the 100-step-suck-dance, but it had served me well in the past. I eventually gave in and sucked. My throat no longer felt like chalk, making it possible for me to breathe without gasping for air. I bent over trying to take a load off my back for a moment and felt myself accidentally kick a rock off the trail. It made loud booming noises, becoming quieter and quieter as it careened down the side of the mountain. I could only hope nobody below got hurt. Once again it was good to be the caboose of a line of hikers.

In between my step-suck-water routine I needed to live in the present. It was a stroke of good luck, prayer, faith, and karma I'd got this far. I knew I'd never pass this way again.

Several people walked by me but nobody had much to offer besides a few nods of headlamps or a quick "good luck." The black sky brightened to blue, and I concentrated on enjoying the dawn of a new day. I knew I was making progress when I looked down and saw the many switchbacks zigzagging below me. I didn't pass anybody but kept moving along, hiking where I felt most comfortable, last in line. Later, we'd be sleeping at Trail Camp with hordes of people and a chemical toilet. Technically this would be my last wilderness day on the trail. I wanted to savor it.

I contemplated all the ways I'd changed as a result of this trip. Some of the things I thought would happen hadn't, and there had been many surprises. I believed I'd get so fit by the end of my journey, hiking would be easy. For some reason it never did. On a positive note, it wasn't as hard for me to get up passes and I hadn't had to use my inhaler in a while. That was huge.

My old knees had even made me appreciate going uphill, they didn't hurt nearly as much as when I went downhill. I wondered what I'd look like when I finally took my hat off as it had become my constant adornment. Often it was accessorized with my bug net over the top. A true wilderness fashion statement. Any vanity I'd had was gone.

Going up, up, and even farther up the trail, I thought of all of the things I couldn't have done without. The first and most important were my trail angels. Many people would call me crazy for believing in them, but they had kept me sane. I'd imagined the wilderness as my biggest teacher, but thinking about everyone I'd met, I realized people had taught me the most. They shined as intensely as the stars of my journey.

The mountains would always be there, stoic and grand. Human beings, including me, were only visitors in a sacred place. I wondered if climbing Whitney would be the day I cherished most in the years to come.

With the aid of my hiking poles, I clicked off the equipment that had served me best. Top of the list was my backpack fitted for a woman. It was as comfortable as anything could be carrying forty-five pounds of gear. My water filter, the water bladder I sucked on continually, the Citrucel I'd finally got, hormone cream, hiking poles to keep some weight off my knees, kneepads that gave my knees some support, flagging tape that Jenny used to mark our campsites, small pieces of paper brought to journal on, sunhat, mosquito net hat and of course sunscreen that served as lotion and hair moisturizer. Then there was my lightweight tent, ensolite pad, compact stove, moleskin, Susie's Shoe Goo, and lastly, and most importantly my camera.

I would be ever grateful to the manufacturers of Emergen-C, the powdered drink that got me over so many passes. I was quite sure I'd never eat another power bar for the rest of my life and it would be a long time before I could look oatmeal in the face again. Gorp was very well a food of my past.

Smiley had been with me the whole trip and I could hardly wait to see him in the flesh. I thought about what fun we had and how many times I could love and be angry at him at the same time. On my interim day at home he had filled our large jacuzzi tub with water and invited me to take a bath with him. Scented candles and classical music were part of the deal. It might have been perfect, but he'd added. "I need you to take a bath with me so I can displace some water." Hmmmm…

Trudging up the trail in relative darkness and watching the day dawn filled me with awe and gratitude. I couldn't believe my good luck in feeling so lifted in both body and mind.

Thinking happy thoughts made even the hardest task easier. I was getting close to the trail junction that would lead me to Whitney. I'd pretty much decided to leave my backpack there and take only the small one that detached from it. I'd put as much of my food in it as possible and leave the rest in the bear canister. I hadn't wanted to bring the canister when we first started the trip, but it'd been a relief not having to hang my food at night. Debra had talked about taking her whole pack up Whitney because people might steal things. I was willing to take my chances. Who in the world would be out backpacking and want to steal my gear?

Everybody had enough stuff of their own.

The sun rays tickled my skin, while silver edged cotton ball clouds shimmered in the sky. Two hikers approached and stopped, "You heading to the top of Whitney?" asked the pretty young girl with clean golden hair.

I looked at her and nodded. Feeling like I was in someone else's body, for the first time I truly believed I was going up Whitney and replied, "I am."

"You're gonna love it," said the brawny, long-haired man. We had some problems with the altitude but we made it. How long have you been out?"

"Three weeks this time, and we were out for two short trips before."

"Then it'll be a piece of cake. You look in great shape and you're acclimated," said the girl.

"Thanks," I was pleased someone thought so. "I'm really excited."

"Looks like the weather might hold for you. Rumor is a big storm's coming in. Hope you miss it," said the man.

"Me, too. Happy trails." I waved at them as they took off. I felt like a real long-distance backpacker. For a lot of the trip it seemed I'd been the *great pretender.* I remembered the words, *as you think you are, so you shall become.*

This last day was a gift from God. The sky was filled with the most amazing beams of light shooting from the heavens like gigantic flashlight rays splaying to the earth. I'd never seen the sky so beautiful in the late morning. It was part of the gift I got on this last day in the wilderness.

My breathing came easy, my feet didn't hurt, and my pack and heart were light. Swinging my poles, I found myself again singing "Climb Every Mountain." I laughed when I thought what my boys would say to me now. "Oh, Mamma, you're so corny. Always finding a song to fit your mood."

It seemed like no time at all until I reached Trail Junction. Nobody else was there. I flung my pack down anticipating the joy of reaching the top without it. I could hardly believe I'd climbed over 100 switchbacks to get where I was.

I took out as much food as possible and ate a hearty lunch. I made small talk with two or three groups that were in a hurry to head up Whitney. Then I took out what I intended to bring with me and left the rest in my backpack.

I looked around for a place to store it. The area was so exposed, there wasn't anywhere to put it but next to the seven other backpacks right in view on the trail. Debra's pack was there, but not Jenny's. I placed mine beside hers. I was ready, and it felt right to be finishing alone. My toes tingled, my heart beat rapidly. I was headed for the top!

Before continuing I looked around for a place to sit and reflect. I found an outcropping of rock resting above the wilderness I'd hiked. I lowered myself onto it. Humbleness and an overwhelming happiness engulfed me as I closed my eyes and offered up a prayer. My breathe became air.

"Thank you, God, and dear majestic Mt. Whitney, for allowing me to visit. To all of you who are here with me, who are part of me, who surround me, thank you. Because of you, I'm here today. I hope you're proud of me. I'm proud of myself. Without all of you I'd never have made it. My heart's full."

I'd read in my guide book that when you start up the trail to Whitney the wilderness experiences you had enjoyed since leaving Yosemite would probably be over. It also said I'd meet hordes of hikers. That was certainly true. In the first quarter mile I'd seen twenty or more. They traveled in groups and appeared jovial and fit.

I obviously wasn't the only one hoping to get to the top. It was an experience to be shared. If I'd wanted to be alone, there were many other hiking areas I could have chosen. Nevertheless, all of us aspired to climb the highest mountain in the continental USA. The round trip to the top of Mt. Whitney and back was approximately four miles with about a 1,000-foot ascent and descent. I moved onward.

Now and then patches of snow appeared along the steep trail. Thousands of boulders filled the talus slope. If those huge rocks decided to fall I could be critically hurt or even killed, but they'd been there a long time and many other hikers had made their way safely across them.

Scampering across the rocky slope I spotted two sleek marmots. They were not nearly as fat as the ones I'd seen previously. Life was tougher up here. I thought of Jun, Kathy, Jenny, and Debra. I hoped they'd made it safely to the top and had taken time to enjoy their awesome accomplishment.

Even without a backpack, I felt the effects of the high altitude. I stopped and slipped my inhaler out of my pocket. Puffing on it, I looked at the sky filling with clouds at an alarming rate.

Continuing climbing the rocky ridge, weaving in and out of a narrow path amongst uneven talus, I tried to not look down at the steep drop-off below me. It was a good thing I wasn't afraid of heights. I figured I'd come about a mile or more of the two needed to reach the top.

Walking steadily, I approached a lone hiker hunched on a rock, his head in his hands. I wasn't sure what to do so I stupidly asked him, "How's it going?"

He looked up, shaking his head, face ashen and contorted in pain. "Not so good."

"What's wrong?"

"Everything. This is the third time I've tried to get up Whitney and the last. I guess I'm not supposed to do it."

"Why not?"

"Not to brag or anything, but I'm in great shape, ride bikes all over, even run marathons. But, this is the closest I've been to the top. Every time I try I get altitude sickness and can't go on."

"Are you here alone?"

"I told my three friends to go ahead. They shouldn't have to skip the top because of me."

"How bad do you feel?"

"Mildly nauseated with a slight headache. We forgot to bring any pain relievers. What about you? Have you hiked the whole John Muir Trail, or are you just trying to do Whitney from Lone Pine, like me?"

"I've been out three weeks hiking the JMT or the altitude would be getting me, too. I've got some aspirin." I handed him three. "Why don't you take these and see how you feel in a few minutes. If you want we can hike together."

Taking long gulps of water from his canteen, he swallowed the pills. "I'd feel awful holding you up. Everybody here has their own agenda, and yours sure doesn't include helping some dumb guy who gets altitude sickness. Still, it's nice of you to offer."

I began to laugh. He glared at me and asked, "What's so funny? This isn't a joke. I realize hiking from Whitney Portal in two days and not acclimating isn't the best way to do it, but some of us don't have the time or money to take three weeks to do the JMT."

"Oh, I'm not laughing at you. I'm laughing because you think you're holding me back. Nobody slows me down. I've been hiking this trail with a woman and her teenage daughter and I'm always at the tail end of the group. My trail name is Caboose. Honestly, I like being last. I may not be fast, but I'm here. And so are you. So, if you want, I'll wait for you. I could use a break."

"I'm starting to feel a lot better. I think the aspirin's working and drinking lots of water seems to have helped. If you wouldn't mind waiting, I'll see how I feel in a few minutes."

I sat and looked at the spectacular view. I could see back toward many of the massive peaks I'd hiked over. "This is amazing! I can't believe I'm here."

"Why not?"

"I'm just an ordinary fifty-one-year-old mom, wife, and teacher, almost at the top of Whitney. I'm so excited!"

"You don't look that old. You need to tell your husband, kids, and students that maybe part of you is ordinary, but you did a very extraordinary thing."

"That's nice of you to say."

"It's true and waiting for me is really decent of you. It'd mean a lot to me to get to the top of Whitney. I'm only thirty-three, and you're in better shape than I. What made you decide to hike the JMT?"

I hoped I wasn't making a mistake encouraging him to go on. Altitude sickness can be a dangerous thing. It makes it so you are unable to get enough oxygen to the brain. It could even lead to death.

But he had some color in his face and wasn't sweating nearly as much. His breathing became less shallow, his speech clearer. "I turned fifty last year and felt like life was passing me by. I wanted to do something to make me feel alive, so when a friend asked me to hike the JMT with her, I jumped at it."

"Are you glad you did?"

"Yes." I replied, and realized I really meant it.

"My name's Chris. What's yours? I should at least know the name of the woman who's making it possible for me to go up Whitney. If you don't mind walking slowly, I think I'm ready to go."

"My name's Lori and Slow is my middle name. I like taking my time. It'll be nice to have company."

After we reached the ridge the trail was mostly flat but still not easy. It wasn't so much a trail as a series of pieces of granite to scramble over. We didn't talk much as we both seemed to want to save our energy. Looking down I noticed a cushioning green plant that was close to the ground. It was covered in purple flowers. "Do you happen to know the name of this plant? It sure is a hardy little thing."

"I think it's called a Sky Pilot. It looks like it's about the only vegetation here," Chris replied, his breathing steady.

We began climbing some short and steep switchbacks. Soon a speck looking like a building appeared in the distance. "Hey, Chris, my guidebook said we should see the hut a long time before we get there and I think that's it." I pointed.

"You're right."

For some reason the walking was easy for me. It felt wonderful to be unencumbered by a large pack. The breeze caressed my face, and my breathing held steady and even. Many hikers passed us climbing up and trekking down. Almost everyone was laughing and talking animatedly. I saw a group of three people I thought I recognized.

As they approached me, I knew for sure it was Debra, Jenny, and Kathy. I noticed Jenny had a loaded backpack and Debra carried nothing. Kathy came running toward me and hugged me. "I was starting to worry about you. We've been on top a long time. What happened?"

"I happened," Chris explained. "This's my third time trying Whitney, and I got altitude sickness. She waited for me."

"I needed a break. You guys know what a slow hiker I am. How was the top?"

"Absolutely glorious. You're really close. We'll all go back with you. Right Debra?" Kathy asked.

"I don't know. Jenny's ankle's hurting, and you took our picture up there. You'll send us a copy, won't you? I think we should go on."

Jenny looked at me and tried to smile. She was limping, leaning to the side, and the backpack seemed to weigh her down. She looked down at her boots and mumbled, "I could wait here for you guys."

"I've got Chris and Kathy, so if you don't want to go back with me that's OK. You two go ahead."

Debra took out a freeze-dried meal from Jenny's backpack. "Here's some food for you in case we don't see you at Trail Camp. We're going down as quickly as we can and try and beat the storm."

She tossed me the food and hurried off. Jenny shuffled along behind her then turned around and waved. Debra continued on without a backward glance.

"Boy, she's a real sweetheart. I can see why you prefer hiking alone." Chris seemed to be gathering more strength the farther we went. I was relieved I hadn't brought him this far just to see him get sicker.

Kathy led the way talking a mile a minute. "Jun is on the top waiting for you. He's been reciting prayers and is planning to spend the night up there. He'll be so happy to see you." Her excitement was contagious, and Chris and I followed her quickly and easily.

About fifty feet in the distance, we could see people waving, clapping, and cheering. "Those are my friends," said Chris.

One young woman slim and tan came running toward us and put her arms around him. "You made it! That's great. You've got to see the view."

"I wouldn't be here without Lori," he said, patting me on the shoulder. "She gave me some aspirin and convinced me to come with her. Wow, I'm sure glad I did!" he said as we reached the hut.

Chris's friends gathered beside the tiny mortared granite shelter smiling and fist pumping in congratulations. Kathy and I stood back, eager to go join Jun. I went over to say goodbye.

"I don't know how to thank you," Chris said.

"Then don't. We helped each other." I leaned over, and we gave each other a quick hug. I turned around toward the actual top of Mt. Whiney, a short distance away. His friends all shouted a warm thank you as we left. Kathy and I raised our poles in response. I couldn't help but notice no one in Chris's group sported a pair of hiking poles.

The last 300 feet to reach the top of Whitney looked like one big rock slide. It's called The Scramble. There is no actual trail, and each person's summit is unique. I was grateful for that. My journey had been my own, as was my summit.

There was a gathering of people near the National Park Service plaque that states we were atop Mt. Whitney, 14,496.811 ft above sea level. I threw my poles down and sat beside the marker. I joined the frenzy of tourists surrounding it and felt proud to be part of a group that'd worked so hard to reach a summit of such grandeur.

"Could you take my picture?" I asked Kathy. "Or better yet, take lots of pictures of me, please."

My clothes were covered with dirt, and my hair hadn't been combed in days. But I couldn't remember a time when I'd ever smiled as widely or felt as beautiful.

After the photo shoot we headed to the rim of the mountain and its 360-degree view. I did my spin dance again, viewing massive mountaintops, deep valleys, even a dusty road far off in the distance. In addition to Sequoia and Kings Canyon, I could look east to Lone Pine and see the White Mountains and Death Valley.

The clouds lurked dark and angry. I was on top of the world, and I could see forever. In the distance a solo eagle rode the currents through the crags of rock. My spirit soared to the heavens, in tune to the eagle's flight.

Jun, removed from the crowd, stood alone. He held his

silence, his arms, and hands reaching high. He wore a radiant smile, lighting up his face from within like a blazing fire. I ambled toward him. He gently placed my hands in his and looked into my eyes. "This is sacred place. My uncle he see me here. My ancestors with me and I am One." We grew still, listening to the heartbeat of Whitney.

The John Muir trail technically ended at the top of Whitney. I couldn't figure out who made that call. There was no public transportation to use from the summit back to civilization if you wanted to call it quits. The only way out was by foot.

After an hour or so of enjoying the view, Kathy, Jun and I formed a small huddle and held each other tightly. I'd miss Jun but would never forget him. We exchanged addresses, and Kathy and I headed away, each tired and happy, one foot following the other. I tried to etch the view on my mind as I descended but knew sometime in the future it would become fuzzy and unclear. My mother's voice whispered in my ear, "Live in the present. It's yours for only a short time."

We stopped and picked up our packs at Trail Junction. Nobody or nothing had bothered them, and once more I wondered what had possessed Debra to make Jenny hike to the top wearing her backpack. They were long gone. Kathy and I headed to Trail Camp, about four miles away. My feet started to throb, and I looked down at my boots-each of them with a gaping hole in the sole. Thoughts of six-year-old Sean calling his comfortable tennis shoes his holy shoes went through my mind. God, I loved my boots.

I was mildly pissed that the trail went up steeply instead of down for a few hundred yards. It irritated me, as I panted for air. Finally, we reached Trail Crest, the last pass on our trip. We had to go over it to go down to Whitney Portal. At 13,600 ft it's the highest point on the JMT except for Whitney. I could see all the way down to the Owens Valley. I stopped for a minute. The view was breathtaking. The dusty brown desert area and green trees were visible. Buildings and roads dotted the landscape. I was surprised to realize it was the view that had taken my breath away and not my asthma.

Looking over at Kathy, I smiled. "I can't thank you enough for giving me those antibiotics. I never would've made it without them. I feel great."

"Glad to help. That's what friends are for," she said as we continued walking.

The next four miles were some of the easiest I'd hiked the entire trip. My whole body felt fit. Hiking over 200 miles in the high Sierra probably had a little something to do with it.

The crowded trail camp was a letdown after Whitney. Campsites were jammed together, and I could smell human sweat all around. A chemical latrine had been provided. There had been times on the trail I'd wished for a *real* toilet. The old saying *be careful what you wish for* spun in my head.

The bathroom stank. Signs posted everywhere told people to only poop in it, not to pee. I tried unsuccessfully to envision how it would be possible to do that. As a woman, was it anatomically possible? I decided not to think about it.

Kathy and I located Debra and Jenny's campsite. Debra stuck her head out of her tent, looking like she'd sucked on a lemon. "Jenny and I've already cooked supper. We might take our tent down and leave. There's nothing much left to see, and we're ready to go home."

We set up camp in a spot away from them and I proceeded to lie down and rest. A heated argument issued from Debra and Jenny's tent.

"I don't want to hike anymore today, Mom." Jenny's voice was the loudest I'd heard all summer. "I'm tired and want to stay in a hotel tomorrow."

"We might go home tomorrow. I don't have money for a

hotel. We could have Todd pick us up," Debra shouted.

"I need a break, Mom. I hiked the whole trail for you. Why can't I rest?"

I got out of my tent, and Kathy and I tried to have a louder than usual conversation. I think we were both embarrassed about the sharp words between mother and daughter. Regardless of the fight, Jenny loved her mom and I believe the feeling was mutual, but I was still surprised she hadn't rebelled long ago. It had been a long trail.

"Well, do you want to walk out with me in the morning?" Kathy asked.

"That'd be great. It's all downhill. Who knows, maybe I can keep up."

"I have a friend coming to get me, not tomorrow but the next day. You guys can hitch a ride if you want to camp and wait. She'd take you to Lone Pine if you'd like."

"That'd be fine with me, but I need to confirm it with Debra."

Our campground was beautiful in spite of all the people. A small waterfall spilled nearby, and craggy cliffs added grandeur to the scene. Kathy and I cooked dinner then decided to bed down early. We looked up at the menacing sky before turning in.

"We'll be lucky to get out dry. I hope Jun is all right on Whitney," Kathy said.

"Me too. If anyone deserves a phenomenal night on top of Whitney, he does. I can hardly believe he packed enough food for nineteen days and did the whole JMT without a resupply."

"Yeah, he's really something. Sleep tight." Kathy crawled into her tent

Dear Diary,

Not even Debra could spoil today for me. When Kathy and I arrived at Trail Camp she asked me if Debra was pissed at her or me or what? Told her I didn't know what she was pissed at and I didn't care.

Getting to the top of Whitney changed me. I no longer feel like being older than fifty is the end of my life's adventures but rather the beginning of a different stage. Have danced in the Sierra wilderness and felt its sweet breath. The rest of my life can be filled with excitement and fun. Getting older can mean getting better or at least smarter about some of the stuff that really matters and letting go of the stuff that doesn't. Proud of myself for helping Chris up the mountain. In helping him, I found another piece of myself. Maybe I'm a trail angel, too? I'd like that.

With everything that went wrong on this trip, so much went right. The moment I lifted my hiking poles on top of Whitney will be forever etched on the emulsion sheets of my mind reminding me to believe in myself and in something or someone much bigger than me. Being in the wilderness I found more than myself, I found God's light, and it will shine in me forever.

Last Part of Journey: Day 27
August 11, 2004

In the morning, the rain we'd managed to avoid pounded the tent. I jumped out and rushed around, breaking down camp and hastily stuffing equipment in my pack. I wouldn't need to use it again on this trip. Kathy was up and doing a similar dance.

Looking over to where Debra and Jenny's tent was last night, I noticed they'd already left. Panic constricted my chest. I'd thought nothing else Debra did could surprise me. Her abandoning me on our last day not only bothered me, but also made me sad and frightened.

We hadn't discussed if we would stay and wait for Kathy's ride or go into Lone Pine and book a hotel room. The last time we talked about it Debra said maybe we'd just go on and ride a shuttle bus to the Mobil station at the entrance to Yosemite. She'd try and call Todd and see if he could come get us. She'd asked me if I had cash to cover the gas and told me to give it to her and she'd pass it on to Todd. I told her I wanted to hand him the money so he'd know it was from me. She hadn't liked that.

I didn't want to spend time or energy to cook oatmeal so I took out my dried fruit and gorp and passed some to Kathy. We gulped it down. There was a rumor of a small store at the bottom of the trail that sold burgers. I could sense my taste buds coming alive and feel the saliva in my mouth. I licked my lips thinking about a thick juicy burger and greasy, salty fries.

Thoughts of civilization peeked into my mind and a lot of those thoughts had to do with food. I could tell I'd lost quite a bit of weight by how my clothes fit. I wondered how long the weight would stay off. I hoped permanently but didn't believe it.

I knew when I got home I would have food in my fridge enticing me to eat. I wouldn't be hiking ten plus miles a day at an elevation of over 9,000 ft with forty-five pounds on my back. It'd been a forced diet, one that would be impossible for me to maintain in civilization.

I opened my guidebook and tried to shield it with my poncho. It said there was a 6.8-mile hike down to Whitney Portal. It was too windy and rainy to talk. Turning my thoughts to the present I cinched the belt of my pack tightly and followed Kathy. The trail continued to slope steadily downhill past Mirror Lake. I'd been looking forward to seeing it, but we went on by as quickly as possible.

The rain pelted into my eyes, making it difficult to read and walk. It turned the trail to a gooey mud, so I stashed the book in my pocket. I spent most of my energy watching my feet and making sure I didn't slip and fall. I hadn't come that far to stumble and break a body part.

I was a much better downhill hiker than uphill and found myself striding ahead of Kathy. Knowing how it felt to be left behind and grateful she'd always waited for me, I stopped at the boundary of the John Muir Wilderness and Inyo National Forest. I realized it was the first time I'd ever been in the Inyo. I wished I could see more of the trail and enjoy it but immediately felt guilty.

The rain was a God thing. The wilderness was drying out and desperately needed the summer storm. I could almost hear the trail sighing and saying, "About time."

Hardly anybody was going down, but many people were going up. Nobody stopped to talk. We kept scurrying on our separate paths.

We were getting closer to the end of the trail when my nose picked up the smell of fast food. The rain let up and I looked back at Kathy, who raised her poles in the air. "We're almost there and I can't wait for a burger!" she shouted.

"Me too." I lifted my poles back at her.

Rounding the bend, a small building appeared. I assumed it was the general store. There was also a huge parking lot filled with vehicles. Feeling repulsed, my body stepped back involuntarily letting me know I wasn't sure I wanted to return to civilization. The altitude was a little over 8,000 ft and we'd descended over 6,000 ft from the top of Whitney.

My knees shook as if they'd seen a ghost and sent pain howling through my body. I looked down at my braces that were now in tatters. I realized they and my hiking poles and shoes belonged at the top of my *best friend list* for this trip.

Before I had a chance to take off my pack or process the fact I'd survived the John Muir Trail, I saw Debra emerging from the store.

"Wow, we made it!" Kathy exclaimed, "We're ready for a burger. Did you get one?"

"We already ate. Where've you guys been?" Debra looked up at the sky. "We need to get going and hitch a ride into Lone Pine so we can get home tonight."

"I'm starved and want a burger. Where should we meet?" I asked.

"We're going to the road to hitchhike. You better come along if you don't want to be left behind."

"You guys can camp overnight with me," Kathy said, "Remember I have a friend coming tomorrow. She can take you to the entrance of Yosemite. I could use a rest and a burger."

"I'm ready to go home. Suit yourself. We'll be down the road and wait awhile but then we'll start trying to get a ride." Debra headed off. Jenny didn't say a word, just followed her mom. I couldn't blame her.

"Do you think Jenny had any fun on the hike?" Kathy asked.

"Yeah, I do," I replied, going inside the store. "I often heard her and Debra laughing uproariously and at times felt envious. I think there'll be a time she'll be really proud of herself and have some great memories. It couldn't have been easy. I'm sure glad her ankle held out."

I ordered a burger with all the trimmings, fries, and a giant Coke. Nothing ever tasted so good. We didn't talk much, just ate with gusto. We looked over at each other about half way through and started to laugh. "I think we're inhaling," I mumbled.

"Yep, and it's delicious," Kathy replied with her mouth full.

In no time at all we finished. I took a few minutes to pick up some postcards and a touristy shirt with *I hiked the John Muir Trail* on it. I was glad I still had my debit card.

Almost everything got misplaced at some time on the trip, but it was right where I'd left it in a small pocket encased in a sandwich baggie. Kathy and I exchanged phone numbers and addresses. I knew I'd better head down the road, though it wouldn't surprise me if Debra had already gotten a ride and left me.

"I'll be staying in the campground, so ask for my site at the office if you need to stay," Kathy said as we hugged.

"You're a brave and remarkable woman. Thanks for being my friend."

"Same to you. Let's keep in touch," she said over her shoulder as we departed in opposite directions.

It felt weird to walk on pavement. Lots of things seemed strange. I'd come to terms with the wilderness on my trek, being amongst so many people and things assaulted my senses. After a quarter of a mile or so, I started to worry, and wondered if maybe I should return to the campgrounds. Two shapes emerged on the side of the road. One of them jumped up and down waving at me.

"Hey, it's good to see you," shouted Jenny, as I approached. By the look on her mom's face, the sentiment wasn't shared.

"We're having a hard enough time getting a ride out of here without you. With three of us, it'll be nearly impossible." Debra frowned and shook her head. "Go over and hide in the bushes. When we get a ride, we'll signal you."

I was annoyed and hurt. "Damn it, Debra. I've done lots of things on this trip I thought I'd never do or at least never do again. Begging for food was awful, but I did it. I haven't hitchhiked since I got married twenty-five years ago, but I'm putting my thumb out now. I'm unwilling to crawl out of the bushes like a bandit when you and Jenny get a ride. I think it's only fair people know what they're up against when they pick us up. So, like it or not, you're stuck with me."

Without a word she went and stood in the middle of the road with her thumb out. I had to give her credit for tenacity. I stood to the side with the backpacks. A couple of cars swerved around her, then a new model sedan approached. Debra waved frantically and they pulled over.

A good-looking man with a young woman next to him poked his head out the window. "Are you guys in trouble?"

"Well, kind of...mmmm actually we are," Debra replied. "We just finished hiking the John Muir Trail and have to get to the Yosemite entrance tonight. Could you please give us a ride to Lone Pine so we can get on the shuttle bus?"

The guy looked over at his passenger then looked at our dirty packs and us. I noticed the car was spotless, and so were they. "I don't think we can fit all of you," he replied.

"We'll squeeze in and hold whatever we can in our laps. Pleeezzz," Debra begged.

"Let's take them." The woman put her arm around him. "After all, they could be me."

"I don't think so." The man laughed. "You don't even like to camp."

We jammed into the car, and I couldn't help but smell the stench coming with us. I thought it was decent of them not to mention it, and the thirteen-mile ride to Lone Pine went quickly. We learned the couple were newlyweds on their honeymoon. They weren't camping but were traveling through the Sierra. They planned to stay in Lone Pine at a nice hotel for the night.

When we arrived in town, the man looked at us, "Where would you like us to drop you?"

"Anywhere would be fine," Debra answered. "We'll ask around town and find out about a shuttle."

They left us at a corner with a stoplight. Even though Lone Pine was a small community, it seemed full of hustle and bustle after my excursion in the wilderness.

We probably looked funny going through town with our backpacks on. I hadn't gazed in a mirror for weeks and I was sure my bright red hair was wild and crazy. It had always been a defining part of me. After years of hating it and going to extremes to straighten it by an iron I'd finally made peace and let it go corkscrew curly and out of control. A woman in her fifties knows which battles are worth fighting, and taming my hair wasn't one I took on anymore.

After walking a block or two, I noticed a sign with *Senior Citizen Center* on it. I walked to the door and opened it. "I'll bet they'd let us go in and wash up."

Inside a lady sat at a table with a badge on that read *Delores.* "Well, you guys look too young to be here for lunch. What can I do for you?"

"We're wondering if we could wash up in your restroom?" I smiled at her. "I know we're pretty dirty, but we'll clean up after ourselves. We just hiked the John Muir Trail."

"Why?" she asked. "I hear there are lots of mosquitoes and bears. You're some gutsy ladies. Go ahead and clean up."

"Thanks," we said, almost in unison.

We left our backpacks in the hall. It felt wonderful to go into a clean restroom with flushing toilets. I didn't have to pee, but forced myself to sit on the porcelain seat. I felt like a queen on her throne. After about five minutes, my body cooperated and I flushed. The sound of the water swooshing down the pipes was musical. I'd never made peace with outdoor toileting.

Debra and Jenny washed up and brushed their teeth. I did likewise. After scrubbing my face, I wet my hair. Looking in the mirror for the first time in weeks surprised me. "Not bad," I told myself. The full-length mirror attested to the fact I'd lost weight, had a golden tan, and my hair wasn't nearly as bad as I'd imagined. I'd survived rather nicely. After fixing ourselves up, we headed out.

"You guys look real good cleaned up," Delores said. "Hey, Frank, these gals hiked the John Muir Trail."

The old man shook his head. "Young people these days are crazy," he growled. "What person in their right mind would want to walk over 200 miles?" He headed toward the door to the lunchroom.

Instead of making me feel bad, his comments made me happy. The best part was he'd called me a young person. It dawned on me I felt that way. Fifty-one no longer seemed ancient. My body looked and acted better than it had in years.

"You guys are welcome to eat," Delores said. "I'll be glad to pay for you."

"Thanks anyway. We've already eaten and need to get going.

Do you happen to know if there's a thrift store in town?" Debra asked.

Delores walked outside with us and pointed across the street. "There's a pretty good one over there."

"Thanks for everything," I said.

"You're more than welcome. Good luck."

We waited for a red light to turn green and proceeded to cross the street. For the first time my back ached instead of my knees or feet. I couldn't wait to release myself from my burdensome pack.

"How about we go in and see if we can buy some underwear and clothes for cheap?" Debra asked as we approached The Good Luck Thrift Store.

"Sounds great," I replied. I'd never worn used underwear before, but I was doing lots of things I'd never imagined. At least they'd be clean, which was a lot more than I could say for the clothing I had on.

We dropped off our packs and decided to take turns watching them. Luckily it had stopped raining. "I'll watch first," Jenny plopped down on top of her pack.

"We've just hiked the John Muir Trail," I said to a burly spiked-haired woman at the counter with a pierced lip and tattoos covering her arms. I couldn't seem to help myself from telling everyone. I still couldn't believe I'd done it.

"Lots of people do that," she replied, returning to the body building magazine she was reading.

"We need some new, well, I mean used—new to us—clothes," I told the woman.

She looked at me with very little interest. "Feel free to browse."

I found a shirt, some shorts, and underwear I was pretty sure would fit. The shorts had an elastic waist because I had no idea what size I needed. "Can I put these on in your dressing room and throw my clothes away?" I asked.

"Be my guest. Put your old stuff in this bag." She handed me a brown sack. "You can take it out back to the dumpster."

The clothes fit, and I eagerly tossed my foul-smelling rags. It was hard to remember ever having such a good time trying on things. I felt refreshed and strangely pretty in a way that didn't only entail my appearance. The minimal $5.67 total price of the clothing was a bargain. I went outside and turned around in place, showing off my new duds.

"You look great. You really have lost weight," Jenny said.

"You have, too, and you didn't need to. Now go inside with your mom and find yourself something to wear. I'll watch the packs."

I had to admit we looked darn good sauntering away from the thrift store. It's amazing what eating a hamburger, washing up, and wearing clean clothes can do for a girl's morale. "We could attract men now if we wanted to," Debra said. We giggled, put our hands on our hips, and tried to look sexy with our backpacks on. Jenny rolled her eyes. We were more than ready to catch the shuttle.

About twenty minutes later, we pushed and shoved our packs into the shuttle. "I can't wait to eat at the Whoa Nelly Deli," Jenny said. "I need to decide if I want a hamburger or fish tacos."

"I'm going for the tacos," said Debra.

"All I can think about is an ice-cold Coke." I looked around and chose a seat, lifting my backpack into the one next to me.

The feeling of comradeship buoyed my spirits until Debra started harassing the shuttle driver about stopping at places not on the route. Most of the time the driver was letting off local Native Americans at their homes. One guy she complained about walked with a crooked wood cane. He was at least eighty and would have had to walk four or five blocks if the bus driver didn't take him to his house.

Debra seemed to be the only one having a problem with it. She kept mumbling under her breath, "We'll never get there." She jumped out of her seat and marched to the front of the bus. "We're going to be late if you keep going out of your way to drop people off. I'm in a hurry."

"Are you going to a fire?" the driver asked.

"We've hiked the JMT, and we're tired."

"So, what?" hissed a pimpled teen, "Lots of people have hiked the friggin' trail and don't think they're all that."

Debra shut up and returned to her seat. I silently agreed with the kid. I didn't feel hiking the trail gave us license to be rude.

Clouds gathered in the sky, and it looked like we could be in for another drenching. I said a silent prayer thanking God for helping me be off the JMT before another big storm hit. The Sierra needed water badly, but I couldn't help feeling grateful it hadn't rained on my parade for most of the trip.

Debra called Todd. He agreed to pick us up at the Whoa Nelly Deli-part of the Mobil Gas Station situated near Mono Lake by Yosemite's entrance station. They sold hearty, yummy, nutritious food, and since it was Saturday night, it was possible there would be live music. I was excited about the prospect of a band, eating fish tacos, and drinking a giant Coke and wine.

I hoped Debra's mood would improve once we got there. For the life of me, I couldn't figure out why she was grumpy. Regardless of the fact many thousands of people had hiked the John Muir Trail, I still felt a great sense of pride, accomplishment, and joy. I couldn't wait to get home to share my journey with family and friends.

I'd finished the trail by trudging along, finding pieces of myself throughout the journey. Placing a hand in my pocket I caressed the heart rock. It had become my talisman and reminded me of Smiley's love and belief in me. He was right. I'd become a different person. I was ready to let him get to know her.

By the time we arrived at the deli the clouds had stacked on top of each other like football players in a tackle. A band was set up outside on the lush green lawn. I hoped to hear some music before the storm hit.

Debra and I went inside and ordered our tacos and wine. Jenny got a burger. I downed a large Coke before eating. Outside we sat under an umbrella devouring our food while the band played bluegrass. A group of young people danced and my feet developed a life of their own, tapping to the beat.

"Excuse me," said a deep male voice over my shoulder. "Your feet tell me you'd like to dance. Would you?"

Looking up I saw a middle-aged man with shoulder length curly white hair, bright blue eyes, a muscular tanned body, and sparkling white teeth. A tie-dyed shirt and faded denim jeans hugged him tightly. I found his look very appealing. He reached out his hand and I took it while he lead me to the grassy area. Debra cleared her throat, making disapproving noises. I no longer cared what she thought.

The dancing helped the transition back into civilization. Moving with wild joyful steps, arms spread wide, I swung my head from side to side. I swayed in time to the music, in tune with my jubilant heart. After the third song, we stopped, both sweating. Amidst our ragged breaths we attempted to converse. I could tell by the way he looked at me he was interested. The pounding in my heart wasn't only from the dancing.

"You're quite a dancer. Took my breath away. Name's Ben. What's yours?"

"Lori. It's been a long time since anyone said I took their breath away. Thanks."

"A good name for a woman with crazy red hair and wild dancing feet to match," he teased, stroking my hand.

I was interested in him, too, but only for a dance. The person my heart beat for was Smiley. I pulled my hand away.

"What brings you here?" Ben asked.

"I just finished hiking the JMT."

"You hiked the John Muir Trail? I've always wanted to do that."

Looking up at him, gentle raindrops, slid down my face. They bounced off my chin, adding moisture to the parched ground.

Reaching for my left hand, he looked down at my wedding ring. "I see you're married."

"Very."

"How could your husband let you go?" He tried to pull me close. "Wasn't he worried he'd lose you?"

Pushing away, I laughed. "My husband doesn't own me. I needed to discover what I'm made of. I think he hoped I'd find out where I belong."

"And did you?" He placed my hand to his lips and kissed it lightly.

I stepped back, forcing him to release my hand, and looked into his sultry blue eyes. "Yes. The JMT helped me know who I am."

"And who is that?"

"A woman who follows her heart." I reached into my pocket. Pulling out my rock and cupping it lovingly, I turned and walked away, ready to go home.

ACKNOWLEDGEMENTS

It took a band of angels to help me write this memoir. Trail angels, family angels, friend angels, and creative angels. All were there for me when I needed them. I want to express my gratitude to numerous kindhearted souls.

First, thank you to Debra, although that isn't her real name. Her expertise facilitated both my dream of hiking the John Muir Trail and this book. Then, there is *Jenny*. You're my hero, and I love you for the profound kindness you displayed each and every day. You were a class-act teenager and often more adult than anyone in our group.

A special thank you to Jessica Therrien and Holly Kammier, authors and co-founders of Acorn Publishing. They were patient and kind, while also nudging me and insisting that I provide readers with a quality book.

A heartfelt thank you to Dane of Ebook Cover Design who made certain I received the perfect cover art.

Thanks to the young talent of Lacey Impellizeri who designed my beautiful bookmarks, business cards, and banners, and to Hayley Lekven who created my awesome map. Zan Strumfeld did a final edit and helped polish my book. Christa Yelich-Koth did an amazing job formatting my manuscript. A shout out of appreciation to my fellow Acorn authors.

Thank you to the editors who generously contributed to my creative process, including Flora Burlingame, Lesley Payne, Ruth Lofsted, Laura Taylor, and Holly Kammier. Critique group members shared laughter, knowledge, and friendship, and I would be remiss not to acknowledge them. They are Vicki Thomas, Elizabeth Adkins, Penny Park, Sandra Alonzo, Ruth Lofsted, Marcia Penner Freedman, Susan Norman, Sheila Boyd, and Jim Kendall. I am deeply grateful for the encouragement and moral support offered to me by Carol Houston, my life-long friend, Karen Fish, and Flora Burlingame who listened and lamented on the trials of writing. They refused to allow me to abandon my book.

A special tribute to my loyal and faithful companion dogs who kept me company in my office cave while I trudged along in the writing and editing process.

My beta readers Astrid Diek, Mandy Urena, and Carol Houston, generously gave their time and offered insightful feedback. You were my posse and I love you.

Special friends Trisha Tomasini, Nan Oswald, Bonnie Little, Jeannine Andre, and my sister Rhonda Fike—the Fabulous Five—thank you for always being there for me.

Deepest gratitude to numerous trail angels along the way, including Susie Hickman, who helped me repair my boots so that I could complete the journey. Kathy Gallagher and Jun became my trail hiking partners late in the hike. I won't ever forget Jane Smith's good humor at the start of the trip.

My family thought I could hike the trail even when I didn't believe in myself. Their love and faith carried me. Special thanks to my husband Smiley (Patrick) Tierney who has never tried to change me, and to Sean and Craig, my two sons, and daughter-in-law Hannah. Their love and faith carried me. Much love to my grandchildren who were dreams in my heart as I hiked.

Last but not least, and in memoriam for those now walking a different trail, I want to celebrate my Dad, Sam Oliver, for helping us to find our way back to each other at the conclusion of his life. My step-father Charlie Baxter lives on in my heart. My dear friend, Connie Rothell, lost her battle with cancer, as did my cherished mother, Maureen Oliver Baxter. Mom showed me how to love unconditionally and to be my best. I miss them and still feel their love and support.

I cherish the lessons of the wilderness. I thought my journey into the wild would be centered on the scenery, but it was equally about the people. They shined like new pennies.

Happy trails to all who assisted me along my path. Not only did you help me to fulfill my dream, you also showed me the way home.

ABOUT THE AUTHOR

At 65 years old, Lori Oliver-Tierney is a wife, mother, retired teacher, and finally the grandma she always dreamed of becoming. She is also still an adventurer who loves to hike. When she grows up, she wants to be a woman of substance, like Susie Hickman, who is 91 years young and living her dream, working at the Muir Ranch in the wild Sierra.